JESSE LIBERTY'S
from scratch
PROGRAMMING SERIES

D0599025

MySQL
and PHP
from scratch

Wade Maxfield

201 West 103rd Street,
Indianapolis, Indiana 46290

MySQL and PHP from scratch

Copyright © 2001 by Que

International Standard Book Number: 0-7897-2440-5

Library of Congress Catalog Card Number: 00-108842

Printed in the United States of America

First Printing: November 2000

02   01   00   4   3   2   1

Trademarks

Warning and Disclaimer

Acquisitions Editor
Gretchen Ganser

Development Editor
Hugh Vandivier

Technical Editor
Tobias Ratschiller

Managing Editor
Thomas F. Hayes

Senior Editor
Susan Ross Moore

Copy Editor
Cynthia Fields

Indexer
Larry Sweazy

Proofreader
Harvey Stanbrough

Team Coordinator
Vicki Harding

Interior Designer
Sandra Schroeder

Cover Designers
Anne Jones
Maureen McCarty

Production
Lizbeth Patterson

Contents at a Glance

Contents

About the Author

Wade Maxfield is president and CEO of Central Telecommunications, an ISP based in Fort Worth, Texas. He has over 15 years experience in the ISP, communications, and consumer software industries. His company runs Linux and employs Apache, MySQL, PHP, and IMP. He is a working consultant. His clients have included Mobil Oil, the State of Minnesota, the U.S. Navy Federal Credit Union, GTE, and RTEC Systems (now Marconi). Wade is currently developing real-time operating systems and data acquisition code for harsh-environment sensors for the Canadian company of Precision Drilling Corporation.

Dedication

This book is dedicated to my wife and family. Without their support, it would not have been possible.

I would also like to extend thanks to Gretchen Ganser, Hugh Vandivier, and Tobias Ratschiller.
They have kept this book on a straight track!

Tell Us What You Think!

As the reader of this book, *you* are our most important critic and commentator. We value your opinion and want to know what we're doing right, what we could do better, what areas you'd like to see us publish in, and any other words of wisdom you're willing to pass our way.

As an Associate Publisher for Que, I welcome your comments. You can fax, email, or write me directly to let me know what you did or didn't like about this book—as well as what we can do to make our books stronger.

Please note that I cannot help you with technical problems related to the topic of this book, and that due to the high volume of mail I receive, I might not be able to reply to every message.

When you write, please be sure to include this book's title and author as well as your name and phone or fax number. I will carefully review your comments and share them with the author and editors who worked on the book.

Fax:	317-581-4666
Email:	quetechnical@mcp.com
Mail:	Associate Publisher
	Que
	201 West 103rd Street
	Indianapolis, IN 46290 USA

Introduction

The Purpose of This Book

I needed to solve a specific problem at low cost. My business required a Web-based email server for my customers. I wanted to use the wealth of open source tools available to any Internet server machine. I also wanted just enough information to get the job done. I didn't need to be buried by extraneous information.

I started looking at the available books. After much searching, I realized many database books are on the market. Many programming language books are on the market. Many Web server books are on the market. However, almost no books give you the opportunity to learn the practical and useful side of Internet services using a hands-on approach.

I decided to attempt such a book. This is it. This is a learning book. You will learn how to customize the most popular applications that provide Internet services. When you are finished, you will have hands-on experience combining several available software components into something very useful.

One note before we continue: The Apache Web server, the MySQL database, the PHP server language, and sendmail are all available on multiple platforms. After reading this book, you will have the basic skills necessary to implement the Web-based email system called IMP on other operating systems, such as Solaris, Windows NT, or Unix.

This book shows you how to implement IMP under Red Hat Linux 6.x. If you want to put IMP on another platform, get it working under Linux first, and then apply that knowledge to another platform. The knowledge and experience gained in doing a successful install on Linux will greatly aid you in the installation of the Web-based email program on a different operating system.

Who Can Use This Book

This book is written with the novice programmer or power user in mind. If you have ever written a batch file for MS-DOS or a shell script for Unix or programmed in any language, you have the skills necessary to do this project. If you have tinkered with the settings on your Linux box, you are ready.

If you have never done any of these things, you are welcome to read this book and give it a try. I hope to give you enough information to help you accomplish the goal.

I do expect you to know how to log in to Linux, start the X Window System, bring up terminal windows, and move around in the directories on your computer. You need to know how to get directory listings. You also need to know how to use a text editor under Linux.

What You Will Learn

After working through the chapters in this book, you will learn

- How to make your Linux system more secure while staying connected to the Internet 24 hours a day, 7 days a week.
- What tools to use to add new software to your Linux system. You will learn how to determine whether software is installed on your system and how to install it.
- The basics of configuring the Apache Web server. You will add modules to extend its functionality.
- sendmail configuration basics, with an emphasis on the Red Hat version of Linux.
- MySQL installation and configuration basics, along with general database design concepts.
- PHP installation and configuration basics. You will learn the basics of using PHP, which can provide ASP-(Active Server Pages) like capability on any popular platform.
- The basics of how to get help from people on the Internet who share similar interests and needs.

What You Will Accomplish

When you are finished with this book, you will have a fully functional, Web-based email server application similar to Netscape's WebMail or Microsoft's Hotmail.

This server application will save user-specific information in the MySQL database. It will be accessible through any browser that supports Java, such as Netscape Navigator or Internet Explorer.

A user will be able to download file attachments to his computer and send files to friends. A personal address book will keep his most commonly used addresses.

If you want, this application can serve interoffice email to a small group of people. Alternatively, it can be attached to the Internet and serve hundreds of people wherever they happen to be.

You will have the source code available for all of the software presented in this book. If you want, you can customize the Web pages to display your logo. You can enhance its functionality, or change it to suit your tastes.

You will have the tools necessary to build an e-commerce application. The main ingredients of an e-commerce solution are as follows:

- Internet-Capable OS
- Web Server
- Database Engine
- Web Browsers

I want you to enjoy using this book. However, please follow the chapters in order, unless told to do otherwise. Each chapter builds upon the previous chapter. Some things you do in one chapter require you to complete the previous chapter properly. I am doing the same steps on a freshly installed Red Hat Linux machine as I write this book, so I am able to experience and solve most of the problems you will have.

Conventions Used in This Book

Some of the unique features in this series include

 An icon in the margin indicates the use of a new term. New terms appear in the paragraph in *italic*.

> You'll see an icon set in the margin next to a box that contains a technical term and how it should be pronounced. For example, "cin is pronounced *see-in*, and cout is pronounced *see-out*."

 An icon in the margin indicates code that can be entered, compiled, and run.

EXCURSION

What Are Excursions?

Excursions are short diversions from the main topic being discussed, and they offer an opportunity to flesh out your understanding of a topic.

Concept Web—With a book of this type, a topic can be discussed in multiple places as a result of when and where we add functionality during application development. To help make this all clear, we've included a Concept Web that provides a graphical representation of how all the programming concepts relate to one another. You'll find it on the inside front cover of this book.

Notes give you comments and asides about the topic at hand, as well as full explanations of certain concepts.

Tips provide great shortcuts and hints on how to program in C++ more effectively.

Warnings warn you against making your life miserable and to avoid the pitfalls in programming.

In addition, you'll find various typographic conventions throughout this book:

- Commands, variables, and other code appear in text in a special `computer font`.
- In this book, I build on existing listings as we examine code further. When I add new sections to existing code, you'll spot it in **`bold computer font`**.
- Commands and such that you type appear in **boldface type**.
- Placeholders in syntax descriptions appear in an *`italic computer font`*. This indicates that you will replace the placeholder with the actual filename, parameter, or other element that it represents.

Chapter 1

Prerequisite Operational System and Software

To put together a successful IMP (Web-based Internet Mail Program) system, you need several software packages installed on your system. Together, we will explore your system and make changes.

In this chapter, you will learn how to determine which software is installed on your system and how to install new software packages. You will also learn how to determine which version of operating system you are running.

Red Hat Linux 6.0 or Greater Recommended

The version of Red Hat 6.x that you can download over the Internet contains only GNU GPL-licensed software, or software that can be freely distributed. All the software in this project falls in this category. Even the Linux version of MySQL is freely distributed, requiring a modest licensing payment for its use under a limited set of circumstances. I assume the unofficial Red Hat 6.1 release as the base platform. *Unofficial* means it was not manufactured by Red Hat and is not supported by them.

Note

The company doing MySQL recently formed a strategic alliance with VA Linux. The MySQL versions 3.23 and greater have been released under the GPL license. As of this writing, MySQL version 3.23 is in Alpha test and is not yet ready for full deployment. I fully expect it will be stable and suitable for production by the time you read this book.

The latest version of PHP is most easily customized on Red Hat Linux 6.0 or later. Because of this, this book uses Red Hat Linux 6.1. I initially installed IMP on Red Hat Linux version 6.0. The two versions have very few differences as far as this project is concerned.

Whenever Red Hat Linux displays the login prompt, it tells you which version of software and which version of kernel you have. If your system starts in graphical mode, you are running the X Window System by default. In this case, you don't see the information displayed by the login prompt.

To see the information displayed by the login prompt, switch to a console mode. To do this, press the Ctrl, Alt, and F1 keys simultaneously.

 Note This will be designated using the plus (+) sign. For example: Ctrl+Alt+F1 indicates to press these keys simultaneously.

This gives you a login screen if you boot into the X Window System by default.

If you run startx to run the X Window System, this will put you into the status screen for the X Window System. If that is the case, you will see several messages that the X Window System outputs because it can or can't find things it would like to have. In this case, you need to press Alt+F2. This will give you a login screen. You should see something like this:

```
Red Hat Linux release 6.1 (Cartman)
Kernel 2.2.12-20 on an i686
winbook login:
```

 Note The keystrokes Ctrl+Alt+F1 through Ctrl+Alt+F4 take you from the X Window System to one of four nongraphical virtual console screens. The first console screen accessed with F1 is where all kernel and debugging messages are printed. To return to the X Window System, press Alt+F7.

This shows we are running Red Hat Linux version 6.1. Let's walk through how this information was generated.

The information displayed comes from the /etc/issue file. The /etc/rc.d/rc.local file creates this file during the boot process. The release information comes from the /etc/redhat-release file, which the Red Hat installation program placed. The kernel information comes from running the uname program with the -r option.

If you don't have Red Hat version 6.0 or greater, many specific details I talk about will not be correct. For that reason, I recommend that you get Red Hat 6.1 and install it. After a successful install, you can try your hand on another platform.

How to Check for the Presence of an Installed Package

To make IMP work, you will need certain software packages. Determining which software packages are installed used to be difficult under the Linux operating system.

Fortunately, the programmers at Red Hat provide a utility to help you manage this: the *RPM Package Manager*. Every file produced by the package manager ends in .rpm. This program provides an easy way for you to determine what software is on your computer. To execute the package manager program from a command line, enter rpm.

> It is best to use this program from a command line. Under the Gnome GUI, which is one of the default installs for the Red Hat X Window System environment, a utility called GnomeRPM is found. You can use this utility for graphically determining whether the packages are installed. You can also use it to install packages. It does not give you as much control over the information you obtain. You also cannot manipulate it in a bash script file. You can run the rpm utility from a script.

The rpm utility uses a local database to manage packages. This database enables you to find out what package versions are installed and keeps track of dependencies between packages. It does not enable you to install a package that requires another package. It also does not enable you to remove a package that is required by another package currently installed in your system.

To find out what program is installed on a system, use the rpm's query command. You can query for all packages or for some packages. I find the query for all packages very useful when I almost know the name of what I am looking for.

For example, suppose I am looking for all the packages I have installed for XFree86, but I'm not sure of the names of each of the packages. I can execute rpm and pipe its output to the grep program. For this example, I ran an xterm program and entered the command

```
rpm -qa | grep -I xf
```

Output

```
[root@mail maxfield]# rpm -qa | grep -i xf
```

Output

```
XFree86-3.3.5-3
XFree86-libs-3.3.5-3
```

```
XFree86-xfs-3.3.5-3
XFree86-75dpi-fonts-3.3.5-3
XFree86-SVGA-3.3.5-3
XFree86-devel-3.3.5-3
XFree86-doc-3.3.5-3
xfm-1.3.2-13
[root@mail maxfield]#
```

 Note   The grep program is an acronym for the General Regular Expression Parser. It searches for text strings in text streams piped to it or in files.

As you can see from the output of rpm, it found XFree86 version 3.3.5, matching libraries, fonts, documents, and the super vga driver. It also found the xfm program. Running a quick man xfm shows this is the X file and application manager, so we can safely ignore it.

```
[root@mail maxfield]# man xfm
```

Output

```
XFM(1)                                                          XFM(1)


NAME
       xfm - X file and applications manager


SYNOPSIS
       xfm [options ...]


DESCRIPTION
       Xfm  is  a file and applications manager program for the X
       window system.  It provides virtually all of the   features…
```

To query for a single package, you generally ask for the package without the version number attached. Here is a query for XFree86:

```
[root@mail maxfield]# rpm -q XFree86
XFree86-3.3.5-3
[root@mail maxfield]#
```

The rpm package also enables you to remove a package, install a package, or upgrade a package. To illustrate this, I queried secure shell, looked for all secure shell packages on my system, and then removed and reinstalled the secure shell clients on my system. I also upgraded the ssh clients package in this example.

```
[root@mail rpms]# rpm -q ssh
ssh-1.2.27-5us
[root@mail rpms]# rpm -qa | grep ssh
ssh-clients-1.2.27-5us
ssh-1.2.27-5us
```

```
ssh-server-1.2.27-5us
ssh-extras-1.2.27-5us
[root@mail rpms]# rpm -q ssh-clients
ssh-clients-1.2.27-5us
[root@mail rpms]# rpm -e ssh-clients
[root@mail rpms]# rpm -i ssh-clients-1.2.27-5us.i386.rpm
[root@mail rpms]# rpm -U ssh-clients-1.2.27-5us.i386.rpm
[root@mail rpms]#
```

Note that not all software installed on your Linux system must come from rpm packages. Many open-source developers provide tarballs for you to use for installation. These tarballs generally don't update the rpm database and must be installed differently.

A tarball refers to the result of the command `tar cvf`, which wraps up an entire directory and its subdirectories in one huge file. It also preserves the permissions of all the files.

Tar is often used to archive data onto tape or another storage device. Hence the name, taken from *Tape ARchiver*.

The process of extracting files from a tarball is often called *untarring*.

To illustrate using a `tar` file, consider the php tarball. This tarball has been compressed using the GNU Zip program, `gzip`.

Two ways are available to unzip and untar this tarball. The first way is to run `gunzip`. To do this, execute the following:

```
[root@mail /root]#gunzip php-3.0.16.tar.gz
```

This leaves the tarball in the current directory without the `.gz` ending. Run an `ls` command. You will see the following:

```
[root@mail /root]#ls php*
php-3.0.14.tar
```

After this, run the `untar` command. An interesting feature of the GNU tar program is a command-line option that allows you to unzip and untar in one step.

Only the GNU version of tar allows you to use the z option while untarring a file. Other versions of tar, such as the one on Solaris, lack this feature. For those versions, you must first unzip the file before untarring.

```
To use this option, enter:[root@mail /root]#tar xvzf php-3.0.16.tar.gz
```

This unzips the `tar` file and untars it. In this case, the directory `php-3.0.16` is created in the current directory. Inside that directory are all the files in the tarball. Note that to untar an already unzipped tarball, you leave the z out of the option list. If you were to untar the unzipped php tarball, you would type

```
[root@mail /root]#tar xvf php-3.0.16.tar
```

Finally, to create a tarball from a directory, use the option cvf. To tar the php3 directory, enter the following:

```
[root@ /root]#tar cvf php-3.0.16.tar php-3.0.16
```

How to Install a Needed Package from a CD

Unlike DOS or Microsoft Windows, Linux does not have drive letters. Disk drives, including CD-ROMs and floppies, have their contents listed under directories rather than under drive letters. Handling file systems this way gives no practical limit to the number of drives that can be used by Linux at any one time. The following sections guide you through the process of using CD-ROMs under Linux.

Mounting the CD

The packages and tarballs necessary to install this project on your computer are located on the CD. To access the CD, use the mount command and attach the CD underneath a directory on your hard drive. Historically, the proper location to do this is under the /mnt/cdrom directory.

The standard installation of Red Hat 6.x that includes the Gnome desktop automatically mounts the CD-ROM for you when you insert it. However, this does not happen if you are running in the console mode and not running the X Window System. For that reason, let's review the mount command and how to use it.

The mount command has a manual page. You can examine it by bringing up a terminal window and entering man mount. The options can be a bit confusing, but you generally use only one or two options. To mount the CD-ROM under the /mnt/cdrom directory, enter

```
[root@mail /root]#mount -t iso9660 /dev/cdrom /mnt/cdrom
```

This tells the mount program to look for a CD-ROM in the CD-ROM device that is formatted with the iso9660 CD-ROM file system. If it finds that CD-ROM and that file system, it then places all the files on that CD-ROM under the /mnt/cdrom directory. At that point, you can do an ls /mnt/cdrom and see all the files on the root directory of the CD.

To mount a floppy disk in drive A: under the /mnt/floppy directory, you would enter

```
[root@mail /root]#mount -t vfat /dev/fd0 /mnt/floppy
```

Another possibility in a dual boot system is to mount a Windows 95 or Windows 98 file system under a directory. If you create a directory called `cdrive` under the `/mnt` directory and the Windows drive C: is on `/dev/hda1`, you can mount it. For example

```
[root@mail /root]#mkdir /mnt/cdrive
[root@mail /root]#mount -t vfat /dev/hda1 /mnt/cdrive
```

After this, you can run `ls /mnt/cdrive` and list all the files in the root directory of drive C. This works for all the recognized file systems listed on the man page for the mount command.

Installing rpms and Copying Files

After you have the CD mounted under the `/mnt/cdrom` directory, you are ready to copy the packages and tarballs onto your computer. I recommend you create a directory under your home directory. This directory will hold all of the rpms and tarballs while we work on this project. For the sake of this project, I'll assume the name of this directory is *imp*.

We have to do a lot of work as root while installing packages and creating and compiling, so put the imp directory under `/root`. Be sure you are logged in as root when you create the directory.

Copy all of the `.rpm` and `.gz` files from the CD into this `imp` directory. The list of files you will have in the `imp` directory follows:

Output

```
MySQL-3.22.32-1.i386.rpm
MySQL-client-3.22.32-1.i386.rpm
MySQL-shared-3.22.32-1.i386.rpm
apache-1.3.12-1.i386.rpm
apache-devel-1.3.9-4.i386.rpm
freetype-1.2-7.i386.rpm
freetype-devel-1.2-7.i386.rpm
horde-1.0.11.tar.gz
imap-4.7a-4.i386.rpm
imap-devel-4.7a-4.i386.rpm
imap-utils-4.7a-4.i386.rpm
imp-2.0.11.tar.gz
php-3.0.15.tar.gz
```

The important rpms here are the `Apache`, `imap`, and `freetype` files. Whenever you install a development rpm, its version must match the standard rpm file's version. If you don't have that exact version of Apache, Imap, or Freetype installed, you must uninstall them first. Then you can install these rpms.

You can obtain all of the latest rpms from the Internet and install them. However, if you do that, you can get a version of software that does not work properly with the other software packages we are about to use.

Standalone Usage: How to Verify Required Services Are Installed and Working

You must have several system services and packages installed to continue. First, check your network functionality. You must at least have the loopback device installed. If you are going to test this over a network, you must also have a network card installed.

As the root user, bring up a terminal window (or log on to a console), and enter the command `ifconfig`. If you have a network card installed and set up, you will see something displayed similar to the following:

```
[root@wmaxlaptop root]# ifconfig
```

Output

```
eth0      Link encap:Ethernet  HWaddr 00:E0:98:76:EB:F2
          inet addr:172.16.13.70  Bcast:172.16.13.255  Mask:255.255.255.0
          UP BROADCAST RUNNING MULTICAST  MTU:1500  Metric:1
          RX packets:98094 errors:1 dropped:99 overruns:0 frame:432
          TX packets:10214 errors:0 dropped:0 overruns:0 carrier:0
          collisions:4662 txqueuelen:100
          Interrupt:3 Base address:0x300

lo        Link encap:Local Loopback
          inet addr:127.0.0.1  Mask:255.0.0.0
          UP LOOPBACK RUNNING  MTU:3924  Metric:1
          RX packets:6 errors:0 dropped:0 overruns:0 frame:0
          TX packets:6 errors:0 dropped:0 overruns:0 carrier:0
          collisions:0 txqueuelen:0
```

You are interested in the lo device. Every machine using TCP/IP has a local *loopback adapter*, which is an imaginary network card that enables you to test your own TCP/IP stack. The address is always 127.0.0.1. You can ping your computer and connect to services on your computer with this address. You don't have to be connected to a network to test the system we are installing.

If you don't have this adapter installed, you need to go back through the Red Hat install. This time, indicate you are upgrading your system, and select a Server Install.

To verify the loopback adapter, you need to use `ping`. `ping` will go on forever, and you can stop it with a Ctrl+C, or you can tell it how many pings to send when you run it. Let's try for five pings.

```
[root@wmaxlaptop root]# ping -c 5 127.0.0.1
```

Output

```
PING 127.0.0.1 (127.0.0.1) from 127.0.0.1 : 56(84) bytes of data.
64 bytes from 127.0.0.1: icmp_seq=0 ttl=255 time=0.0 ms
64 bytes from 127.0.0.1: icmp_seq=1 ttl=255 time=0.0 ms
```

```
64 bytes from 127.0.0.1: icmp_seq=2 ttl=255 time=0.0 ms
64 bytes from 127.0.0.1: icmp_seq=3 ttl=255 time=0.0 ms
64 bytes from 127.0.0.1: icmp_seq=4 ttl=255 time=0.0 ms

--- 127.0.0.1 ping statistics ---
5 packets transmitted, 5 packets received, 0% packet loss
round-trip min/avg/max = 0.0/0.0/0.0 ms
```

If you get the preceding printout, you are in business. Otherwise, try reinstalling your Red Hat system using the guidelines mentioned previously.

Note ping tests about 95% of a TCP/IP network's connectivity. Generally, if ping works, everything else will work. This rule of thumb applies to all machines and TCP/IP stacks that I know of.

If you are going to test using only your computer, you need to have XFree86 installed and working. If you have a graphical user interface using Gnome or KDE, you are ready. If you don't, you need to install that package. The best way to do this is reinstall Red Hat and choose a Gnome Workstation Upgrade.

The other packages you need to check for being installed are sendmail and Netscape Navigator:

```
[root@wmaxlaptop php-3.0.15]# rpm -q sendmail
sendmail-8.9.3-15
[root@wmaxlaptop php-3.0.15]# rpm -q netscape
package netscape is not installed
[root@wmaxlaptop php-3.0.15]# rpm -qa | grep netscape
netscape-common-4.61-12
netscape-communicator-4.61-12
```

As you can see, I tried to query for Netscape, and I received no answer. So I ran `rpm` with the `-qa` option, which gave me everything. I then used `grep` to locate everything with Netscape in it. If you don't have these packages, install them from the Red Hat installation CD. You don't have to install Netscape if you are not running the X Window System on your computer.

Network Functionality

If you are going to use this system on the Internet, you need to set up a small local area network. The smallest practical local area network you can have is two computers connected to a small hub with 10BaseT connecting cable. You will also need two network cards that are supported by Windows and Linux.

Note   Actually, if you get what is called a crossover cable, you can connect the two machines directly to each other. However, this network cannot be expanded. It will be limited to only two machines.

Everything required can be purchased at a local computer store. Most of the smaller shops can help you set up the Windows machine. You need to choose a network card that is supported by Red Hat Linux for your server. Most 3Com or NE2000 compatible cards are supported by Linux.

It is beyond the scope of this book to go into the details of installation of various network cards. If you installed Red Hat Linux before you installed your network card, the best thing to do is to reinstall Red Hat Linux, choosing the Server option. If it recognizes your network card, it will ask you to fill out the IP address information for the card. If it does not recognize the card, that part of the install will be skipped.

If you will be setting up a small local area network, you need to read the next two sections. I show you how to pick the IP addresses and names you will give your machines. After you have gone through this exercise, you will have the general information necessary to set up a private network of practically any size.

General Network Connectivity Guidelines

You must assign unique IP addresses to each machine on an IPV4 network that hosts Internet services such as Web pages. If you are connected to the Internet, you must have your addresses assigned to you. If you are on a private network, you get to choose your addresses.

Three sets of addresses are reserved for private networks:

```
10.0.0.0 through 10.x.x.x (where x is anything from 0 to 255)
172.16.0.0 through 172.31.x.x
192.168.0.0 through 192.168.x.x
```

These addresses fall into the three classes of IPV4 address ranges available on the Internet. After you have chosen a set of addresses, all machines on your local network must use the same netmask and network address set, with unique IP address numbers for each machine.

EXCURSION

Internet IP Addressing

The IPV6 networking scheme will arrive within a few years, and will allow over 3,000 addresses per square meter of earth's surface. It will require changes in current TCP/IP stacks. These changes, for the most part, have already been made in all currently produced operating systems.

**how too
pro nouns' it**

IPV4 is pronounced *eye pee vee four.*

TCP/IP is pronounced *tee cee pee eye pee.*

Three classes of network addresses exist in the IPV4 TCP/IP addressing scheme. These network classes are called A, B, and C, and they allow easy configuration of routing schemes between networks. The number of machines you are deploying on the network determines the class of addressing you will use; it can also be referred to as the addressing range.

The first address range is called a class A address. You have almost 16,777,216 addresses from which to choose.

 Note This value is calculated from 256×256×256. Two hundred and fifty six possible address values are in each dotted section, called a quad.

It has a class A netmask value of `255.0.0.0`.

The second address range is called a class B address. You have almost 65,536 addresses from which to choose.

 Note The value is calculated from 256×256.

It has a class B netmask value of `255.255.0.0`.

The third address range is called a class C address. You have almost 256 addresses from which to choose. It has a class C netmask value of `255.255.255.0`.

You don't have all the addresses to choose from in any of the address classes because of how two of the address values in a network are used. These two addresses play significant roles in network design.

One of the numbers used is 0. It denotes the base network in the netmask value. No machine can have an IP address of 0 if it coincides with the 0 in the netmask.

The other number is 255. No machine can have an IP address that contains 255 because 255 is reserved for the broadcast address on a network. All machines will receive any message sent to address 255 on the local network.

This 255 must be within the 0 part of the network mask. For example, let's assume the network is 192.168.1.0. Every machine on the network has three numbers in common: 192.168.1. Each machine has a unique last number, from 1–254. For example, one machine could have an IP address of 192.168.1.10, and another one could have an IP address of 192.168.1.20. You cannot give two different computers the same IP address. Each machine on a network must have a unique address.

Testing Your Network Connection

To connect your machine to a network, you must connect one end of one 10BaseT cable to one computer and the other to the hub. Do the same for the other computer. Most hubs have an uplink port. This port is used to connect two hubs together without using an uplink cable. Do not use this port!

Now you must assign IP addresses to each machine. I picked two numbers from the 172.16.1.0 network. I decided to name my Windows machine *win*, and my Linux machine *lin*. The address of the Windows machine is 172.16.13.66, and the address of the Linux machine is 172.16.13.70. These decisions were arbitrary. Now you are ready to set up a local method of resolving machine names to IP addresses.

On the Windows machine, you need to edit the c:\windows\hosts file. If it does not exist, create it. In that file put the IP addresses and the names of the machines. Your file will look something like this:

```
127.0.0.1       localhost                      # the loopback adaptor address
172.16.13.66    win  win.mydomain.com          # our test name
172.16.13.70    lin  lin.mydomain.com          # the Linux test name
```

On the Linux machine, edit the /etc/hosts file and place the same type of information in it. It will look like this:

```
127.0.0.1       localhost.mydomain.com localhost
172.16.13.70    lin winbook lin.mydomain.com
172.16.1.66     win wmaxlaptop win.mydomain.com
```

Note that you can refer to the Linux machine as lin or winbook. When the TCP/IP stack looks up the machine name from the address (called a reverse lookup), the name returned will be lin because it is first in the list.

Bring up a DOS prompt on the Windows machine, and run the command ping lin. You should see something similar to the following:

```
C:\WINDOWS>ping lin
```

Output

```
Pinging lin [172.16.13.70] with 32 bytes of data:
Reply from 172.16.13.70: bytes=32 time=21ms TTL=255
Reply from 172.16.13.70: bytes=32 time=2ms TTL=255
Reply from 172.16.13.70: bytes=32 time=1ms TTL=255
Reply from 172.16.13.70: bytes=32 time=1ms TTL=255

Ping statistics for 172.16.13.70:
```

```
      Packets: Sent = 4, Received = 4, Lost = 0 (0% loss),
Approximate round trip times in milli-seconds:
    Minimum = 1ms, Maximum =  21ms, Average =   6ms
```

Your ping times should be much better. I am running Windows under VMWare on my laptop, which makes the ping times longer.

On your Linux machine, bring up a terminal window and run the command `ping -c 5 win`. This will provide a provide a printout similar to this:

```
[root root@winbook]#ping -c 5 win
```

Output

```
PING win (172.16.13.66) from 172.16.13.70 : 56(84) bytes of data.
64 bytes from 172.16.13.66: icmp_seq=0 ttl=128 time=7.3 ms
64 bytes from 172.16.13.66: icmp_seq=1 ttl=128 time=0.8 ms
64 bytes from 172.16.13.66: icmp_seq=2 ttl=128 time=1.8 ms
64 bytes from 172.16.13.66: icmp_seq=3 ttl=128 time=0.9 ms
64 bytes from 172.16.13.66: icmp_seq=4 ttl=128 time=1.2 ms

--- win ping statistics ---
5 packets transmitted, 5 packets received, 0% packet loss
round-trip min/avg/max = 0.8/2.4/7.3 ms
```

If you don't get these results, something is wrong with your network setup. You might need to get someone who has set up small networks to help you. You cannot expect to log on to your Linux server from your Windows machine and use any services until this works.

If you want to continue on a standalone basis, without network support, you can. However, the ping of the loopback adapter must work.

System Security

System security is a way of thinking coupled with action. We put locks on our doors to prevent entry by uninvited people. For those locks to be effective, we must use them. Having an unlocked door is equivalent to having no locks.

Three prevalent mindsets exist in the security world. The first is security through obscurity. This mindset says "I'm too small, I won't advertise my presence, they will never find me." This thought process had some validity when there were very few machines on the Internet.

Today, with script kiddies abounding, security through obscurity never works. You must actively lock down your system, and keep it up-to-date with the latest packages that have been updated for security reasons.

Script kiddies is the name given to people who run automated tools that probe all possible addresses on the Internet. They usually download these tools and have no idea how they work. If the automated toolkit identifies an exploit, simple additional security measures usually stop the attack.

These tools identify systems that have not been updated properly, and automatically install root kits. These root kits allow crackers to take over your machine as root and do whatever they want. If this happens to you, you have been rooted.

Another mindset is permissive security. This security thought says "I will only deny people who have proven to be a problem." This is as bad as the obscurity mindset. Don't think this. The mindset of "Deny all, allow some" provides the best general security. You only allow people into your equipment who, in your opinion, are worthy of trust.

The tcp_wrappers package that is installed with Red Hat provides the locks needed to implement the deny all, allow some system security. We must do a few things to complete locking down a system in addition to enabling tcp_wrappers.

Initial Security Steps

The basic security for a Red Hat Linux server (or any server that uses the tcp_wrappers package) is very simple. This package installs a daemon called inetd, which listens on the standard Internet service ports for a request. After a request comes in, it checks to see whether it is allowed to start a server for that request.

To determine whether a server, such as telnet or ftp, can be started for a request, the inetd server first looks in its /etc/inetd.conf file. If that service is not listed in that file, the service is not started. If the service is listed, it then checks the /etc/hosts.allow file. If this file explicitly allows the service to be started for that client, it is. If no service is allowed at this point, the inetd program checks /etc/hosts.deny. Only if this file explicitly denies service for that client will the service not be started.

The easiest way to use this chain of logic is to allow services in your /etc/inetd.conf that you need to allow. You should not allow finger or rlogin.

Finger will give away usernames that are allowed to log in to your system or use system services. This is the first step in trying to crack a system.

Login, shell, and exec will give crackers remote access to your computer if your security fails. Very few administrators use these services today, and they can almost always be removed or tightly restricted.

The services I recommend you remove are as follows:

```
shell
login
exec
```

```
finger
cfinger
systat
netstat
```

To remove a service, put a # in front of the service name. Your /etc/inetd.conf file
should now look something like this:

```
#
# inetd.conf    This file describes the services that will be available
#               through the INETD TCP/IP super server.  To re-configure
#               the running INETD process, edit this file, then send the
#               INETD process a SIGHUP signal.
#
# Version: @(#)/etc/inetd.conf    3.10   05/27/93
#
# Authors: Original taken from BSD UNIX 4.3/TAHOE.
#               Fred N. van Kempen, <waltje@uwalt.nl.mugnet.org>
#
# Modified for Debian Linux by Ian A. Murdock <imurdock@shell.portal.com>
#
# Modified for RHS Linux by Marc Ewing <marc@redhat.com>
#
# <service_name> <sock_type> <proto> <flags> <user> <server_path> <args>
#
# Echo, discard, daytime, and chargen are used primarily for testing.
#
# To re-read this file after changes, just do a 'killall -HUP inetd'
#
#echo           stream  tcp     nowait  root    internal
#echo           dgram   udp     wait    root    internal
#discard        stream  tcp     nowait  root    internal
#discard        dgram   udp     wait    root    internal
#daytime        stream  tcp     nowait  root    internal
#daytime        dgram   udp     wait    root    internal
#chargen        stream  tcp     nowait  root    internal
#chargen        dgram   udp     wait    root    internal
#time           stream  tcp     nowait  root    internal
#time           dgram   udp     wait    root    internal
#
# These are standard services.
#
ftp      stream  tcp     nowait  root    /usr/sbin/tcpd  in.ftpd -l -a
telnet   stream  tcp     nowait  root    /usr/sbin/tcpd  in.telnetd
#
# Shell, login, exec, comsat and talk are BSD protocols.
#
#shell   stream  tcp     nowait  root        /usr/sbin/tcpd      in.rshd
#login   stream  tcp     nowait  root        /usr/sbin/tcpd      in.rlogind
#exec    stream  tcp     nowait  root        /usr/sbin/tcpd      in.rexecd
#comsat  dgram   udp     wait    root        /usr/sbin/tcpd      in.comsat
talk     dgram   udp     wait    nobody.tty  /usr/sbin/tcpd      in.talkd
ntalk    dgram   udp     wait    nobody.tty  /usr/sbin/tcpd      in.ntalkd
#dtalk   stream  tcp     wait    nobody.tty  /usr/sbin/tcpd      in.dtalkd
#
```

```
# Pop and imap mail services et al
#
#pop-2    stream  tcp      nowait  root    /usr/sbin/tcpd     ipop2d
#pop-3    stream  tcp      nowait  root    /usr/sbin/tcpd     ipop3d
#imap     stream  tcp      nowait  root    /usr/sbin/tcpd     imapd
#
# The Internet UUCP service.
#
#uucp     stream tcp       nowait  uucp    /usr/sbin/tcpd /usr/lib/uucp/uucico -l
#
# Tftp service is provided primarily for booting.  Most sites
# run this only on machines acting as "boot servers." Do not uncomment
# this unless you *need* it.
#
#tftp     dgram   udp      wait    root    /usr/sbin/tcpd     in.tftpd
#bootps dgram     udp      wait    root    /usr/sbin/tcpd     bootpd
#
# Finger, systat and netstat give out user information which may be
# valuable to potential "system crackers."  Many sites choose to disable
# some or all of these services to improve security.
#
#finger   stream  tcp      nowait  nobody  /usr/sbin/tcpd in.fingerd
#cfinger  stream  tcp      nowait  root    /usr/sbin/tcpd in.cfingerd
#systat   stream  tcp      nowait  guest   /usr/sbin/tcpd /bin/ps       -auwwx
#netstat  stream  tcp      nowait  guest   /usr/sbin/tcpd /bin/netstat  -f inet
#
# Authentication
#
auth      stream  tcp      wait    root    /usr/sbin/in.identd in.identd -e -o
#
# End of inetd.conf

linuxconf stream tcp wait root /bin/linuxconf linuxconf \http
```

The next step is to default deny services to the world. This makes it very easy to control access to your computer because you only open it to machines you explicitly agree to. In the /etc/hosts.deny file, enter the following:

ALL: ALL

Be sure to press the Enter key after the end of the line. Some versions of inetd will not process the line unless it has an Enter at the end of it.

Finally, you allow machines that are acceptable to you. In /etc/hosts.allow, you can do global allows or allows by service. I like to do allows by service because it permits very tight control. The way to globally allow services for your new local network is to insert the following line:

ALL: 172.16.13.

Again, be sure to press Enter after the end of the line. This setting enables any computer on the local network previously set up to access any service your machine offers.

The best way to configure this file is to use the service name followed by the IP addresses of the machines that are allowed to access that service. If you trust your local network, you can also include the network addresses. To enable imap, telnet, pop3, imapd, and ftp access to the set of machines on your local network, you would end up with something similar to the following. Change your hosts.allow file to look like this.

```
#
# hosts.allow   This file describes the names of the hosts which are
#               allowed to use the local INET services, as decided
#               by the '/usr/sbin/tcpd' server.
#
imapd: localhost, lin.mydomain.com
in.telnetd: 172.16.13.
ipop3d: lin, win
in.ftpd:  172.16.13.
```

Note a few things in passing about this file. First, the telnet and ftp services are provided without restriction to all machines on the 172.16.13 network.

Only two machines on the network are allowed to access the ipop3d daemon: lin and win. No other machines can have access to the ipop3d service. The imapd daemon can only be accessed from the Linux machine.

Because the hosts.deny file has ALL: ALL in it, no other machines will have access to any service on your Linux server. It is important that you set your system up to have the previously mentioned entries in hosts.allow and hosts.deny.

One final note about system security. If you have Red Hat version 6.0 or greater, it enables shadow passwords by default. You know you have shadow passwords enabled if you have an /etc/shadow file. If you do not have an /etc/shadow file, you must run the command pwconv to enable shadow passwords. This is another security precaution you should take, especially if your machine is going to be on the Internet.

The shadow password system came about because the /etc/passwd file must be world readable because of the design of the login process. Some crackers were able to retrieve a copy of the passwd file and run a password-cracking program against it. They could usually decrypt a few passwords. This allowed them to impersonate users, or possibly gain root access to a machine.

The shadow password system stores all passwords in the shadow file. This file is readable only by the root user, and the login process during authentication. This generally prevents crackers from reading this file unless they already have root access.

Application Upgrades

No security is foolproof because fools are too ingenious. You must keep on your toes. New exploits are discovered on a regular basis. New packages are released as these exploits are fixed. You must keep up-to-date.

The Internet hosts several mailing lists regarding security. Red Hat hosts the Linux security mailing list. To join this mailing list, send an email to `linux-security-request@redhat.com`, with the subject line containing the word `Subscribe`. Another good mailing list for security updates is the Red Hat watch list. Send an email to `redhat-watch-list-request@redhat.com`, with the word `Subscribe` in the subject. You will receive confirmation replies with further instructions.

When you are informed a package is updated, get it. For updates to Red Hat software, use an ftp and log in to `ftp.redhat.com`. This site is usually very busy, and you might require several attempts before you are let in.

After you are connected, you will generally go to the `/pub/redhat/updates` directory. There you will find directories that correspond to the version you are using. For Red Hat 6.1, the directory name will be 6.1. Because that is the version I run, I change to the 6.1 directory and then choose the i386 directory. You might be running version 6.0. If so, choose that directory and then the i386 directory.

Now download the files that you need to update your system. When finished, run the `rpm` command with the `-U` option to upgrade those packages.

EXCURSION
System Security and Commercial Applications

If you plan to install a commercial server or intend to use the IMP package in a commercial application, you must get qualified help. Although the security information presented here will be very useful, it is not complete. An expert in security must evaluate your system. You must have constant monitoring of your server to provide a reasonable level of defense against attack.

Even if you do have good security, you are not immune to attack. Microsoft, CNN, and the U.S. government have all had their Web sites attacked in the last few months. If you have not carefully considered the security implications of your whole site, you are taking great risks.

Apache Web Server

The Apache Web server is the heart of the installation. The server runs the PHP scripts that access the user's mail. I will show you how to ensure your Apache server is properly installed.

Verifying Apache Installation

Next, you need to see which version of Apache Web server you are running. Run `rpm` in the query mode for all packages, and `grep` for Apache:

```
[root@wmaxlaptop root]# rpm -qa | grep apache
```

Ouptut

```
apache-1.3.9-4
apache-devel-1.3.9-4
```

If you don't get a printout similar to this, you do not have the Apache Web server installed. If you don't have both the Apache Web server and the Apache development package currently installed, you must make a choice. You must find the development rpm for your version of Apache on the Internet and install it, or remove the current version of Apache and its modules.

 Note   If you will be putting this server on the Internet, it is *very important* that you use the latest stable Apache Web server. It is updated to fix security issues as well as minor bugs.

If you decide to remove your installed version of Apache, shut down the service. To do this, enter the following in a terminal window:

```
[root@maxlaptop root]#/etc/rc.d/init.d/httpd stop
```

Next, remove the current Apache server:

```
[root@wmaxlaptop root]# rpm -e apache apache-devel
```

Note that I included the apache-devel package on the same line as the apache package. The rpm utility allows you to install or remove multiple packages with one command.

Now change to the imp directory and run rpm with the install option for each of the Apache packages you have decided to install.

```
[root@wmaxlaptop impcd]# rpm -i apache-1.3.9-4.i386.rpm apache-devel-1.3.9-4.i386.rpm
```

You should specify the entire package name without using the wildcard character (the asterisk *) when installing an rpm file. This prevents costly mistakes.

After the server is installed, you must start it. This process is similar to stopping the server, only you enter the word start:

```
[root@winbook root]#/etc/rc.d/init.d/httpd start
```

To verify the server has started, run the ps command, and grep for the httpd daemon:

```
[root@winbook root]# ps ax | grep httpd
```

Output

```
 514 ?        S        0:00 httpd
 518 ?        SW       0:00 [httpd]
 519 ?        SW       0:00 [httpd]
 520 ?        SW       0:00 [httpd]
 521 ?        SW       0:00 [httpd]
 522 ?        SW       0:00 [httpd]
 523 ?        SW       0:00 [httpd]
 524 ?        SW       0:00 [httpd]
 525 ?        SW       0:00 [httpd]
 526 ?        SW       0:00 [httpd]
 527 ?        SW       0:00 [httpd]
 975 pts/1    S        0:00 grep httpd
```

You should get a listing similar to this. If you don't, try removing and re-installing the Apache packages. You must have both the Apache and Apache-devel packages installed for this project to work. Both of the Apache packages must be of the same version.

Testing the Web Server Locally

If you are running the X Window System, execute the Netscape program. It will display its default Web page. Enter the following:

```
http://127.0.0.1
```

You should see the "It Worked!" Web page that the default Apache server configuration displays. If you don't, you need to use rpm to remove the Apache Web server (rpm -e) and try installing it again. You can also try a reinstall of Red Hat Linux.

If you are not running the X Window System on your Linux server, log on to a console and enter the following command:

```
lynx http://127.0.0.1
```

This brings up a text version of the "It Worked!" Web page if your Apache Web server is functioning properly. If not, remove Apache and reinstall.

Testing the Web Server from Another Computer

Testing from the network is much like testing from the X Window System. Run Internet Explorer (IE) or Netscape on your Windows machine. Enter the URL as follows:

```
http://lin
```

The browser will contact the server and display the default page. The top line of the page will declare "It Worked!"

If you don't get this page, you can get an HTTP/1.1 404 Not Found error. You can also get an "Unable to locate the server" type of message.

The 404 error message indicated that you were able to communicate with the server, but it did not have the page you were asking for. This indicates your Web server is working, but has configuration problems.

The unable to locate the server message indicates that you have not entered a name the Web browser was able to turn into an IP address. Check the following things:

- Your `c:\windows\hosts` file can have errors in it, or not exist.
- Check the spelling of the machine name in the browser URL line.
- Check the spelling of the machine name in the hosts file.
- Check the IP address on your Linux machine to make sure it matches the address in the hosts file.

sendmail

The sendmail system provides the ability to send and receive mail.

Verifying sendmail Installation

To verify that you have sendmail installed, run the `rpm` query command.

```
[root@winbook root]# rpm -q sendmail
sendmail-8.9.3-15
```

If it does not show information similar to this, you need to install sendmail from the Red Hat CD. Any version of sendmail will work. However, if you want to use your server on the Internet, you need to use version 8.9.3 or greater.

Previous versions have some implementation shortfalls. These versions can allow people to send unwanted email to others, using your machine as a relay. This is true even if you had configured those versions of sendmail not to be a relay.

A *relay* is a machine that is given mail to deliver to someone else. The machine requesting delivery of the mail can then disappear from the Internet. This leaves system operators upset at you if the mail delivered to them is Unsolicited Commercial Email, or UCE for short.

A *smart SMTP host* is a machine that can deliver mail with no other assistance. The sendmail package turns your Linux machine into a smart SMTP host.

sendmail is also known as a Mail Transport Agent (MTA).

Y2K stands for Year 2000.

Here is how a relay works: Mail client software is configured such that it knows your server is a smart SMTP host. Many email messages are created, and the client hands off each one to your server. Your sendmail program then delivers each one of the messages to their final destination. This could occur long after the client software has disconnected from your server.

This is the source of the massive amount of UCE being distributed over the Internet. It is the Y2K version of Post Office-delivered advertisements, also known as junk mail. It has been referred to by a well-known canned meat product name, in spite of objections by that company, some in the form of legal actions. Personally, I don't blame them. Regardless of their objections, *spam* is popularly used to describe junk email.

If your MTA is responsible for sending UCE to servers across the world, you will find your machine blacklisted.

 If your machine is used as a relay too often, you will find that, after awhile, no one will accept any mail from you. This is known as *blacklisting*. You need to run the latest software and have it properly configured!

If you find yourself blacklisted, you can have an expert fix your installation, and ask that your machine be removed from the black list. One of the most used lists is at `http://maps.vix.com`. It is called MAPS, or the Real Time Blacklist (RBL).

sendmail Configuration

You must configure your sendmail to accept mail for relay from clients you approve. You also must configure sendmail to receive messages directed to your machine. Let's do that.

First, for the Red Hat install of sendmail in release 6.0 or greater, the two configuration files we will edit are

```
/etc/sendmail.cw
/etc/mail/access
```

In the `sendmail.cw` file, you need to put the names by which your machine will be known. One name goes on one line.

```
lin
lin.mydomain.com
```

In our case, we are only interested in mail that is delivered to machine lin. We will use our fictitious domain `mydomain.com`.

If your hostname as reported by the hostname program is not `lin.mydomain.com`, run `linuxconf` in the X Window System and set the hostname. Or edit the file `/etc/sysconfig/network` and change the line that starts with `HOSTNAME=` to look like this:

```
HOSTNAME=lin.mydomain.com
```

This will cause Red Hat to pick up the correct hostname the next time you reboot the machine. You can temporarily set the hostname for your machine by running the following command:

```
hostname lin.mydomain.com
```

Now we move on to the /etc/mail/access file. This file governs who can relay through your server. It can also reject email from machines or networks from which you do not want to receive mail. These machines can be sources of UCE, or perhaps you simply don't like the people who send mail from those machines.

Bring up the access file in an editor. Modify it so it is similar to the following printout:

```
# Check the /usr/doc/sendmail-8.9.3/README.cf file for a description
# of the format of this file. (search for access_db in that file)
# The /usr/doc/sendmail-8.9.3/README.cf is part of the sendmail-doc
# package.
#
# by default we allow relaying from localhost...
localhost.localdomain        RELAY
localhost                    RELAY
127.0.0.1                    RELAY
```

You can also add a domain to the relay command. Specific machines, users, or networks can be rejected. In the following example, the user LoansForYou cannot send mail to your machine. That user is rejected. The network 192.168.12.0 is rejected, as well as any messages from the domain badmail.com. The machine mail1.foofoo.com, and the specific address 192.168.22.22 are both rejected.

```
LoansForYou@ REJECT
mail1.foofoo.com REJECT
192.168.12 REJECT
badmail.com REJECT
192.168.22.22 REJECT
```

Modify the access file to include your Linux and Windows machine names. If you need to allow other machines on the network as a test, add your network address also. Here is how your access file should look:

```
lin.mydomain.com             RELAY
win.mydomain.com             RELAY
172.16.13                    RELAY
localhost.localdomain        RELAY
localhost                    RELAY
127.0.0.1                    RELAY
```

After modifying the access file, you must restart sendmail. The process of doing this rebuilds the database file access.db from the information in the access text file. Run the following commands:

```
[root@lin root]# /etc/rc.d/init.d/sendmail stop
```

Output

```
Shutting down sendmail:                                    [  OK  ]
[root@lin root]# /etc/rc.d/init.d/sendmail start
Starting sendmail:                                         [  OK  ]
```

If sendmail takes a very long time to start or appears hung, you probably have not entered your IP address and hostname information in the /etc/hosts file. Also, sendmail needs the information in the sendmail.cw file to be properly presented. Either one of these will prevent its operation.

To verify sendmail is running, use the ps command:

```
[root@lin root]# ps ax | grep sendmail
```

Output

```
  883 ?          S        0:00 sendmail: accepting connections on port 25
```

If you don't have a printout similar to this, go over the setup again. Verify the name and IP address information in the /etc/hosts file and in the sendmail.cw file.

With non-private Internet domain and IP settings in the files just covered, sendmail can send mail to anyone over the Internet. It can also receive mail for delivery to anyone on your Linux machine. With the UCE rejection measures available to you by editing the access file, you can keep undesired mail to a minimum.

The final part of the configuration is setting the startup scripts so Sendmail will automatically run at boot time. In an Xterm, run the setup command.

This command can be run in any kind of terminal. If you are using a non-graphic terminal, the printout will appear as follows. Graphic or color terminals improve the display, but the point is that you can run this command from any machine, even across the network.

Output

```
Text Mode Setup Utility 1.2                    (C) 1999 Red Hat Software


          Pick a Tool
          Authentication configuration
          Keyboard configuration
          Mouse configuration
          System services
          Sound card configuration
          Timezone configuration
          X configuration
```

```
        Run Tool      Quit

<Tab>/<Alt-Tab> between elements  |    Use <Enter> to edit a selection
```

Use the arrow keys to select the System services line, and press Enter.

Testing sendmail

To test the sendmail installation, telnet to the SMTP port, which is port 25. You should see Sendmail respond with a sign-on banner. Then enter the `ehlo` `mydomain.com` greeting and see it respond:

```
[root@lin root]# telnet lin 25
```

Output

```
Trying 172.16.13.70...
Connected to lin.
Escape character is '^]'.
220 lin.mydomain.com ESMTP Sendmail 8.9.3/8.9.3; Thu, 9 Mar 2000 07:11:38 -0600
ehlo mydomain.com
250-lin.mydomain.com Hello IDENT:root@lin [172.16.13.70], pleased to meet you
250-EXPN
250-VERB
250-8BITMIME
250-SIZE
250-DSN
250-ONEX
250-ETRN
250-XUSR
250 HELP
quit
221 lin.mydomain.com closing connection
Connection closed by foreign host.
```

The sign-on banner gives you the hostname and the sendmail version number. Verify these are what you expect. The response to the `ehlo` command gives an indication of what services sendmail can provide. If you see a list similar to the previous one, sendmail is ready.

GNU C/C++ Compiler

Two version of the GNU c/c++ compiler exist. The standard one installed with Red Hat is the egcs compiler. It is a fairly new rewrite of their old standby, gcc.

Both the gcc and the egcs compilers are of high quality. Either one can be used for our project. I assume you have the egcs compiler installed. If you don't, don't worry about it. The project will work exactly the same way.

Verifying GNU C/C++ Installation

To verify the installation of the compiler, bring up a terminal window and enter the following:

```
[root@lin root]# gcc
gcc: No input files
```

The egcs compiler is a bit terse in some circumstances. If you enter gcc --help, you will get over a screen full of information. To find the version of egcs you are using, run the rpm query command. Your version should be the same as mine or higher:

```
[root@lin root]# rpm -q egcs
egcs-1.1.2-24
```

Testing the Compiler

To verify the compiler is working as you expect, you need to create a small file and compile it. Use the "Hello World!" example found in beginning C instruction manuals. Bring p a text editor, enter the following lines, and then save it as test.c.

```
#include <stdio.h>
main()
{
  printf("Hello World!\n");
}
```

Press Enter after the end of the last line. After saving the file, run the following commands to test the compiler and your work:

```
[root@lin root]# gcc test.c -o test
[root@lin root]# ./test
```

Output

```
Hello World!
```

The first time I tried this, I had misspelled stdlib.h as stlib.h. The compiler spit out an error message, and I had to try it again. If you get an error, look carefully at your typing and reread the previous example.

If you get the "Hello World!" printout, you are ready. You have now verified the compiler is properly installed and the basic libraries are installed and working.

If you enter the commands as shown, and get the response "bash: gcc: command not found", you don't have the compiler installed. If you get an error indicating a header file could not be found, or there was a library problem, you either have a damaged egcs or gcc install, or a damaged Red Hat installation.

If you get any of these errors, first try removing and installing the egcs package. If that does not work, I suggest redoing the Red Hat install, and selecting the development packages.

Optional Local Network Usage

I have already covered the basic information required to create a small network. If, however, you are connecting to an existing local network, you need to coordinate with the network administrator.

How to Connect to an Existing Local Area Network

The network administrator needs to assign you an IP address and a machine name. If you are part of an Internet domain, you need to obtain the domain name and put it in place of the `mydomain.com` you previously used. The administrator will know the network mask, the DNS server, and the default gateway.

If some other machines on the network do not run TCP/IP, you and the administrator must decide which of those will need to communicate to your server. Those will require additional protocol configuration and IP address assignments. This can be a very involved task.

Network Usage: Windows-Based Clients

The Windows environment comes with three standard utilities to use for this project—the Web browser, `ping`, and `telnet`. Internet Explorer is the default Web browser installed with Windows 98 or above. Netscape can also be used as your browser, but must be installed separately. The `telnet` and `ping` utilities are installed when you install the TCP/IP protocol.

You can use `telnet` to connect to the Linux server and run any command that you would run from a local xterm under the X Window System. You must connect to the Linux server as a normal individual and use the command `su -1` to become root before you are able to execute some commands.

In the previous sections, "Testing Your Network Connection," and "Testing Your Web Server," I covered the steps necessary to validate a network-based connection. After you are connected to an existing network, try performing these checks on your Windows machine.

When you have validated the Windows machine's connection, you are ready to continue with the IMP installation. After the IMP package is fully functional, you can use Internet Explorer or Netscape on your Windows machine to check your email.

Chapter 2

Obtaining the Software

If you want to follow this book exactly during the installation process, use the files specified by the chapters.

For example, later versions of PHP don't work with the version of IMP we are using, and later versions of IMP don't work with the version of PHP we are using. By using the versions specified in this book, you will keep on track with this project!

 Note   This book assumes you know how to install Red Hat Linux, or have it already installed. A good Linux installation and configuration guide is Red Hat Linux Installation and Configuration Handbook, by Duane Hellums, published by Que.

How to Obtain Red Hat 6.2

The Red Hat Linux software is available over the Internet. If you have a fast enough Internet connection, you can download Red Hat as a series of files, and install from your hard drive. You can also download the ISO image (which is an image of a CD-ROM) and use a CD-ROM writer to write the image to a blank CD-R (a recordable CD-ROM). You can then boot from this CD-ROM and install Linux.

Where to Purchase or Download

Your ability to purchase Linux on CD-ROM has been greatly expanded in the last two years. If you like "brick and mortar" stores, you can go to stores such as Best Buy, CompUSA, or Fry's. Call computer stores in your area to see whether they carry Linux.

Many online stores are available. A *very small* listing of sites that you can purchase from online is http://www.linuxmall.com, http://www.linuxcentral.com, http://www.redhat.com, or http://www.linuxdisk.com, which is a site my company runs. If you purchase directly from Red Hat, you get installation support directly from them.

If you want to download Linux free, Red Hat keeps a list of mirrors that carry their Linux distribution at http://www.redhat.com/download/mirror.html. My favorite sites are ftp.freesoftware.com, and ftp.redhat.com. A new site, http://www.linuxiso.org, might be a bit sluggish.

Currently, Compaq, Dell, and IBM either have or are working on programs that allow you to purchase Linux with their machines.

How to Obtain MySQL, PHP3, and IMP

If you will be following this book exactly, you need to have Red Hat Linux version 6.1 or 6.2 installed on your computer.

If you need to install onto other platforms, or you want to use the very latest software, you can download the software from the following locations:

Software	Location
MySQL	http://www.mysql.com
PHP	http://www.php.net
IMP	http://www.horde.org
RED HAT	ftp://ftp.freesoftware.com, ftp://ftp.redhat.com

When you attempt to download software from an online site, you may find a newer version of the software available. In most cases, you must use the versions of software described in this book and go through the installation procedures at least once using that software. After you have a successful install, you can attempt to upgrade to the next version of software. You may find the new software breaks the installation. Experience is the best teacher!

Required File List

Package File	Location
apache-1.3.12.i386.rpm	ftp.freesoftware.com
apache-devel-1.3.9-8.i386.rpm	ftp.freesoftware.com
freetype-devel-1.2-7.i386.rpm	ftp.freesoftware.com
freetype-1.2-7.i386.rpm	ftp.freesoftware.com
imap-4.7a-4.i386.rpm	ftp.freesoftware.com
imap-devel-4.7a-4.i386.rpm	ftp.freesoftware.com

Continued

Package File	Location
imap-utils-4.7a-4.i386.rpm	ftp://ftp.redhat.com (in contrib/libc6/i386/)
horde-1.0.11.tar.gz	http://www.horde.org
imp-2.0.11.tar.gz	http://www.horde.org
MySQL-3.22.32-1.i386.rpm	http://www.mysql.com
MySQL-client-3.22.32-1.i386.rpm	http://www.mysql.com
MySQL-devel-3.22.32-1.i386.rpm	http://www.mysql.com
MySQL-shared-3.22.32-1.i386.rpm	http://www.mysql.com
php-3.0.16.tar.gz	http://www.php.net

 Note

The Apache, freetype, and imap packages should be obtained from a Red Hat Linux CD-ROM, or downloaded from the Red Hat version 6.2 directory on ftp.freesoftware.com, or ftp.redhat.com. The versions of imap that I used came from the Red Hat 6.2 Linux installation CD-ROM.

If you need to use a Red Hat Linux CD-ROM, you can purchase one at http://www.linuxdisk.com, or pick one up from your local bookstore.

The version of Apache should be 1.3.12 or later. Versions before 1.3.12 have a small security vulnerability and should not be used for this project.

I gathered all the software packages and put them in an imp subdirectory in root's home directory. I recommend you put all your files in a directory of the same name. This will keep things organized, and will enable you to follow along with the examples in the book.

You are now ready to begin the installation of MySQL, PHP, and IMP. Have fun!

Chapter 3

MySQL

In this chapter, I will give you a good overview of MySQL and a brief overview of database design.

I will walk you through installing MySQL on your system. You will be installing the freely available RPM package file, version 3.22. Because MySQL is always improving and changing, I strongly recommend you install the 3.22 version. After your project is up and working, you can experiment with different versions of MySQL. Later versions might introduce some features that will cause problems with your project.

how too pro ñouns it	MySQL is officially pronounced "*my ess queue ell.*" It is not pronounced "*my sequel.*"

I will also introduce you to some database design concepts and give you some rules of thumb to use during database design and implementation. The concepts introduced will help you understand how IMP uses MySQL. (IMP uses MySQL to store user preference settings and an address book for each user.)

You will learn enough of MySQL to enable you to examine the tables and data that IMP uses on your machine. You will be given ideas to use in future enhancements of your system. As you work through these possible enhancements, you will be shown common problems in using MySQL and solutions to those problems.

A Brief History

MySQL started out as a tool to fulfill an internal requirement. The authors of MySQL wanted to use mSQL to connect to some tables using its very fast ISAM routines. However, mSQL turned out to be too slow. They started working on their own solution.

ISAM is short for *Indexed Sequential Access Method*. Very simply, and very briefly, the data is stored sequentially in a file on the disk, with one piece of data following another. The retrieval of the data is through an index that specifies the offset in the data file to begin retrieving the data. If done correctly, the data retrieval routines can be very fast.

Mini SQL is the name of the mSQL database engine. The mSQL engine can be found at `http://www.hughes.com.au/`. It is not free for commercial use. The license can be found in the mSQL download. If you are an educational institution, a non-commercial research institution, a registered charity, a registered not-for-profit institute, or a full-time student, you can use mSQL without payment.

The result was an interface that had an API very similar to mSQL. This allowed easy porting of third-party tools and code. The developers of MySQL have continued stretching MySQL. It now has many more features than mSQL, and is typically much faster. According to benchmarks at `http://www.mysql.com/information/benchmarks.html`, MySQL can be over 10 times faster than mSQL. You will find benchmarks on that page that compare MySQL to many other databases. It performs quite well on all platforms.

MySQL has grown in popularity over the years. It is a very fast database. It implements a subset of SQL, so it might not be suitable for all applications. For most applications it is more than sufficient.

MySQL is also changing. It is being constantly improved. If the version you obtain today does not do what you need, check on the MySQL to-do list, and their expected completion date. It might well be that the MySQL crew is implementing the features you need very soon.

Where the name MySQL came from is a mystery, even to the authors. The most visible driving force behind MySQL, Michael "Monty" Widenius, had a daughter named My. However, MySQL has been around a little longer than his daughter, so even they are not sure of the connection.

Regardless of the source of the name, MySQL is very dependable. It is very fast. I have not yet had a loss of data because of MySQL in three years of use. I would be willing to use it in a mission-critical application. I have read some comments on the Web that indicate you should shut down and restart MySQL about once a month on heavily trafficked sites.

What Is MySQL?

MySQL is a database engine that supports the SQL database query language. SQL is a standardized way of talking to databases of any sort, regardless of the underlying methods of saving and retrieving data.

SQL is pronounced multiple ways. I have seen colleges teach it pronounced *sequel*, and I have read books written by early pioneers of databases insist that it is pronounced *ess-queue-ell*.

I tend to pronounce it *ess-queue-ell*, because the MySQL creators pronounce each letter. I have found that everyone knows what I mean when I pronounce the letters. Some give me questioning looks when I say *sequel*.

MySQL saves the database in files on your hard drive. For best performance, these files must exist on a local hard drive. If you share drives across a network and place your database files on those drives, you will pay a significant performance penalty.

For your IMP project, you should put the database files on the same machine as the MySQL server. The load that IMP puts on the database is very small, but existing network traffic can cause remote drive access to be very slow.

MySQL can support large databases. The creators of MySQL are using databases as large as 50 million records. A maximum file size limit under Linux's ext2 file system is about 2GB. Therefore, each database is limited to 2GB when running on that file system. Future file systems for Linux will probably lift this limitation.

With your project, the 2GB limit allows for several tens of thousands of users. This is because of a good database design. IMP is well thought out in terms of data storage requirements.

MySQL Description

MySQL is a database server. It is fully multithreaded using kernel threads.

The term *multithreaded* refers to the capability to divide a job into small pieces to work on. Each piece is called a *thread*. Each thread can operate independently of other threads. When an application uses kernel threads on a multiple CPU machine, it can put some work off onto other CPUs for simultaneous execution. The term *CPU* is a brief way of referring to the processor, such as an Intel Pentium processor or an AMD K6 processor, the main computation unit in your computer.

MySQL has a robust API set supporting multiple programming languages. The languages supported are C, C++, Eiffel, Java, Perl, PHP, Python, and TCL. IMP uses the PHP API to communicate with MySQL.

API is short for *Application Programming Interface*. The MySQL API provides a short list of routines you can call within a program to talk to the database to save data to it or retrieve information from it. An API can be written for any type of server or operating system. For instance, the Apache Web server has a set of APIs for people who write Apache modules.

MySQL works on multiple platforms. The operating systems supported so far are as follows:

- AIX 4.x
- BSDI 2.x
- BSDI 3.0, 3.1, and 4.x
- DEC UNIX 4.x
- FreeBSD 2.x
- FreeBSD 3.x
- HP-UX 10.20
- HP-UX 11.x
- Linux 2.0+
- NetBSD 1.3/1.4 Intel and NetBSD 1.3 Alpha
- OpenBSD
- OS/2 Warp 3
- OS/2 Warp 4
- SGI Irix 6.x
- Solaris 2.5, 2.6, and 2.7 on SPARC and x86
- SunOS 4.x
- SCO OpenServer
- SCO UnixWare 7.0.1
- Tru64 Unix
- Win95
- Win98
- NT

 Note

The Win95, Win98, and NT versions of MySQL version 3.22 require licenses for use. A shareware version of MySQL (version 3.22.30) has been released for a "try before buy" experience. MySQL 3.23 does not have these restrictions because it is released under the GPL license.

Read your Microsoft license agreement carefully. You might be prohibited from running MySQL on Win95, Win98, and NT workstation if more than 10 users are able to connect simultaneously.

Because IMP uses MySQL, PHP, and JavaScript, it can be installed on the platforms that support both MySQL and PHP running under a Web server. The user can be on any machine that hosts a browser capable of running JavaScript.

MySQL supports many data types. The supported data types include signed and unsigned integers in lengths of 1, 2, 3, 4, and 8 bytes. Other data types supported are floating-point numbers, variable character data, text fields, and binary data sets (called *BLOBs*). Also supported are date, time, and year fields. Two interesting data types supported are SET and ENUM fields. These types enable you to create lists of data that are stored in fields in the database.

You can have up to 16 indexes per table. *Indexes* are special lookup tables that MySQL maintains. Indexes enable you to get to data without having to do a row by row search for the data. In a large database, indexes can mean the difference between a very fast application and a disaster. You can use up to 16 columns or parts of columns for each index. Normally, MySQL uses a length of 256 bytes for each index. When creating a table, you can explicitly specify an index using fewer bytes.

All columns are created with default values with MySQL. You can use INSERT to insert a subset of values into columns. The columns you set to Null or leave out of the INSERT are set to their default values.

MySQL enables you to join tables into pseudo tables for efficient lookup of data. This is done using what is described as "an optimized one-sweep multijoin."

Under MySQL, the SQL statements SELECT and WHERE can have mathematical operators. They can also include functions. You can also mix tables from different databases in the same query.

If not being run using the --ansi flag, MySQL treats the || symbol as an OR, rather than the ANSI SQL concatenate feature. Instead, you use the CONCAT() function.

Here is an example to demonstrate some of the elements I have described. To print the first, middle, and last names for all people with monthly incomes greater than $3,000.00 and older than 29 years of age you could run this statement from the mysql command-line utility:

```
mysql> SELECT CONCAT(FirstName," ",MiddleI," ",LastName)
mysql> FROM TheNameTable WHERE AnnualIncome/12 > 3000 AND Age >= 30;
```

MySQL fully supports SQL GROUP BY and ORDER BY clauses. The group functions AVG(), COUNT(), COUNT(DISTINCT), MAX(), MIN(), STD(), and SUM() are supported. Also included is ODBC and ANSI SQL syntax for LEFT OUTER JOIN.

MySQL has a privilege and password system based on system tables. This system is very flexible and requires some thought to implement more than simple rules. You can allow only certain users from certain machines to connect. The allowed users can be denied connection from other machines. Certain machines can be denied altogether, including the local machine. It is possible to lock your running programs out of the MySQL database if you get the permissions wrong.

You might find you have locked yourself out of MySQL during installation of IMP. I have done that myself. Don't worry! There is a way to get into the MySQL database, even if you have locked yourself out using the permissions tables.

If you start the `mysqld` server using the `--skip-grant-tables` command-line option, everyone is allowed access to all tables without passwords. This lets you fix the grant tables in the mysql database. You then restart the server to apply the new permissions.

MySQL fully supports the ISO-8859-1 Latin1 character set. This allows you to insert foreign language character sets into the database or into table names. All comparisons for normal string columns are not case sensitive. The sort order is also in the ISO-8859-1 Latin1 character set, although you can change that.

A few miscellaneous features are worth mentioning. MySQL also supports aliases on tables and columns. The row affecting commands (`DELETE`, `INSERT`, `REPLACE`, and `UPDATE`) returns the number of rows affected. You can also name a table the same name as a function. This requires that you not put a space between the function name and the parenthesis that follows it. For example: `ABS()` will work and `ABS ()` will not work, if you have a table or column named ABS. Finally, MySQL can return error messages in many languages.

EXCURSION

You Should Not Use Confusing Features

Even though MySQL enables you to use function names as table names, you should not use this feature unless absolutely necessary. I have strong opinions about this from my 20 plus years of experience. Do not use confusing features!

I saw an email tagline that I loved. It said "eschew obfuscation." That is proper English. I had to use a dictionary to understand it. The term means, in its simplest form, "avoid making things hard to understand." The colloquial term is "Keep It Simple, Stupid" (KISS).

If I had not explained the above tagline, most of the population would not have understood it without going to a dictionary. When you design tables and databases and write programs, make them as simple and understandable as possible. This will help you months or years later when you must make changes.

With the power available to today's computer, it is reasonable to make the computer do most of the work, not the programmer. When you optimize for speed, only 10% of your program will need to be optimized. So, make everything you do crystal clear, even if there is another, more clever way to do it. Clever ways have a tendency to be hard to understand when a problem occurs and you are under pressure to fix the problem.

As you examine the IMP database structure, you will find the creators of IMP followed this tenet. The IMP database is a very simple database.

How It Works

The MySQL database server consists of a daemon that waits on a predetermined TCP/IP port for a client request. When a request comes in on that port, Linux runs the MySQL daemon.

 A *daemon* is the name of a program that runs in the background. The Linux operating system has a program scheduler that checks to see which programs need to run for a little bit of time. This time period is typically in slices of 1/100th of a second (also called 10 milliseconds). That means that Linux checks for what software needs to execute 100 times a second.

how too pro ñouns it

Reality is different from academia. I suspect that *daemon* needs to be pronounced with a long *a* sound, but every use of the word I have heard uses a long *e* sound. The dictionary backs this up, proclaiming daemon is a variant of *demon*, and gives the same pronunciation.

When a program needs to run, it is given a minimum of 10 milliseconds to execute. A well-designed 300MHz-Pentium system can execute around 100,000 computer instructions in 10 milliseconds.

Daemons are not allowed to run unless they need to do something. The *process list* is the list of daemons that the operating system has in its scheduler. The ps command gives information about the list of processes.

A TCP/IP port is a number tacked onto the end of a TCP/IP address. A real-world analogy is a suite number at an office building. If your mail is addressed to 1111 Office Blvd., Suite 3303, the mail is first delivered to your building. Then it is delivered to suite 3303. The 1111 is analogous to the TCP/IP address, and the suite is analogous to the port number. You have 65,536 possible ports available at every TCP/IP address under the IPV4 protocol.

After the MySQL daemon is executing, it holds a small dialog with the client. The client is authenticated against the MySQL authentication database. If the client is authorized, MySQL handles the request and feeds the requested data to the client. To free up the initial port to accept further requests, MySQL and the client program negotiate another port number on which to continue their conversation. After that port number is in use, the original port number is available for another connection.

You can use the ps command to determine if MySQL is running. The command ps ax | grep mysql should show you four processes running under Linux. The first one shown is the safe_mysql script that starts the server. One process shown is the one used by the Linux thread manager. Another process is to service connections from clients. The last process is to handle alarms and signals.

Whenever a program requests services from MySQL, it contacts MySQL through the network software layer, even if no physical network connection exists to the computer. When the connection stays on the local machine, it is often done through Unix sockets, which don't go through the network card drivers. The requesting program is called a *client*. The program being asked for a service is called a *server*.

MySQL reads and writes files to store its data. This means that copying all the data files to another storage device will totally back up your database. Note that the MySQL server must be shut down to do this. A raw disk storage system is under development. This storage system would not store data in files, and would require another backup method.

For your project, the simplest approach is to use a `cron` job to shut down the `mysqld` server in the early hours, copy the database file to the backup device, and then restart the `mysqld` server. The best way to shut down `mysqld` with `cron` is to use the system `init` script as follows:

```
/etc/rc.d/init.d/mysql stop
```

What It Does for You

MySQL hides the mechanics of the database storage mechanism from you. You interface to the database through the standardized SQL interface. There are very few SQL commands to learn. After you learn these commands, you can write database query applications that work regardless of the underlying database.

If you are careful to use only the SQL standard commands, the portability of your application is very high. I have used my knowledge of SQL to query databases from Informix, Oracle, Microsoft, and MySQL without having to worry about which database was running at the time.

All database engines extend the SQL standard slightly. If you study the documented extensions, you can make notes of what to avoid if portability is your main concern. Otherwise, the extensions are there to make your life easier. Don't be afraid to use them if portability is not your main goal.

Getting Online Help for MySQL

Every application in the MySQL suite responds to the `--help` command-line syntax. For example, running the command `mysql --help` prints out the list of command-line switches available to you.

Help is also available through the World Wide Web. If you go to `http://www.mysql.com`, you will find a documentation link. This link takes you to online Web pages that provide full documentation for MySQL. The Web pages are a bit terse at times, but every time I have checked on something the information there is correct.

The MySQL Web site also has links to several mailing lists. These mailing lists include people who understand MySQL, along with people just like you who are learning more about MySQL. These are an excellent source of help.

Installation

To prepare for installation, make sure you have plenty of room on your root partition. When you install MySQL server rpm, MySQL client rpm, MySQL shared rpm, and the MySQL development rpm, it requires over 26MB of space.

In addition to the space MySQL needs, the database files themselves require room. The default database storage directory is /var/lib/mysql. In that directory, you will find files and directories. The database files are stored in directories.

If you have a partition on which you want to store the database files, you will need to do some work after install. I will cover moving the entire MySQL database files to a new location after installation.

Installing the RPM

Copy all the MySQL rpm files into one directory. Run the rpm install command with all the MySQL rpms listed, putting a space between each one. You will get a printout similar to Listing 3.1.

Listing 3.1   Initial MySQL Installation

```
[root@winbook imp]# rpm -i MySQL-3.22.32-1.i386.rpm MySQL-client-3.22.32-1.i386.
rpm MySQL-shared-3.22.32-1.i386.rpm MySQL-devel-3.22.32-1.i386.rpm
Creating db table
Creating host table
Creating user table
Creating func table
Creating tables_priv table
Creating columns_priv table

PLEASE REMEMBER TO SET A PASSWORD FOR THE MySQL root USER !
This is done with:
/usr/bin/mysqladmin -u root password 'new-password'
See the manual for more instructions.

Please report any problems with the /usr/bin/mysqlbug script!

The latest information about MySQL is available on the web at http://www.mysql.c
om
Support MySQL by buying support/licenses at http://www.tcx.se/license.htmy.

Starting mysqld daemon with databases from /var/lib/mysql
[root@winbook imp]#
```

Now select a password for the root user. The root user has full access to MySQL by default. The initial password for the root user is blank. Choose something you will not forget and that is difficult for other people to guess. For this book, I'll be using the password mypass. It is a terrible password and should not be used under any circumstance.

Run the command as shown. Note that MySQL does not prompt you to re-enter the password. You must get it right the first time!

```
[root@winbook /root]# mysqladmin -u root password 'mypass'
```

A Quick Test of the Install

Three things must be done to verify that MySQL installed correctly. First, run the rpm query (rpm -qa) command and make sure all the packages installed. Because I want to see all the packages installed, I have rpm dump the entire list and then grep for the packages I want. I use the search option -i, which is not case sensitive.

```
[root@winbook /root]# rpm -qa | grep -i mysql
```

Ouput

```
MySQL-3.22.32-1
MySQL-client-3.22.32-1
MySQL-shared-3.22.32-1
MySQL-devel-3.22.32-1
```

After this checks out, I look to see that the mysql daemons are running. I run the ps commmand with the ax command-line switch, and grep for mysql. You should get a printout similar to the following:

```
[root@winbook /root]# ps ax | grep -i mysql
```

Output

```
  529 ?        S      0:00 sh /usr/bin/safe_mysqld --user=mysql \pid-file=/var/
  563 ?        SN     0:00 /usr/sbin/mysqld --basedir=/ --datadir=/var/lib/mysql
  621 ?        SN     0:00 /usr/sbin/mysqld --basedir=/ --datadir=/var/lib/mysql
  622 ?        SN     0:00 /usr/sbin/mysqld --basedir=/ --datadir=/var/lib/mysql
```

Finally, I run the mysql command-line program and take a look at the mysql database. The mysql database contains information about permissions and other databases in the system.

```
[root@winbook /root]# mysql mysql
```

Output

```
ERROR 1045: Access denied for user: 'root@localhost' (Using password: NO)
[root@winbook /root]# mysql -pmypass mysql
Reading table information for completion of table and column names
You can turn off this feature to get a quicker startup with -A

Welcome to the MySQL monitor.  Commands end with ; or \g.
Your MySQL connection id is 5 to server version: 3.22.32
```

```
Type 'help' for help.

mysql>
```

The first time I attempted to use the `mysql` program, I got an error message because I did not enter the password. If you don't get an error message, it is because you did not set a password! The second time, I entered the password and it let me in. Note the password is entered immediately after the `-p` option with no spaces in between.

Now, show the table information. You must put a semicolon (;) at the end of every command. This signals to MySQL that you are finished entering the command, and to begin acting upon that command. If you press Enter before putting in a semicolon, simply enter the semicolon on the next line and then press Enter:

```
mysql> show tables;
```

Output

```
+-----------------+
| Tables in mysql |
+-----------------+
| columns_priv    |
| db              |
| func            |
| host            |
| tables_priv     |
| user            |
+-----------------+
6 rows in set (0.00 sec)

mysql>
```

 Note

The `mysql` program allows commands to span multiple lines. You usually let the `mysql` program know that you are ready for it to interpret the command line(s) just entered by entering a semicolon as the last character in the line before pressing Enter. You can also use `\G` or `\g` as the signal to the `mysql` program to interpret the command line(s). These endings format the output a different way when using the `mysql` program.

The `mysql` utility also uses the `readline` library. This library enables the up arrow and down arrow keys to be used to recall previously entered command lines. These lines can be edited using the right and left arrow keys to move the cursor. After you press Enter, the new line is entered into the `readline` buffer and handed to the `mysql` program for interpretation.

When you use SQL statements in PHP, do not use the semicolon to signal the end of the statement. If you do, you will get an error. The semicolon is only used by the `mysql` utility to tell it to start processing your command.

You can show information from all the tables in the mysql database. The most interesting table in a new mysql database is the user table (see Listing 3.2). Let's look at the columns in the user table:

Listing 3.2   MySQL System User Table

```
mysql> show columns from user;
+-----------------+----------------+------+-----+---------+-------+
| Field           | Type           | Null | Key | Default | Extra |
+-----------------+----------------+------+-----+---------+-------+
| Host            | char(60)       |      | PRI |         |       |
| User            | char(16)       |      | PRI |         |       |
| Password        | char(16)       |      |     |         |       |
| Select_priv     | enum('N','Y')  |      |     | N       |       |
| Insert_priv     | enum('N','Y')  |      |     | N       |       |
| Update_priv     | enum('N','Y')  |      |     | N       |       |
| Delete_priv     | enum('N','Y')  |      |     | N       |       |
| Create_priv     | enum('N','Y')  |      |     | N       |       |
| Drop_priv       | enum('N','Y')  |      |     | N       |       |
| Reload_priv     | enum('N','Y')  |      |     | N       |       |
| Shutdown_priv   | enum('N','Y')  |      |     | N       |       |
| Process_priv    | enum('N','Y')  |      |     | N       |       |
| File_priv       | enum('N','Y')  |      |     | N       |       |
| Grant_priv      | enum('N','Y')  |      |     | N       |       |
| References_priv | enum('N','Y')  |      |     | N       |       |
| Index_priv      | enum('N','Y')  |      |     | N       |       |
| Alter_priv      | enum('N','Y')  |      |     | N       |       |
+-----------------+----------------+------+-----+---------+-------+
17 rows in set (0.00 sec)

mysql>
```

The user table has many columns. The column names are fairly obvious. This table controls most of the ability to access this database system. For now, let's look at the first four columns for all the rows in the database:

```
mysql> select host,user,password,select_priv from user;
```

Output

```
+-----------+------+------------------+-------------+
| host      | user | password         | select_priv |
+-----------+------+------------------+-------------+
| localhost | root | 6f8c114b58f2ce9e | Y           |
| winbook   | root |                  | Y           |
| localhost |      |                  | N           |
| winbook   |      |                  | N           |
+-----------+------+------------------+-------------+
4 rows in set (0.00 sec)

mysql>
```

Briefly, the root user can access the database from the localhost (on loopback address 127.0.0.1) using a password. If the root user accesses the database from the winbook host, no password is needed.

 Note

> Even though winbook and localhost are the same machine in this case, any command-line invocations of programs use the loopback adapter by default. This means that you will always require a password to access MySQL. However, if someone is able to spoof and pretend they are coming from the winbook host, MySQL does not require a password.
>
> To fix this problem, you need to run mysql as root and enter an update command where you update the password for all occurrences of the root user:
>
> ```
> mysql> select Host,User,Password from user;
> ```
>
> **Output**
>
> ```
> +-----------+--------+------------------+
> | Host      | User   | Password         |
> +-----------+--------+------------------+
> | localhost | root   | 6f8c114b58f2ce9e |
> | winbook   | root   |                  |
> | localhost |        |                  |
> | winbook   |        |                  |
> | localhost | impmgr | 5567401602cd5ddd |
> +-----------+--------+------------------+
> 5 rows in set (0.00 sec)
>
> mysql> UPDATE user SET Password=PASSWORD('mypass') where User='root';
> Query OK, 1 row affected (0.12 sec)
> Rows matched: 2  Changed: 1  Warnings: 0
> mysql> select Host,User,Password from user where User='root';
> +-----------+------+------------------+
> | Host      | User | Password         |
> +-----------+------+------------------+
> | localhost | root | 6f8c114b58f2ce9e |
> | winbook   | root | 6f8c114b58f2ce9e |
> +-----------+------+------------------+
> 2 rows in set (0.01 sec)
> ```

The root user also has select privilege to databases. Any other user has no select privilege, whether coming from the localhost or from the winbook host. If you examine the rest of the columns in the user table, you will see that root has full privileges, and other users have no privileges. This is the default security setup for MySQL.

To exit the mysql command-line utility, enter **quit** and press Enter. For some reason, no semicolon is needed at the end of this command.

Troubleshooting the Install

I have never had the MySQL install fail unless I was installing it on an early version of an operating system. If you attempt to install this on a stock Red Hat 5.x system then MySQL might very well not work. If you must do this, be sure to upgrade your glibc package. If this library is too far out of date, MySQL will not function.

The other possibility for an install failure is lack of disk space. You must have plenty of room in the partition that holds the /usr and /var directories. If you don't then MySQL might install, but fail to work properly. I strongly recommend that you have 100MB of free disk space in the partition that holds the /var/lib/mysql directory after you have installed MySQL. If you don't you might have a surprise failure after a short time, unless you monitor your disk usage carefully.

Configuration for Use with IMP

You can configure MySQL by hand, or you can use the script that the IMP software package includes. I will show you how to configure MySQL for IMP by hand, and then I will show you how to do it using the script. To get to the MySQL script, you must unpack the IMP tarball.

As you go through this exercise, if you make a mistake, you can use the SQL DROP command to drop the table or database you created. You can then start over. Please don't DROP any table in the mysql database. Don't DROP the mysql database! If you do, you will have to reinstall MySQL!

First, let's look at the disk storage issue. I have decided I want to store the MySQL database files in the /home partition because I have plenty of free space on that partition. Because I won't have many users who can log in through telnet or secure shell on this machine, it is safe to do this.

Before you move things around, you need to stop MySQL. When you installed the rpm, an init script was stored in the /etc/rc.d/init.d directory. It is called mysql. It is a convention for all init scripts to obey the commands start and stop. Most also obey the restart command. So, to stop the MySQL server, run the following:

```
[root@winbook imp-2.0.11]# /etc/rc.d/init.d/mysql stop
Killing mysqld with pid 622
```

The script will always respond with the process ID of the mysqld server. It also places a message in an error log file in the data directory. The logfile name is made up of the local machine's hostname, obtained by running the hostname command, with .err tacked on the end. If you run cat on the .err file in the /var/lib/mysql directory, you will see the startup and shutdown of the MySQL server:

```
[root@winbook mysql]# ls /var/lib/mysql
```

Output

```
mysql  test  winbook.err
[root@winbook mysql]# cat /var/lib/mysql/winbook.err
mysqld started on  Sat Mar 18 08:31:42 CST 2000
/usr/sbin/mysqld: ready for connections
000318  8:31:57  /usr/sbin/mysqld: Normal shutdown

000318  8:31:57  /usr/sbin/mysqld: Shutdown Complete

mysqld ended on  Sat Mar 18 08:31:57 CST 2000
```

Now that MySQL is stopped, you will move the database directory to where you want it.
Linux will not allow you to move directories across file systems. Therefore, you must copy
the directory. If you use the -a command-line option for cp, it will preserve permissions
and directory structure. Follow these commands, and notice the results in Listing 3.3.

Listing 3.3 Moving MySQL's Database To Another Location

```
[root@winbook lib]# cd /var/lib
[root@winbook lib]# cp -a mysql /home/mysql
[root@winbook lib]# ls /home
Office51  httpd  lost+found  maxfield  mysql  root
[root@winbook lib]# ls /home/mysql
mysql  test  winbook.err
[root@winbook lib]# ls -l /home
total 36
drwxr-xr-x  26 root      root       4096 Feb 18 16:26 Office51
drwxr-xr-x   5 root      root       4096 Feb 28 18:11 httpd
drwxr-xr-x   2 root      root      16384 Feb 18 12:38 lost+found
drwx------  12 maxfield maxfield   4096 Mar  7 19:23 maxfield
drwxr-xr-x   4 mysql     root       4096 Mar 18 08:31 mysql
drwxrwx---  26 root      root       4096 Mar 19  2000 root
[root@winbook lib]# pwd
/var/lib
[root@winbook lib]# mv mysql mysql.old
[root@winbook lib]# ln -s /home/mysql mysql
ls[root@winbook lib]# ls
cddb  dosemu  games  mysql  mysql.old  nfs  rpm  slocate  svgalib  texmf  xkb
[root@winbook lib]# ls -l mysql
lrwxrwxrwx   1 root      root         11 Mar 18 10:14 mysql -> /home/mysql
[root@winbook lib]# cd mysql
[root@winbook mysql]# ls -l
total 12
drwx--x--x   2 mysql     root       4096 Mar 18 11:14 mysql
drwxr-xr-x   2 mysql     root       4096 Mar 18 11:14 test
-rw-r--r--   1 root      root        960 Mar 18 08:31 winbook.err
[root@winbook mysql]# pwd
/var/lib/mysql
[root@winbook mysql]# df .
Filesystem          1k-blocks     Used Available Use% Mounted on
/dev/hda7             7178940  1101984   5712284  16% /home
[root@winbook mysql]#
```

What happened? First, I copied the mysql data directory, which is under /var/lib/ to the /home directory, using the -a option. Then I made sure it was there, with the proper permissions. After that was verified, I made sure I was still in the /var/lib directory, and moved the mysql directory to mysql.old. If I make a mistake, I still have the original directory. I then created a soft link to the new mysql data directory, and did a cd to that directory. I verified that directory was indeed on the /home partition by using the df command.

If you have plenty of room on your root partition, you don't have to do this. If you have a partition mounted under a directory other than /home that you would like to put the data directory on, you can use it instead.

Finally, if you want to create an /etc/my.cnf file or modify the safe_mysql startup script to place the data directory elsewhere, you can. However, this can require modifying MySQL every time you upgrade it, and at the least requires additional study. It is a matter of personal taste. I believe in the motto "If it ain't broke, don't fix it." I recommend you become familiar with MySQL's default behavior before you take any such action.

To start MySQL after you have moved the database, enter the following:

```
[root@winbook /root]# /etc/rc.d/init.d/mysql start
[root@winbook /root]# Starting mysqld daemon with databases from /var/lib/mysql

[root@winbook /root]# ps ax | grep my
```

Output

```
 1145 pts/1    S       0:00 sh /usr/bin/safe_mysqld --user=mysql \pid-file=/var/
 1162 pts/1    SN      0:00 /usr/sbin/mysqld --basedir=/ --datadir=/var/lib/mysql
 1164 pts/1    SN      0:00 /usr/sbin/mysqld --basedir=/ --datadir=/var/lib/mysql
 1165 pts/1    SN      0:00 /usr/sbin/mysqld --basedir=/ --datadir=/var/lib/mysql
[root@winbook /root]#
```

You will have to press Enter after the "Starting …" message is displayed. Running the ps command gives you total assurance that MySQL has started. You can check the error file in the /var/lib/mysql directory for a final cross check.

Now that MySQL is started, run the mysql command-line utility and start creating the IMP database.

```
[root@winbook /root]# mysql -pmypass mysql
```

Output

```
mysql> INSERT INTO user ( host, user, password )
    ->     VALUES (
    ->         'localhost',
    ->         'impmgr',
    ->         password( 'impmgr' )
    ->     );
Query OK, 1 row affected (0.45 sec)
```

This SQL statement created a row in the user database that allows the `impmgr` user access. The password for `impmgr` is `impmgr`.

```
mysql> INSERT INTO db (
    ->      host, db, user,
    ->         Select_priv, Insert_priv, Update_priv, Delete_priv,
    ->         Create_priv, Drop_priv )
    ->      VALUES (
    ->      'localhost',
    ->      'imp',
    ->      'impmgr',
    ->      'Y', 'Y', 'Y', 'Y',
    ->      'Y', 'Y'
    ->         );
Query OK, 1 row affected (0.00 sec)
```

The `INSERT INTO db` statement sets the privileges for the `impmgr` user. That user is allowed to run the following SQL commands on the `imp` database: `SELECT`, `INSERT`, `UPDATE`, `DELETE`, `CREATE`, and `DROP`.

```
mysql> CREATE DATABASE imp;
Query OK, 1 row affected (0.00 sec)
```

This statement actually creates the database. If you bring up an `xterm` and do an `ls` of the `/var/lib/mysql` directory, you will see a new directory named `imp`. This directory contains all of `imp`'s database files.

```
mysql> use imp;
Database changed
```

The `use imp` command tells the `mysql` utility to apply all the following SQL statements to the `imp` database, unless specifically overridden.

```
mysql> CREATE TABLE imp_addr (
    ->   user text,
    ->   address text,
    ->   nickname text,
    ->   fullname text
    -> );
Query OK, 0 rows affected (0.46 sec)
```

```
mysql> CREATE TABLE imp_pref (
    ->   user text,
    ->   fullname text,
    ->   replyto text,
    ->   lang varchar(30),
    ->   sig text
    -> );
Query OK, 0 rows affected (0.00 sec)
```

The `CREATE` commands created the `imp` tables. If you run the `'show tables;'` command under `mysql`, it will list the two tables just created. The command `'show columns from imp_addr;'` will show the columns for that table. Give it a try.

```
mysql> quit
Bye
[root@winbook /root]# mysqladmin -pmypass reload
```

The mysqladmin program is used to reload the grant tables so that you can use the new database privileges without taking the server down.

The easy way to accomplish this is to run the mysql_create.sql script, which is placed in the imp directory. The easiest way to run this script is to cd into the imp-2.0.11/config/scripts/ directory and run the following command:

```
[root@winbook /root]#mysql -pmypass <mysql_create.sql
```

This will interpret the statements in that text file as if they had been typed from the command line. This is a very powerful feature of MySQL. It enables you to build useful queries and keep them for future use.

Web-Based MySQL Administration

At http://phpwizard.net/phpMyAdmin/ you will find a PHP Web application that can help you manage MySQL. It enables you to manage a MySQL database using a browser and makes administrative work much simpler.

After you have installed PHP and MySQL, you are ready to install phpMyAdmin. The work done while preparing for IMP has also prepared the system for phpMyAdmin. You do have to edit one of the .php3 files in phpMyAdmin to enter the MySQL database name and password.

With phpMyAdmin, you can create and drop databases and tables. You can also add and remove fields and perform other administrative chores.

I have found phpMyAdmin to be very useful when trying to create or delete tables. After you have filled out a form that describes the table, it generates the SQL for you. You can use this information to create script files for later use.

For now, phpMyAdmin has some bugs. I have had it crash on me several times. However, its usefulness is good enough for me to ignore the occasional crash.

From a security point of view, phpMyAdmin is terrible. After it is installed, everyone who uses that Web page has unrestricted access to the MySQL database. I strongly recommend that you do not put your server on the Internet with phpMyAdmin active. If you do, you must configure your Web server to serve only the phpMyAdmin Web pages to your local network. You should also protect the Web pages with a password. Be careful!

Database System Concepts

The next few sections cover database theory and implementation. These concepts will help you understand what was and was not done with the IMP database. This section can give you some ideas for future modifications. If you are interested only in installing IMP, skip to the next chapter.

Database Design Tips

After you have used IMP for awhile, you will probably want to change it. In this section, I will give you a brief overview of database design and use. The lessons learned here will give you concepts to use as you decide what information to capture.

You will also be shown how to query a database for specific information. The skills learned here will help you troubleshoot installation problems and future user problems.

System Design Overview

About 15 years ago, I learned a truth that has had a profound effect on my abilities as a designer. It is basically this: If you define every piece of data in a system and what you do to each piece of data, you have defined the system, and you know what your software must do.

This flew in the face of what I knew about flow charts and design documents. It turned out to be absolutely correct. After you have identified every piece of data, you can generate the design.

Even today, I often start the design first, and then realize I need to define my data. I then backtrack and nail down all the data. You need to do the same, especially in database design. Let's cover data definition and grouping issues.

General Database Design Issues

A good database design requires grouping the data element types together in certain ways. I will explore the methods involved using plain language and examples.

After you have IMP running, you might decide to provide a free service with IMP. There is no such thing as a free lunch, so the system has to be paid for. The most common way of financing free online services is to sell advertising space. For this to succeed, you usually need demographic data. The following examples don't have a direct bearing on the current IMP database. However, they do provide you with some concepts that will give you a handle on collecting useful data on users.

You will be taken through a database design scenario. This scenario has been chosen to illustrate database design concepts in the simplest fashion.

Let's assume that your customers live in an area famed for its best of breed dogs. You need to collect information regarding these customers and their pets for advertising demographics. We will start from the beginning concepts, and pretend we have the base information from the local veterinarian.

To begin with, let's take a brown dog. The dog is an animal of a certain type, or breed. The data are as follows:

- Animal Type—dog
- Breed—Black Lab

The data element types are `Animal` and `Breed`. The information concerning these types is `dog` and `Black Lab`. To store this information in a database, we could create a column named `Animal`, and a column named `Breed`. The attributes `dog` and `brown` go into the rows. With this database design, we can also insert Persian cats.

Relational Databases

Now assume you have decided to narrow the database to dogs and have expanded the information you are collecting to include owner name and phone number plus the ID tag number attached to the dog's collar.

In our example, we are dealing with dogs and owners. Therefore, it makes sense to create a dog_info table and owner_info table. Generally, you need to create as many tables as you have classes of information. This is a very intuitive process. In this case, we can classify the information by dogs and owners.

This is the beginning of a relational database. The dogs are part of the pet owner's life. In real life, a veterinarian gives the dog the owner's last name. The data in the tables is related in real life, and the information in the tables reflects that relationship. Now let's work on the tables.

Data Identification Techniques

A good way to begin on a table design is to get a notepad (electronic or otherwise), and start listing all the data element types that will be in it. A data element type is a piece of information that you can describe. The data element type is usually put into a database as a fixed-name column. The description of the data element is usually put into the database as a variable piece of information stored in a row.

In database design, a data element type is referred to as an *entity*, a *data field*, or a *data column*.

A data element is referred to as an *entity attribute* (or simply *attribute*), a *data record*, or a *data row*.

A data table can be called a *database*. The description's data table and database are used interchangeably in many books. For our use, a *data table* (or simply *table*) is a collection of data columns, and a database is a collection of data tables.

The definitions used in database theory and design have evolved over the years, and will probably continue to evolve.

It is important to determine the level of detail and the type of information covered by your data element types. It makes sense to create a column named Breed because we are doing a table that consists solely of dog families. It would not make sense to do such a column if we were doing a table cataloging all earth animals. It is generally best to hold off determining the table names until you have most of the data described.

After you have done this, you can begin naming tables and columns with confidence. After the tables are done, you can start defining keys.

As far as the IMP database is concerned, we find we do not need much relational information. The user column provides the glue between the preferences table and the address table. The preferences table contains the user-settable options for his IMP usage. The address table contains the list of all that user's contacts.

Database Design Helpers

Ironically, one of the best tools for developing a database is a database! The column names for such a database could possibly be item_name, item_description, item_use, item_group, when_modified, and rules_for_modification. These can also be headings on a paper worksheet or electronic spreadsheet.

Very carefully fill in all the fields for each data item you have identified. The item_use field would contain a description of when this item would be used, such as "When dog tag number is assigned." The item_group field can simply be a number or a group description. In our example, you could group information by "dog" or "dog owner." The when_modified field would contain information such as "when dog received." The rules_for_modification field could be something such as "when payment is made."

All this information helps you decide how to arrange the data. You make up the rules, and you determine when the information is correct. Try to use very similar or the same language in the same columns whenever possible.

After you have filled in the database information, try printing it out, sorted by various columns. Sort by group, sort by modification time, and sort by rules of modification. This will give you a head start on a good database design.

Another useful tool with a free evaluation download is called *dezign*. It is a visual tool that runs on the Windows platform. It is available from http://www.heraut.demon.nl/dezign/index.html. The registered version removes the limits on the number of entities and attributes you can deal with during the design process. It knows about MySQL, and it holds your hand as you work with tables. It can also generate SQL scripts.

Keys

A *key* is a unique item. In real life, you have a key to a door. In general practice, we assume a specific key only unlocks a specific door. A key in a database works much the same way. A unique key value in a database refers to only one row. Non-unique keys are analogous to master keys that unlock more than one door. Non-unique database keys will refer to more than one row.

It is a good idea to have at least one key in every database table. Keys are used to make data lookup in databases much faster. Keys are kept in special index tables that are managed by the database, in a specific sort order. This ordering of key information allows the database engine to do lookups for specific information quickly.

In our database example, a good key would be the dog tag ID number. This number is guaranteed to uniquely identify one dog. This number will never change for the life of the dog, or most likely even after death. It is a unique key. Only one instance of that value exists.

Another key could be an owner's name or a dog's name. However, you could have many dogs named Spot, or many owners named John Smith. These would be non-unique keys. Many rows could exist containing John Smith.

Finally, we can arbitrarily decide to create a unique key. We can give each owner an ID number that is guaranteed to be unique. It is unique because we say so. The term for that is *by definition*. It can be an automatically incrementing number, managed by the database. Only one instance of any particular number would ever exist in the database.

A unique key managed by the auto-increment feature of the database can be considered unique. It might not be, in the strictest sense. Let's assume our database is extremely active, and our key is an auto-increment integer with an upper limit of about 4 billion. If we were putting 1 billion pets a year into the database, we would run out of unique keys in 4 years. However, if we put in one dog per hour, 24 hours a day, we would only put in about 9,000 pets per year. It would take somewhere around 500,000 years (a very rough approximation) to use all the keys in the database.

For all practical purposes, auto-increment keys can be considered totally unique and infinitely large. In this case, infinity is a relative concept.

In our example, the dog tag ID number is the key for the dog_info database. We will put a unique ID number in the owner_info database and make it a key.

Correct Utilization of Data

Now we need to determine how to relate the dogs to the owners. We can store the owner's name with each dog. We can also store the dog ID numbers with each owner. However, each of these solutions presents problems.

If we store the owner's name with each dog, we are taking up a lot of space in the database for each dog we enter. If we store the tag ID number for each dog with the owner, we have to worry about leaving enough room in the owner table to make sure we cover any number of dogs for that person. This is clearly very difficult.

Each of these solutions provides duplicate information. Also, if an owner should legally change her name, the amount of work necessary to correct the information in the database is quite large. *Normalization* is the name for the technique of correcting duplication of data.

Normalization is a term used for minimizing data duplication in a database. In other words, don't put the name "John Smith" in more than one database table. As you start considering the issues in handling this concept, you will begin to see it is simply the use of common sense. However, professors who teach database theory have come up with terms to describe this common-sense approach.

This leads to confusion for the people who have never heard this term. Also, unless you have thought through the ramifications of normalization, some surprises are in store. I use plain English to explain normalization. You might find that different database books explain normalization using different languages. Some books explain better than others.

To start normalizing, you must group the data properly. Generally, put the highest level concept into its own table. (Examples are dog_info and owner_info.) After that, create columns to hold data element types (or entities). The attributes of these entities are the entries (rows) in the database.

After you have done this, go over the database and look for duplicate information. In our example, let's assume the owner's name is initially stored in the dog_info table and in the owner_info table. Our table information looks something like this:

```
TABLE: dog_info        TABLE: owner_info
OwnerName              OwnerName
Breed                  Phone
DogName                OwnerIDNumber (KEY)
OwnerIDNumber
IDTagNumber (KEY)
```

Because we have the owner's name in two tables, we have duplicate information. If we consider the type of data carefully, we also realize we have a one-to-many relationship between the two tables. One owner can own many dogs. However, for the sake of illustration, one dog belongs to only one owner.

The problems we find in the sample tables illustrate the reasons for normalization. Several named normalization steps exist. The steps have technical terms not covered here. To do further study, a good book is Codd's *Further Normalization of the Data Base Relational Model*, 1972.

The first step in normalizing data is achieved when we have identified all data element types properly. In its simplest case, we have not achieved this step if we have made a table name a column. If we had made owner_info a column name, we would have a normalization problem. The problem is obvious when we realize the owner has several attributes. In our example, they are the owner's name and the owner's phone number. We can say, "The phone number is owner information." We can also say, "The owner's name is owner information." Both statements are true. However, this would lead to having multiple values for an owner info column.

After we realize this, we realize the `owner_info` belongs in a table. We then set separate columns for the attributes. This solves the problem of trying to stuff a table into a column. Removing all these types of problems is our goal.

The next step is to see that data is not duplicated across tables or within a table. In our example, because an owner can own multiple dogs, putting the owner's name in the `dog_info` table along with the reference ID pointing to the owner info table causes duplication of information in that table and in the `owner_info` table.

The name is repeated for each dog owned, and occurs once in the `owner_info` table. Errors can creep in, and misspellings of the owner's name can cause confusion. The data is also redundant because following the reference ID gives you the ability to recover the Owner's name.

To solve this, we place the name in one location where it appears once. The interesting thing about an owner is there is only one owner for a dog. Therefore, the owner name is relatively unique, and should show up in the database system only once. We handle this by removing the owner's name from the `dog_info` table.

This leaves us with another possible problem. For example, if we were to put State Name and a two-letter State Abbreviation in the address in `owner_info`, we would have a future problem. Whenever the State Name changed, the State Abbreviation would also have to change. At the same time, having both pieces of information in the `owner_info` table adds nothing to the `owner_info` table's data store.

The solution is to create a new table that lists State Name for State Abbreviation. You then would use either a State Abbreviation in the `owner_info` table, or an ID in that table to look up the State Name.

Finally, note that the rules in the second step are technically broken in our final design. There are two problems. The first problem is that the Breed column is the name of the Breed, rather than a Breed ID. Because Breed names repeat, and can be misspelled, this is not a good thing. To finish out the design, the Breed column needs to be an ID that references to a Breed table. If you decide to create this table, you should modify the database design to accommodate this change.

The second problem is that the owner's ID number is in the dog table, and it repeats for each dog the owner owns. This will always happen in a one-to-many relationship. Note, however, that the database design is clean, because changing information such as the phone number of the owner will affect all dogs owned. When you look up the dog's table entry using the `IDTagNumber`, you can then look up the owner's table entry by the using

`OwnerIDNumber`. At this point you have the correct phone number. You can also find all dogs owned by the owner by finding all rows that have that specific `OwnerIDNumber`.

Our final database looks like this:

```
TABLE: dog_info          TABLE: owner_info
FKOwnerIDNumber (KEY)      OwnerName
Breed                      Phone
DogName                    OwnerIDNumber (KEY)
IDTagNumber (KEY)
```

You will see that the `FKOwnerIDNumber` in the `dog_info table` is defined as a key. This will be a non-unique key. Telling the database that it is a key will speed lookups of which dogs an owner has. This is a perfectly legitimate use of a key.

Modifications to the IMP Database

These concepts can be applied to your study of the IMP database design. As you examine the IMP tables, you find they are very short and very easy to understand. This is the KISS principal at work. There is one duplicate piece of data (the user-name is repeated between tables), but this is not a fatal mistake.

The IMP tables can be improved and enhanced. The most obvious enhancement is to change the user column to a key column in one of the tables. You would need to create a unique ID column and reference this in the other table. This would provide faster lookup. However, in personal experience, the IMP table supports about one thousand users very well. The amount of re-work of the PHP code to accomplish this could cause you much grief and cost time.

If you decide to store extra information in the IMP database, I recommend that you place your changes in separate tables using a key loosely based on the username. A username must be unique within an email system. Alternatively, because a Social Security Number is unique, it is a good key for identifying individuals. Another fairly unique ID is the username linked with the user phone number, though this can repeat in rare circumstances. Unless you really want to do a lot of rework of the PHP code, leave the current table structures alone and enhance the database with separate tables.

In other words, break the database design rules for simple changes! This will cause fewer problems in the long run, because the only code that will break is the new code you added. That is part of the KISS principal. When modifying an existing system, change as little of the current system as possible, unless the gain outweighs the pain. This is true even if the current system is poorly designed.

Graphical Database Representations

Many ways exist to design databases graphically. I like to use rectangular boxes with lines connecting them. The name of the table is at the top of the rectangular box, enclosed with lines to set it apart.

Each data element in the table is listed below the table name. A bullet or asterisk indicates which element is a key. A line goes from one table to another table where a relationship exists. I like to draw a line from the data element in one table to the corresponding data element in the next table.

Our sample database is shown in Figure 3.1. The good thing about this particular graphical approach is that it can be worked on the back of a napkin! When done, it will transfer easily into a drawing program. It is a matter of taste. You should feel free to look for a table representation method you prefer.

Figure 3.1

The sample database in graphic form as created in Dezign.

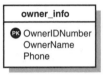

The IMP Database Structure

The IMP database is very simple. It consists of two tables. The first table, named imp_addr, holds the name and address information for user contacts. The other table, named imp_pref, holds the user preferences.

All the fields except for one are text fields. This allows unlimited length for these fields. MySQL handles the storage issues. The lang field in the imp_pref table is a varchar field of length 30, because its length requirements are well known by the designers.

The IMP database is shown in Figure 3.2. It is a very simple database, easily understood. This shows that simple databases can be very useful.

The imp_addr table stores the username in the user field. Because all user logon names on a Linux machine are unique, all searches are done on this field. The address field contains the full email address of the contact. The nickname field contains a brief name by which you can remember the user. The fullname field contains the user's full name. This table is not indexed. If it were indexed, a non-unique index could be put on the user column.

The imp_pref table stores the username in the user field, identical to the imp_addr table. The fullname field contains the user's full name. The replyto field contains the reply address the user requires his email to display. The lang field contains the language preference. The sig field contains the user's signature text to be placed at the end of his email.

Figure 3.2

The IMP database graphic structure as shown by Dezign.

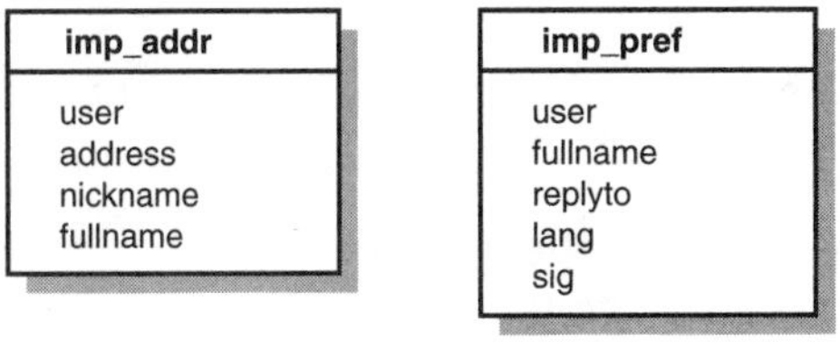

imp_addr
user
address
nickname
fullname

imp_pref
user
fullname
replyto
lang
sig

SQL Overview

SQL, or *Structured Query Language*, is not really a language. It does not follow all the rules of the typical computer programming language. There are no constructs in SQL to allow decision branches. You can't go to a specific piece of code or execute that code if a decision has been made.

On the other hand, SQL is ideal for getting data out of a database using complicated rules. If you team SQL with other languages such as PHP or C/C++, the combination is very powerful. With this kind of combination, you can accomplish any programming task.

SQL is inherently simple. The most commonly used commands in SQL are CREATE, DROP, GRANT, INSERT, SELECT, and UPDATE. The modifiers for most of these commands are WHERE, AND, OR, LIKE, GROUP BY, or ORDER BY. A few helper functions such as, but not limited to, COUNT(), AVG(), MIN(), MAX(), and SUM() also exist.

After you have mastered this list of commands, you are ready to use SQL for most tasks. In almost all cases, by using some thought, complex statements can be boiled down to simpler statements. Very rarely do you require some of the more complex constructs.

MySQL Implements a Subset of SQL

Not all ANSI SQL features are implemented in MySQL. As of the 3.22 version of MySQL, the following features are left out:

- -- is the start of a comment only if followed by a whitespace. SQL allows it to be a comment in any case.
- In VARCHAR columns, trailing spaces are removed when stored in the database.
- In some cases CHAR columns are changed to VARCHAR columns without notification.
- Privileges stay after a table is deleted. They must be explicitly revoked using the REVOKE command. This is because privileges are stored in the mysql database tables.
- NULL and FALSE both evaluate to NULL.
- Sub-selects do not yet work in MySQL.

Because sub-selects are not allowed, you cannot use the following syntax:

`SELECT * FROM MainTable WHERE MyID IN (SELECT MyID FROM SecondTable).`

You can rewrite the command to look like this:

```
SELECT MainTable.* FROM MainTable,SecondTable
WHERE MainTable.MyID = SecondTable.MyID;
```

The following syntax is also not allowed:

`SELECT * FROM MainTable WHERE MyID NOT IN (SELECT MyID FROM SecondTable).`

Instead, use the following syntax:

```
SELECT MainTable.* FROM MainTable LEFT JOIN SecondTable
ON MainTable.MyID = SecondTable.MyID WHERE SecondTable.MyID is NULL;
```

- MySQL 3.22 doesn't support transactions. However, it does do its work using "atomic operations." The authors of MySQL believe this provides "equal or better integrity," with better performance. MySQL version 3.23 is having transactions added to it.
- MySQL does not support stored procedures or triggers.
- The FOREIGN KEY statement mostly does nothing.
- Views are not supported.
- COMMIT and ROLLBACK are not supported.

You can simulate COMMIT and ROLLBACK. A COMMIT on an operation is a way of saying all the conditions are good, store the data. To do this in a multiuser environment, you LOCK the tables to prevent any other user from changing them. You then make your changes and test all the conditions. If the conditions look good, you UNLOCK the tables, simulating a COMMIT.

During the process of testing and making changes, you must keep enough information to put the tables back to their original condition if the test for all the conditions fails. This simulates the ROLLBACK.

SQL Keywords

Now is a good time to review the list of SQL keywords. I also include all MySQL keywords. These keywords should not be used in any table or column name, even though MySQL will allow you to do this under certain conditions. Some keywords are reserved for use in future versions of ANSI SQL or MySQL.

If you decide to modify the IMP database, or create your own database, do not use any of these keywords as column or table names. MySQL will permit you to do this, but it is a very bad idea. It also prevents portability to other databases.

3

action	add	aggregate	all
alter	after	and	as
asc	avg	avg_row_length	auto_increment
between	bigint	bit	binary
blob	bool	both	by
cascade	case	char	character
change	check	checksum	column
columns	comment	constraint	create
cross	current_date	current_time	current_timestamp
data	database	databases	date
datetime	day	day_hour	day_minute
day_second	dayofmonth	dayofweek	dayofyear
dec	decimal	default	delayed
delay_key_write	delete	desc	describe
distinct	distinctrow	double	drop
end	else	escape	escaped
enclosed	enum	explain	exists
fields	file	first	float
float4	float8	flush	foreign
from	for	full	function
global	grant	grants	group
having	heap	high_priority	hour
hour_minute	hour_second	hosts	identified
ignore	in	index	infile
inner	insert	insert_id	int
integer	interval	int1	int2
int3	int4	int8	into
if	is	isam	join
key	keys	kill	last_insert_id
leading	left	length	like
lines	limit	load	local
lock	logs	long	longblob
longtext	low_priority	max	max_rows
match	mediumblob	mediumtext	mediumint

middleint	min_rows	minute	minute_second
modify	month	monthname	myisam
natural	numeric	no	not
null	on	optimize	option
optionally	or	order	outer
outfile	pack_keys	partial	password
precision	primary	procedure	process
processlist	privileges	read	real
references	reload	regexp	rename
replace	restrict	returns	revoke
rlike	ruow	rows	second
select	set	show	shutdown
smallint	soname	sql_big_tables	sql_big_selects
sql_low_priority_updates	sql_log_off	sql_log_update	sql_select_limit
sql_small_result	sql_big_result	sql_warnings	straight_join
starting	status	string	table
tables	temporary	terminated	text
then	time	timestamp	tinyblob
tinytext	tinyint	trailing	to
type	use	using	unique
unlock	unsigned	update	usage
values	varchar	variables	varying
varbinary	with	write	when
where	year	year_month	zerofill

Typical SQL Statements

Let's examine a few SQL statements. I will assume that you need to create a demographic information table to store the information that advertisers most want to see. The potential advertisers have told you they want to see the age, income level, cost of housing, and type of automobile for our customer pool.

We will use a fictitious table called demographics to store this information. This table has a list of incomes, ages, automobile types, and housing costs for each of our customers. We have decided not to identify the particular customer in this database. The advertisers will be presented with composite information not targeted to an individual.

First, the demographics table will be created. Then, the table will have a few items added to it. Finally, we will pretend the table is full, and do several data retrievals on it. We will use MySQL features where possible. You will see how many common problems that arise during the use of MySQL are handled.

In creating the table, we want to add columns named income, age, auto, and housing. The age column is a TINYINT, because we don't need to register an age greater than 127. The other two columns are dollars and cents, and we will make them DECIMAL columns. The auto column will be a text column. I will make a few mistakes along the way so you can see what happens.

First, we create the demographics database. Then we create the demographics table. Note that the database and table have the same name.

```
mysql> create database demographics;
Query OK, 1 row affected (0.00 sec)

mysql> use demographics;
Database changed
mysql> create table demographics(DECIMAL(9,2) income, TINYINT age,
mysql>DECIMAL(10,2) house_price, TEXT auto_type);
ERROR 1064: You have an error in your SQL syntax near 'DECIMAL(9,2)
➥income, TINYINT age, DECIMAL(10,2) house_price, TEXT auto_type)' at line 1
mysql> create table demographics(income DECIMAL(9,2), age TINYINT,
mysql>house_price DECIMAL(10,2), auto_type TEXT );
Query OK, 0 rows affected (0.00 sec)
```

Notice that MySQL pointed to my error. I had reversed the order of the column named income and the description of the column. It printed the string beginning where it found the error.

Now it is time to add the user(s) who are allowed access to the database and give them the privileges necessary to run the database. The user myname will have full access, including the ability to set up other users. The user part will have partial access. We will use the SQL GRANT command. Notice that when the entire table_priv table is dumped, a wrap-around of information occurs on an 80-column screen. Listing 3.4 is a little messy, but decipherable.

Listing 3.4 Providing Access to Demographics Databaseresume

```
mysql> use mysql
Database changed

mysql> GRANT ALL ON demographics.* TO myname@localhost IDENTIFIED BY 'mypass'
    -> WITH GRANT OPTION;
Query OK, 0 rows affected (0.21 sec)

mysql> select host,user,password from user;
+-----------+--------+------------------+
| host      | user   | password         |
+-----------+--------+------------------+
| localhost | root   | 6f8c114b58f2ce9e |
| winbook   | root   | 6f8c114b58f2ce9e |
```

Listing 3.4   continued

```
| localhost |         |                  |
| winbook   |         |                  |
| localhost | impmgr  | 5567401602cd5ddd |
| localhost | myname  | 6f8c114b58f2ce9e |
+-----------+---------+------------------+
6 rows in set (0.00 sec)

Query OK, 0 rows affected (0.08 sec)
mysql> select * from tables_priv;
+------+--------------+--------+-------------+---------------
➥+---------------+--------------------------------------------
➥-----------------------+-------------+
| Host | Db           | User   | Table_name  | Grantor
➥| Timestamp    | Table_priv
➥| Column_priv |
+------+--------------+--------+-------------+---------------
➥+---------------+--------------------------------------------
➥-----------------------+-------------+
| %    | demographics | myname | demographics | root@localhost
➥| 20000325085822 | Select,Insert,Update,Delete,Create,Drop,Grant
➥,References,Index,Alter |             |
+------+--------------+--------+-------------+---------------
➥+---------------+--------------------------------------------
➥-----------------------+-------------+
1 row in set (0.30 sec)
```

Notice that the output from the `mysql` program wraps. This is the worst part about using the command-line program. The only solutions that I like are to use small character fonts and make a very wide `xterm` window, or to do small selects that only show part of the database at a time.

At this point, quit `mysql`. As the superuser, in the same terminal window, use the `adduser` command to add the user `myname`. You can give this user any password you choose. While you are at it, add the user `part`. Then use the `su -1` command to assume the identity of the user `myname`.

 Note

You are not required to create the users as described in the previous paragraph to log in to the MySQL system as those users. I am showing you how MySQL uses the authentication system of the host operating system, and assumes that user is the one logging into MySQL.

MySQL picks up the current logged in user's context when determining what access to give, when using tools such as `mysqladmin` or `mysql`. This can cause you problems if you tend to use the database as one user, and connect to it remotely as a different user. You might not understand what is going wrong when you connect to the database remotely. The easiest way to discover what is wrong is to log in to the system as that user and use the database tools at their default settings.

Let's work through the following example for user myname. First, we will look at the tables and insert some values. Then we will insert a user-called part with only SELECT, INSERT, and DELETE privileges. Finally, we will add a single table called test to the demographics database.

Then the user part will modify the demographics database. The user part will also try to modify the test table we have created (see Listing 3.5).

Listing 3.5   Attempting to Modify Table Demographics Without Enough Permission

```
[root@winbook root]# su -l myname
[myname@winbook myname]$ mysql
ERROR 1045: Access denied for user: 'myname@localhost' (Using password: NO)
[myname@winbook myname]$ mysql -pmypass
Welcome to the MySQL monitor.  Commands end with ; or \g.
Your MySQL connection id is 8 to server version: 3.22.32

Type 'help' for help.

mysql> use demographics;
Reading table information for completion of table and column names
You can turn off this feature to get a quicker startup with -A

Database changed
mysql> show tables;
+-----------------------+
| Tables in demographics |
+-----------------------+
| demographics          |
+-----------------------+
1 row in set (0.00 sec)
mysql> show columns from demographics
    -> ;
+-------------+---------------+------+-----+---------+-------+
| Field       | Type          | Null | Key | Default | Extra |
+-------------+---------------+------+-----+---------+-------+
| income      | decimal(9,2)  | YES  |     | NULL    |       |
| age         | tinyint(4)    | YES  |     | NULL    |       |
| house_price | decimal(10,2) | YES  |     | NULL    |       |
| auto_type   | text          | YES  |     | NULL    |       |
+-------------+---------------+------+-----+---------+-------+
4 rows in set (0.00 sec)

mysql> insert into demographics ( income, age)
    -> values (
    -> 32756.32, 42 );
Query OK, 1 row affected (0.15 sec)

mysql> select * from demographics
    -> ;
+----------+------+-------------+-----------+
| income   | age  | house_price | auto_type |
+----------+------+-------------+-----------+
```

Listing 3.5 continued

```
| 32756.32 |   42 |       NULL | NULL      |
+----------+------+------------+-----------+
1 row in set (0.00 sec)

mysql> GRANT SELECT,INSERT,UPDATE ON demographics
mysql>TO part@"%" IDENTIFIED BY 'mypass';
ERROR 1044: Access denied for user: 'myname@localhost' to database 'mysql'
```

The error that user `myname` received when trying to assign a password to user `part` shows an interesting side effect of the MySQL security system. Because user `myname` was not given global access to all databases by the root user, no password can be assigned to user `part`.

With no password assigned, user `part` is allowed to access the database from anywhere with no password. This is a very undesirable side effect. Unless you are dealing with a totally open, noncritical database, you should never give a user GRANT options on a single database.

To allow user `myname` to assign passwords when granting access to a database, the user must be given global access to the `mysql` database. This allows modification of privileges for all databases. This side effect might not be what you intended, so be careful.

The GRANT command to give global access would look like this:

```
mysql> GRANT ALL ON *.* TO myname@localhost IDENTIFIED BY 'mypass'
    -> WITH GRANT OPTION;
```

There should only be one database system superuser. Be very careful to whom you give superuser privileges.

```
mysql> GRANT SELECT,INSERT,UPDATE ON demographics TO part@"%";
Query OK, 0 rows affected (0.03 sec)

mysql> GRANT SELECT,INSERT,UPDATE ON
mysql>demographics.demographics TO part@localhost;
```

Whenever you GRANT privileges to a user from anywhere (represented by `username@"%"`), you must also GRANT privileges to the same user `@localhost` (represented by `username@localhost`) if you want to grant command-line access privileges. This is because of the anonymous user that is in the `mysql` user database.

If you don't create a `username@localhost` entry, the default user's privileges will apply when the user is using `mysql` from the command line. This will prevent use of the database as you intended.

```
mysql> delete from demographics;
```

Output

```
Query OK, 0 rows affected (0.08 sec)

mysql> select * from demographics;
Empty set (0.00 sec)
mysql> insert into demographics ( income, age)
    -> values (
    -> 32756.32, 42 );
Query OK, 1 row affected (0.15 sec)

mysql> CREATE TABLE test (TEST INTEGER);
Query OK, 0 rows affected (0.01 sec)

mysql> show tables;
+-----------------------+
| Tables in demographics |
+-----------------------+
| demographics          |
| test                  |
+-----------------------+
2 rows in set (0.01 sec)

mysql>quit
```

When you use GRANT, your privilege changes take effect immediately. If you use a tool such as mysqladmin to add or modify a user, the database privileges must be flushed (or reloaded) by the superuser. An example of reloading the privilege table is shown in Listing 3.6. Note that the mysqladmin flush-priv command is not necessary in our case.

Listing 3.6 Using the Demographics Database

```
[root@winbook /root]# mysqladmin -pmypass flush-priv

[part@winbook part]$ mysql demographics;
Reading table information for completion of table and column names
You can turn off this feature to get a quicker startup with -A

Welcome to the MySQL monitor.  Commands end with ; or \g.
Your MySQL connection id is 27 to server version: 3.22.32

Type 'help' for help.

mysql> select * from demographics
    -> ;
+----------+------+-------------+-----------+
| income   | age  | house_price | auto_type |
+----------+------+-------------+-----------+
| 32756.32 |  42  |        NULL | NULL      |
+----------+------+-------------+-----------+
1 row in set (0.01 sec)
```

Listing 3.6   continued

```
mysql> show tables;
+-----------------------+
| Tables in demographics |
+-----------------------+
| demographics          |
+-----------------------+
1 row in set (0.00 sec)
```

The user part cannot even see the database test. This hiding of information is good to know about from a database design point of view. You must be careful to ensure that tables visible to a user in a database do not require information from hidden tables. If you do this, errors will occur. Now let's try to access the test table as user part.

```
mysql> select * from test;
ERROR 1142: select command denied to user: 'part@localhost' for table 'test'
```

To round out the demonstration of SQL statements, let's add a few rows to the demographics database, create an index, and print out some sorted information (see Listing 3.7). We will have to be user myname to do this.

Listing 3.7   Inserting and Retrieving Demographics Table Data

```
mysql> insert into demographics (income, age) values (11111.11, 22);
Query OK, 1 row affected (0.00 sec)

mysql> insert into demographics (income, age) values (21111.11, 25);
Query OK, 1 row affected (0.00 sec)

mysql> insert into demographics (income, age) values (31111.11, 35);
Query OK, 1 row affected (0.00 sec)

mysql> insert into demographics (income, age) values (41111.11, 45);
Query OK, 1 row affected (0.00 sec)

mysql> select * from demographics where income < 30000;
+----------+------+-------------+-----------+
| income   | age  | house_price | auto_type |
+----------+------+-------------+-----------+
| 11111.11 |  22  |        NULL | NULL      |
| 21111.11 |  25  |        NULL | NULL      |
+----------+------+-------------+-----------+
2 rows in set (0.03 sec)

mysql> select * from demographics where income < 30000 and age > 22;
+----------+------+-------------+-----------+
| income   | age  | house_price | auto_type |
+----------+------+-------------+-----------+
| 21111.11 |  25  |        NULL | NULL      |
+----------+------+-------------+-----------+
1 row in set (0.01 sec)
mysql> update demographics set house_price=75000+age where income > 30000;
```

Listing 3.7   continued

```
Query OK, 3 rows affected (0.00 sec)
Rows matched: 3  Changed: 3  Warnings: 0

mysql> select * from demographics;
+----------+------+-------------+-----------+
| income   | age  | house_price | auto_type |
+----------+------+-------------+-----------+
| 32756.32 |  42  |    75042.00 | NULL      |
| 11111.11 |  22  |        NULL | NULL      |
| 21111.11 |  25  |        NULL | NULL      |
| 31111.11 |  35  |    75035.00 | NULL      |
| 41111.11 |  45  |    75045.00 | NULL      |
+----------+------+-------------+-----------+
5 rows in set (0.00 sec)
```

Note

A very powerful feature of MySQL is the capability to do math in the SET or WHERE clauses. In the updates example shown, the database engine found the row we requested, pulled the information from that row's age column, and added it to the number we supplied for the house price.

```
mysql> update demographics set house_price=100000+age where income < 30000;
Query OK, 2 rows affected (0.00 sec)
Rows matched: 2  Changed: 2  Warnings: 0

mysql> update demographics set auto_type='miata' where age > 40;
Query OK, 2 rows affected (0.00 sec)
Rows matched: 2  Changed: 2  Warnings: 0

mysql> update demographics set auto_type='ford' where age < 40;
Query OK, 3 rows affected (0.00 sec)
Rows matched: 3  Changed: 3  Warnings: 0

mysql> update demographics set auto_type='chevy' where age < 25;
Query OK, 1 row affected (0.00 sec)
Rows matched: 1  Changed: 1  Warnings: 0

mysql> select * from demographics where income < 40000 ;
+----------+------+-------------+-----------+
| income   | age  | house_price | auto_type |
+----------+------+-------------+-----------+
| 32756.32 |  42  |    75042.00 | miata     |
| 11111.11 |  22  |   100022.00 | chevy     |
| 21111.11 |  25  |   100025.00 | ford      |
| 31111.11 |  35  |    75035.00 | ford      |
+----------+------+-------------+-----------+
4 rows in set (0.00 sec)
```

The previous SELECT statement produced a listing that had no ordering to it whatsoever. This is the natural order of the database. If we want the information to be ordered, we must impose order on it using the ORDER BY statement, as shown by Listing 3.8.

 Note

The natural order of a database is the order in which the data was entered into the database, combined with deletions and additions to the database. It is not a predictable order, and cannot be used in any predictable fashion. It does provide the fastest retrieval of data in most database systems, but even that is not guaranteed.

Listing 3.8   Using an Order-By Clause

```
mysql> select * from demographics where income < 40000 order by income;
+-----------+------+-------------+-----------+
| income    | age  | house_price | auto_type |
+-----------+------+-------------+-----------+
| 11111.11  |   22 |   100022.00 | chevy     |
| 21111.11  |   25 |   100025.00 | ford      |
| 31111.11  |   35 |    75035.00 | ford      |
| 32756.32  |   42 |    75042.00 | miata     |
+-----------+------+-------------+-----------+
4 rows in set (0.00 sec)
```

In the following command, note that the initial index creation failed. Indexes cannot be created on columns that can contain null values. We must modify the index column to make sure it cannot contain null values. To do this, the ALTER TABLE command must be used. Following the application of this command, the index can be created.

```
mysql> create index age_index on demographics (age);
ERROR 1121: Column 'age' is used with UNIQUE or INDEX but is not defined as NOT
NULL

mysql> alter table demographics modify age TINYINT NOT NULL;
Query OK, 5 rows affected (0.02 sec)
Records: 5  Duplicates: 0  Warnings: 0

mysql> create index age_index on demographics (age);
Query OK, 5 rows affected (0.00 sec)
Records: 5  Duplicates: 0  Warnings: 0
```

The information we have covered gives you a brief overview of SQL. It is by no means an exhaustive example of use.

MySQL's License

The MySQL server version 3.22 and below is under the MySQL Free Public license, which is applicable to non-Microsoft platforms, and is included at the end of this book. It is a very liberal license, requiring payment under limited circumstances.

Some parts of the MySQL tools are under the GNU public license. Some parts of the MySQL tools are in the public domain. The MySQL server itself is not under the GNU license or in the public domain. On Microsoft platforms, the license for version 3.22 and below is a different license and requires payment after a trial period. Check their Web site for details concerning the Microsoft licensing details.

MySQL server version 3.23 is now released under the GPL license. Version 3.23 is still in alpha as of this writing, but should be released soon. It is in your best interest to upgrade to version 3.23 as soon as it is stable because the GPL license is less restrictive than the MySQL license.

Free Use Within Limitations

MySQL version 3.22 is generally free for use on Unix and OS/2 platforms. On the Microsoft Windows platform, you must pay for a license after a trial period of 30 days.

You must pay for a license for MySQL version 3.22 if you include MySQL in a product or service for which you charge. You must pay for a license if you bundle MySQL with a distribution that is not redistributable by others.

One MySQL license goes with one machine. It covers an unlimited number of customers and CPU's on that machine. It covers an unlimited number of users on that machine. This license is the most generous license for an SQL database that exists, in my opinion.

If you are using MySQL version 3.23 or later, the GPL license applies. It is free to use for any purpose, commercial or otherwise. You do not need to pay for a license to put it on any machine, or to use it for any purpose.

Implications and Examples

A few example situations covered under the MySQL license for version 3.22 are as follows:

- You install MySQL on a server and charge for that service. You must pay for a license.
- You install MySQL on an office machine in the company you work for. You build an intranet Web-based email application. No payment is necessary.
- You decide to distribute MySQL for Linux on a CD with some other free applications. You include the source code to MySQL. No payment is necessary.
- You bundle MySQL with an application and sell the application to others. MySQL is installed as a normal part of the installation process. A payment is necessary.

- Your customer already has a non-OEM version of the MySQL license for a machine. You install MySQL and charge a fee. You do not have to pay for an additional license.

It is always a good idea to pay for a MySQL license for version 3.22 or below, for any kind of installation where you expect problems. With the MySQL paid license, you get support from the creators of MySQL. They are very responsive, and handle problems quickly. I've seen their support efforts in the past, and their help far outweighs the amount of the license fee. It is a very good deal.

If you use MySQL version 3.23, these rules do not apply because of the GPL license. You can bundle MySQL with any application or provide any service with MySQL. However, you must provide the end customer with the source code or the ability to obtain the source code.

Onward!

You now have a working MySQL server that supports the IMP Web application. The next step is to configure your Apache Web server to run the IMP application. Let's do that now.

Chapter 4

Apache Web Server

The Apache Web server is the most popular Web server on the Internet. As I am writing this, it occupies over 60% of the market and last quarter added over a million Apache Web servers to the Internet. It is not the fastest Web server available, but it is very stable. It is highly expandable through the use of modules. This feature allows it to support all computer languages and formats used on the World Wide Web today.

One of the greatest features of the Apache Web server is that it is free. You can purchase support for it from http://www.apache.org, and the Apache license is included in the back of this book.

In this chapter, I will show you how to configure the Apache Web server to host the PHP language module. The PHP module will be required for the IMP email system to work. The following sections cover the modifications to the Apache server to allow PHP and IMP to function properly.

With this language module installed, you will be able to create Web pages that are executed as programs on the server. The reader of the Web page will only see the result of your Web page program, depending on how you write it. (In some cases, the reader of the Web page can show the code you placed on that page.)

Apache License

The Apache license is a very generous license. It enables you to redistribute the Apache server in modified or unmodified binary or source form, as long as the copyright notice is included. Other restrictions regarding use of the name Apache in advertising or promoting a modified product apply. No payments are required for its use. It is available online at http://www.apache.org/LICENSE.txt.

PHP Configuration Overview

To allow your Web server to correctly respond to the PHP commands entered in the Web page, you must change its configuration files. On the Red Hat system, the Apache configuration files are in directories below the /etc/httpd directory.

Whenever you make a change to the Web server by editing the text configuration files, you must restart it. This forces it to reload its settings. You must be the root user. In a terminal window, run the httpd restart command as shown:

```
[root@winbook root]# /etc/rc.d/init.d/httpd restart
```

Output

```
Shutting down http:                                      [  OK  ]
Starting httpd:                                          [  OK  ]
```

If you don't get an [OK] after the Starting httpd printout, something is wrong with your configuration files. Recheck the last thing you edited. You will see clues to what is wrong in the /var/log/messages file and in the /var/log/httpd/error_log file. The easiest way to check these log files is with the tail command:

```
[root@winbook httpd]# tail /var/log/messages
```

Output

```
Mar 27 07:12:48 lin gnome-name-server[763]: name server starting
Mar 27 07:12:48 lin gnome-name-server[765]: starting
Mar 27 07:12:48 lin gnome-name-server[765]: name server was running
➥on display, exiting
Mar 27 07:27:27 lin cardmgr[377]: executing: './network suspend eth0'
Mar 27 07:27:27 lin kernel: eth0: interrupt from stopped card
Mar 27 01:27:34 lin cardmgr[377]: executing: './network resume eth0'
Mar 27 01:54:35 lin httpd: httpd shutdown succeeded
Mar 27 01:54:36 lin httpd: httpd startup succeeded
Mar 27 01:55:57 lin httpd: httpd shutdown succeeded
Mar 27 01:55:58 lin httpd: httpd startup succeeded
```

 Note   At around version 6.2 of Red Hat, the Apache Web server configuration files started merging into one file, httpd.conf.

To support PHP, Apache's /etc/httpd/conf/srm.conf file must be modified. In that file, at around line 164, find the lines that look like the following

```
#AddType application/x-httpd-php3 .php3
#AddType application/x-httpd-php3-source .phps
```

and remove the comment symbol (the #) so they look like this:

```
AddType application/x-httpd-php3 .php3
AddType application/x-httpd-php3-source .phps
```

Note
PHP version 3 uses the .php3 file extension. PHP version 4 uses the .php file extension (which was also used by PHP/FI). IMP version 2.0.11 uses PHP version 3. For the sake of our project, we will focus on the IMP 2.0.11 setup features.

Now you must edit the /etc/httpd/httpd.conf file. Locate the AddModule section at around line 176, and remove the comment symbol on the mod_php3.c line. The line should look like this:

```
# Extra Modules
#AddModule mod_php.c
AddModule mod_php3.c
#AddModule mod_perl.c
```

 Note
The LoadModule section is being ignored for now. This allows Apache to keep working, even if the PHP RPM file is installed. During the install of PHP3, the PHP installation script modifies the LoadModule line.

IMP Configuration Overview

The Apache Web server needs to know to run the PHP interpreter when the IMP main page is requested. This page is index.php3. To do this, edit the /etc/httpd/conf/srm.conf file. Change the default DirectoryIndex from the following

```
DirectoryIndex index.html index.shtml index.cgi
```

to the following:

```
DirectoryIndex index.html index.php3 index.htm default.html index.cgi
```

 Tip
Starting with Red Hat version 6.2, the version of the Apache Web server being shipped combined the srm.conf and the access.conf files into the one httpd.conf file. If you have the later version, you need to search for the DirectoryIndex directive in the httpd.conf file.

You can tell whether you need to search the httdp.conf file by looking at the srm.conf file. If it only has a few comment lines in it, all the directives are in the httpd.conf file.

CGI and PHP Server Pages Overview

To understand how IMP works, you need a brief explanation of CGI and modules. You need to know how CGI technology works and how it differs from the method used for the IMP project.

> I have often had people who proclaimed they "know more than you" tell me CGI is the only way to go. They have even offered to "fix" my system for me. Don't let some so-called expert do this to you! With the information covered in this section, you will know why CGI should not be used for this project.

CGI was the first method widely used by Web servers to execute user-provided programs triggered by their Web pages. This method is still available. If you know about this method, you might wonder why IMP uses PHP as a module.

How CGI Works

Common Gateway Interface is abbreviated *CGI*. A CGI script is any program that is run by a Web server when requested by a Web browser. These programs typically run in memory separated from the Web browser. They get information the user put into a Web page through environment variables, or through stdin. (See the explanation of stdin and stdout in Chapter 6, "IMP.")

When CGI scripts use the GET request method for getting data, the data is passed on the URL line and is reflected in the environment variables. This data is visible to the Web browser user. You should not use this method for sensitive data. An example of using the CGI GET method can be found using search engines. Here is a sample search on a fictional search engine:

```
http://www.mm.com/Mamma?lang=1&timeout=4&qtype=0&query=cgi+script
```

The ? symbol starts the information to be given to the CGI script. The & character indicates that a new variable is beginning. The = sign assigns a value to a variable name. The variable name is on the left of the =, and the value is on the right. Any space characters in the text are replaced with the + sign. The receiving script must parse this information to use it.

When CGI scripts use the POST method, the information is sent to stdin using the same format as described for the GET method. The environment variable REQUEST_METHOD is set to the string POST for POST methods, GET for GET methods. Data sent on stdin is not visible to the user of the Web browser. That data can be derived from the Web page the user filled out, or it can be based on computation. The only advantage here is that a casual over-the-shoulder observer might not easily determine what information was sent to the server. Security-wise, both POST and GET are about the same.

CGI scripts are typically much slower than PHP. The slowness comes from the time necessary to allocate system resources, such as memory, and execute the program. The program often must be loaded from disk, which incurs greater time penalties. For small scripts, PHP running as a module is much faster.

You can run PHP as a CGI script if you want. However, to get the best performance from your Web mail program, you do not want to do this. In this project, you will be installing PHP as a module.

How PHP Works in the ESL Mode

ESL stands for *Embedded Scripting Language*. When PHP is run in this mode a CGI script is not called. Instead, the server is given clues through configuration files that the Web page can contain PHP code. When the tags <? and ?> are seen, the server runs the page through the PHP engine before delivering the page to the Web browser.

By running PHP as a module, you cut out a lot of time the user would normally have to wait in the CGI mode. The PHP module is resident in memory, as opposed to being loaded from the hard drive for each use. To achieve the most responsiveness, you never want to use PHP as a CGI script engine.

> To work with Front Page and some XML parsers, you should change the initial tag to read <?php. This is not an issue if you won't be editing with Front Page or using an XML parser.

To avoid calling PHP as a CGI script, it must be installed as a module in your Web server. The configuration file changes you made tell the Web server that PHP is a module. The next step is to install PHP.

> This book covers the free Apache Web server for this project. It must be noted that other Web servers support PHP as a module also. One that comes to mind is the Xitami Web server.

Testing the PHP and IMP Configuration

Red Hat 6.1 has a bug with the PHP RPM file included on its install CD-ROM. Therefore, you must do an install of PHP following the instructions in Chapter 5, "PHP3," before you can test.

After you have installed PHP per the directions in Chapter 5, you can try a simple test. Create a directory named test under /home/httpd/html. In this create a simple Web page with the name index.php3. The contents of the Web page will be as follows:

```
<?php phpinfo() ?>
```

Then, run Netscape or Internet Explorer, and enter the following URL:

```
http://lin/test/index.php3
```

Or, if you are running X Windows on the Linux machine, enter the following:

```
http://127.0.0.1/test/index.php3
```

You should see a Web page similar to Figure 4.1. This figure shows a stripped-down PHP that does not include any of the services we will need. Yours will be different.

Figure 4.1

The standard PHP with no added features.

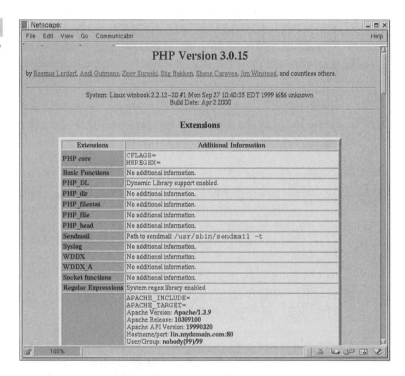

If you do not see this Web page, verify your `httpd` daemon is running. If it is running, revisit the edits in the `httpd.conf` file and check your error messages in `/var/log/messages`, `/var/log/secure`, `/var/log/httpd/error_log`, and `/var/log/httpd/access_log`. In most cases, the information there will tell you what you have done wrong. In some circumstances this will not occur.

Security Issues

Problems arise when users try to make your Web server give them documents or files you don't want them to have. PHP is written with this in view. Let's look at some possible attacks, and how PHP would handle them. Because our project uses PHP, the information here describes how the PHP-based IMP system will respond to some types of attacks.

Note

To add value to your IMP system, you might want to provide a welcome page to your system that has a link to your IMP login screen from one or more places. Your welcome screen could sign up a user and add that user to your system, making IMP immediately available.

To do this, you will need to run another Web application. If you use any helper CGI programs within your IMP system to run that application, you need to know about the issues covered in this section.

I will cover the precautions PHP takes when it is being used as a CGI program. Other CGI programs should also take these precautions. You need to check those programs for compliance to these security issues.

Users that have permission to execute programs in the Web server's cgi-bin directory can sometimes fool a cgi script to send them a file. One attempt could be a URL similar to the following:

```
http://www.servername.com/cgi-bin/php?/etc/passwd
```

If this line succeeds, the CGI script tries to interpret /etc/passwd as a script. In many cases, the CGI script will give you the contents of the file along with error messages. PHP is written to prevent this. PHP will not interpret the command-line argument, which is /etc/passwd, and so won't try to open that file.

Note

Nevertheless, PHP scripts can be vulnerable if incorrectly written. The version of IMP prior to 2.0.11 had a bug in it where it would display any readable file in the system. The 2.0.11 release fixes this problem.

Another attack would be to try to get access to hidden parts of your file server. A username and password normally protect those parts. (The Apache documentation covers these types of Web pages.) This type of URL could look something like this:

```
http://www.servername.com/cgi-bin/php/mysecret/document.html
```

To avoid this, PHP allows you to set a compile-time option `--enable-force-cgi-redirect`. This option tells PHP that you can't trust your Web server. When you use the Apache Web server, the environment variable REDIRECT_STATUS is set. This environment variable is unique to Apache, and tells PHP whether it is safe to use the redirect information on the command line. This is not a concern for your project, unless you decide to run PHP as a CGI program. I guide you through installing PHP to run as a module, so this will not be an issue.

When PHP is included as a module in the Apache Web server, it is run with the privileges of the user that Apache runs as. The Apache Web server typically runs as the user nobody. This user cannot log on to the system. This user is in it's own group. With this precaution, it is easy to protect a document from prying eyes by making it impossible for the user nobody to read it.

> If you have sensitive information on your system, and are paranoid about possible access from other users, you can protect a document by making it unreadable by anyone but the owner of the file. The command line for doing this under Linux is
>
> ```
> chmod o-rw,g-rw,u+rw filename
> ```

Running PHP with Minimal Risk

The best way to run PHP is as a module under Apache. When running as a module, most of your possible security issues fall under the umbrella of the Web server. Apache has proven itself to be very secure.

If you really must run PHP as a CGI script, you should use the `--enable-force-cgi-redirect` compile option. This will provide a minimum level of security.

Apache Configuration Issues

The PHP rpm that Red Hat included on its installation CD with version 6.1 is severely broken. It simply will not let Apache run when it includes PHP as a module. I browsed the Red Hat site at `http://www.redhat.com/errata`, and attempted to find a note or correction about this. No such information was forthcoming. To test the PHP and IMP configuration changes just made, you need to build PHP with the correct options and install your build. These steps will be covered in Chapter 5.

In some cases you might try to restart your server and get the following message:

```
[root@wmaxlaptop php-3.0.16]# /etc/rc.d/init.d/httpd restart
```

Output

```
Shutting down http:                                    [FAILED]
Starting httpd: httpd: cannot determine local host name.
Use the ServerName directive to set it manually.
                                                       [FAILED]
```

This happened to me because I am not on a local network with a DNS server. The best way to handle this is to make sure that the hostname the Linux machine is currently using is in the `/etc/hosts` file along with the correct ip address. Then edit the `/etc/httpd/conf/httpd.conf` file, and change the `ServerName` directive to the name you have chosen for your machine, or its IP address. Be sure to remove the # in front of the ServerName directive, as that turns the line into a comment line:

```
#
# ServerName: allows you to set a host name which is sent back to clients for
# your server if it's different than the one the program would get (i.e., use
# "www" instead of the host's real name).
#
# Note: You cannot just invent host names and hope they work. The name you
# define here must be a valid DNS name for your host. If you don't understand
# this, ask your network administrator.
# If your host doesn't have a registered DNS name, enter its IP address here.
# You will have to access it by its address (e.g., http://123.45.67.89/)
# anyway, and this will make redirections work in a sensible way.
#
ServerName lin
```

Now you can restart the Web server. Note the number of httpd processes that are running:

```
[root@wmaxlaptop conf]# /etc/rc.d/init.d/httpd restart
```

Output

```
Shutting down http:                                     [FAILED]
Starting httpd:                                         [  OK  ]
[root@wmaxlaptop conf]# ps ax | grep httpd
 1414 ?        S     0:00 httpd
 1417 ?        S     0:00 httpd
 1418 ?        S     0:00 httpd
 1419 ?        S     0:00 httpd
 1420 ?        S     0:00 httpd
 1421 ?        S     0:00 httpd
 1422 ?        S     0:00 httpd
 1423 ?        S     0:00 httpd
 1424 ?        S     0:00 httpd
```

The Next Step

You now have a basic understanding of how PHP works with a Web server, and some of the security issues involved with Web applications. Although fairly simple, these changes are crucial to making the IMP project work.

The next step is to build the PHP interpreter and incorporate it into the Apache Web server. After that is done you will have MySQL, PHP, and Apache ready to work together as a team to support the IMP Web application. Let's go!

Chapter 5

PHP

Introduction

PHP is a server-side scripting language. It strongly resembles the C programming language, with Perl flavoring thrown in. It is a very easy language to learn.

PHP supports many databases. We will concentrate on MySQL support. You will learn how to compile PHP to add the features needed for use with MySQL and the IMP email application.

Of the four pieces for your project, MySQL and Apache are already in place. When you are finished with this chapter, you will have a general-purpose system consisting of Apache, MySQL, and PHP. You will be able to access tables in the MySQL database using PHP-embedded scripting language in a Web page, and display the results to a Web browser.

The process of putting code in a Web page for the server to execute is often called *embedding*. Another term for this is *server-side scripting*. Microsoft calls its version of this process *Active Server Pages*.

All these terms refer to the process where the Web server interprets the information or code on the Web page. The server then sends the result of that work to the Web browser. The original Web page is almost never sent to the browser, though pieces of it can be.

A Brief History

Rasmus Lerdorf conceived PHP in 1994. He did some work with the preliminary version to keep track of who was looking at his rèsumè. The first generally available version debuted in early 1995 and was known as the Personal Home Page Tools.

It was a very limited tool set at that time. PHP's parser was rewritten in the middle of 1995, and became known as PHP/FI Version 2, for Personal Home Page Tools/Form Interpreter.

Starting in the middle of 1997, Zeev Suraski and Andi Gutmans rewrote the parser. This became the core of PHP. Several other people have contributed to PHP, some of whom are listed in the online documentation.

PHP Worldwide Use

PHP is shipped with every version of Red Hat Linux, and C2's StrongHold Web Server. As of 2000, PHP was being used in approximately 1,000,000 computer systems worldwide.

The GNU Public License

PHP is licensed under either the GNU Public License (GPL) or the PHP license, according to the Web page at `http://www.php.net/license.html`. You can choose to distribute PHP under either license. I will cover PHP as distributed under the GPL.

What It Means

First, I must strongly state that I am not an attorney, and if you need a true legal opinion on this matter, you should consult one. My opinions as expressed in the following paragraphs are not legal opinions; they are my thoughts about what you can do under Public Domain rules and under the GNU Public License. The GNU Public license (GPL) is in plain language, and I am expressing my views as they come from reading the license in a plain-language sense. These opinions are only mine, and they might be wrong. Only courts of law can rule on the legal nuances of the GPL.

The GPL is included at the end of this book. It is an interesting license. It differs from Public Domain in several critical ways.

In general, Public Domain material is free for use. It is usually widely available. You can take Public Domain information and modify it. The changes you make to Public Domain material might or might not be part of the Public Domain. As author of the changes, it is generally up to you, along with legal counsel, to decide. In some cases you might not have to distribute your changes to public domain material.

Other implications to modifying Public Domain material could be worked out within the legal system. You should consult a licensed attorney before distributing Public Domain material, either modified or not. It is best to consult an attorney who specializes in this field.

The GNU Public License (GPL) is different. Under the GPL, you can take the code and modify it for any purpose, and you can transfer it to any entity.

The GPL says you can charge money for cost of the transfer of any software covered under the GPL. You must also allow the entity that purchases software covered under the GPL to obtain the source code. You can charge money for the transfer of this source code to that entity.

After you have transferred the software or source code, that entity is bound by the GPL. You have no control over what is done to the software or source code you have transferred. That entity can modify it and transfer the modified or unmodified software under the same rules you had to follow.

It also specifies that your changes to any material covered under the GPL are immediately covered under the GPL. You must give these changes to the person or entity that obtains your compiled software if it contained those changes, at their request.

A loophole is possible in the GPL concerning code placed under it. If you have private version 1.0 of code, and generate version 1.1, you can place version 1.1 under the GPL. It appears that you can then take version 1.0 of the code and improve it to private version 2.0. Private version 2.0 of your code is not under the GPL. Nothing prevents someone from taking GPL version 1.1 of the code and modifying it so it matches the functionality of private version 2.0. However, only the version path that went from GPL 1.1 to GPL 2.0 is covered under the GPL.

Use of PHP Under the GNU License

You are free to use PHP on any machine for any purpose without paying for software or making royalty payments to anyone. You can create any application with PHP and distribute PHP with it any way you want. You must provide the source code to PHP, or the ability to get it if you do distribute PHP.

The code you put on a Web page to be executed by PHP is not part of the GNU Public License. You can copyright it and protect it from copying by others by restricting its use through signed agreements. Under certain circumstances, that will be the only way to protect your work.

Any PHP code you write and put on a Web page is "in the clear" if someone has physical access to the machine it is installed on. Most of the code you put on a Web page is also visible to the person who views the Web page with a browser. If they use the View Source option available in all browsers, they will be able to see most of the code you write using PHP for that page.

A Web page that totally consists of PHP instructions might not show any of the underlying PHP code. This is done by creating your Web page using print instructions. This is an excellent way to hide the most critical PHP code.

What Is PHP?

PHP is an interpreted language. It strongly resembles the C language. It also has some flavor of the Perl language. It is available for almost all platforms, including Linux, other versions of the Unix family, and Windows.

PHP enables you to generate Web pages on-the-fly. You do this by pulling data from databases or files, manipulating that data, and then sending that data to a Web browser.

Using PHP, you can update databases, create databases, and perform mathematical calculations (including complex trigonometric functions). You can also create and delete arbitrary files on your system, depending on the level of security at which you have PHP running. You can create Internet network connections and service those connections. It is theoretically possible to write a Web server using PHP. You are limited only by your imagination.

 Languages are either interpreted or compiled. An *interpreter* is a program that reads the file containing the code to be executed, and immediately acts upon it. The code in the file is called *source code*. In general, the code is readable and understandable by a person.

A *compiler* is a program that reads the source code file and compiles the program into binary code that can be executed directly by the computer. This binary code can't be read and understood by most people.

How It Works

The Web server generally runs PHP when a user requests a Web page that contains PHP code. Typically, the Web server is configured to use the filename extension to determine whether to run PHP. For example, a Web server will look at a Web page, and if it ends in `.htm` or in `.html`, the Web server will not attempt to execute any PHP script. If the page ends in `.php` (or in `.php3`, depending on how you have configured the Web server), the Web server looks at the contents of the Web page.

When the Web page contains one of the following escape sequences, it will run PHP to interpret that part of the page:

- `<?   "php code"  ?>`
- `<?php "php code"  ?>`
- `<% "php code"  %>` (Only available when the php.ini setting asp_tags is ON. OFF is the default setting.)
- `<script language="PHP"> "php code" </script>`

The Web page that the user sees is a mixture of the standard HTML commands on the page and the output of the PHP interpreter.

HTML stands for *Hypertext Markup Language*, and is a widely available standard for text documents. The home page for HTML is http://www.w3.org/MarkUp/. Several versions of HTML are available. All recently produced browsers understand at least HTML version 1.1.

PHP can also be built to run as a standalone program executing a file containing PHP code. This allows you to run timed programs using cron, or long-running programs from the command line. Any output from PHP when run in this fashion goes to stdout.

You will often see references to stdout, stdin, and stderr when the behavior of programs is being described. Whenever a program is run under Linux, three standard channels for information are opened.

The stdin channel takes information from an input source and feeds it to the program. This is usually done from the keyboard. You can, by using pipes (the | symbol) or redirection (the > symbol), feed the information from files.

The stdout channel takes information from the program and sends it out to a device. This device is usually the screen on a terminal window. You can use pipes or redirection to send this output to a file or another program's standard input.

The stderr channel is for error messages, and cannot be easily redirected to a file or another program. It is typically reserved for debugging during development, and for indicating very serious errors the program cannot handle. Many programs quit immediately upon sending a message out stderr.

For example, look for all index.html files on your computer in the Web server directory. One way to do this is to run the find command, looking for files that contain html, and screen for index as part of the filename. This can be accomplished with this command line:

```
[root@winbook /]# find /home/httpd/html -name "*.html" -print | grep index
```

What It Does for You

With its capability to execute complex instructions on data inserted into or retrieved from databases, PHP is an ideal format for creating interactive Web sites. It supports multiple databases, including mSQL, MySQL, Informix, and Oracle.

PHP allows you to quickly generate interactive Web pages. Because it is interpreted, you don't have to go through any extra steps to use your program. Changes can be made to your Web page and tested immediately.

This allows you to learn in a stepwise fashion. It is perfectly acceptable to test each line of code as you go, noting the effects of each change.

Because Linux, Apache, and PHP are free, and because MySQL is free on Linux for most uses, you can inexpensively set up a test machine. This enables you to duplicate your production environment and test changes. This is critical when modifying software because it allows you to make as many mistakes as you need to without affecting your customers.

Getting Online Help for PHP

Help for PHP is available at http://www.php.net. Online documentation along with FAQs and mailing lists is available at that site.

The Software Packages to Obtain

This project requires several software packages not normally installed on a system. These packages are the Apache Web server development RPM, the PHP source code, IMP source code, IMAP development RPM, and the Freetype development RPM. All these packages are available on the Web.

Apache Development RPM

The Apache Web server software and the Apache development rpm are included on the enclosed CD. Install the development rpm that matches the Apache Web server you have installed on your computer. If you don't, this project will not work. The latest RPMS for the Apache Web server under Red Hat Linux are available at ftp://ftp.redhat.com. The updated RPMS for Apache for Red Hat 6.1 are included on the enclosed CD-ROM.

PHP3 Source Code

The PHP source code is on the enclosed CD, and is available from the PHP Web site at http://www.php.net. As of this writing, PHP version 4 is almost ready. You will probably be able to upgrade both IMP and PHP after this project is installed and working. I don't recommend you do that at this point.

The philosophy is "make it work." After it works, you can "improve" it. The *just released* version of PHP has problems and does not have a track record. After the project is working correctly, you can upgrade to the new version of PHP. If the new version of PHP fails because of an unexpected bug, you can always backtrack to the version you know works.

If you have not copied the PHP source code tarball into your imp directory, do so now.

IMP Source Code

The IMP source code is on the enclosed CD, and it is also available from the IMP Web site, `http://www.horde.org`. Copy the IMP source code tarball to your `imp` directory. We will untar it later.

IMAP Development RPM

The IMAP development RPM must be installed, and the version must match the IMAP version installed. If you have not already installed the IMAP packages, do so now. The IMAP packages are available at `ftp://ftp.redhat.com`. They are supplied on the enclosed CD-ROM.

Freetype Development RPM

The Freetype Development RPM is not typically installed by the Red Hat installation routines. If it is not installed, install it now. You can download the Freetype development RPM from the ftp site at `ftp.redhat.com`.

5

Installation

You now have installed all the packages necessary for building PHP from source. I will lead you through a step by step build and install of the PHP package, with the options necessary for this project.

Note

Under RedHat 6.1, a bug is introduced with the Apache server. You must either install the updated Apache RPM files, version 1.3.9.8 or later, included on the CD-ROM, or you must edit an Apache configuration file.

If you cannot update the Apache RPM's, then edit the `/usr/sbin/apxs` file. Around line 81 you will see a line similar to the following:

```
my $CFG_LIBEXECDIR = 'modules';              # substituted via APACI
install
```

Change the line to read

```
my $CFG_LIBEXECDIR = '/usr/lib/apache';   # substituted via APACI
install
```

At around line 76, locate the line similar to the following:

```
my $CFG_LDFLAGS_SHLIB = '-shared'; # substituted via Makefile.tmpl
```

Change the line to read

```
my $CFG_LDFLAGS_SHLIB = 'q(-shared)'; # substituted via Makefile.tmpl
```

The next step is to untar the PHP directory. Change into the `imp` directory, and run the `untar` command:

```
root@winbook imp]# tar xvzf php-3.0.15.tar.gz
```

This will create the php-3.0.15 directory. Change to it, and run the `configure` command as follows:

```
[root@winbook imp]# cd php-3.0.15
[root@winbook php-3.0.15]# ./configure --with-apxs --with-xml
➥--with-mysql=/usr --with-imap
```

 Note The latest release of PHP compiles MySQL as a default. However, the installation documentation is misleading. It tells you to put the path to MySQL after `--with-mysql`. That will cause the compile to fail if you read it like I did. Instead, use the `--with-mysql=/usr` command line.

The configure script will start printing the checks it is making. This will take a few minutes. Next, run the `make` command:

```
[root@winbook php-3.0.15]# make
```

This can take several minutes. When `make` is finished, run the `install` command:

```
[root@winbook php-3.0.15]# make install
```

You should see a printout similar to this:

```
apxs -i -a -n php3 libphp3.so
cp libphp3.so /usr/lib/apache/libphp3.so
chmod 755 /usr/lib/apache/libphp3.so
[activating module `php3' in /etc/httpd/conf/httpd.conf]
```

The last line of the printout tells you that the install script modified the Apache `httpd.conf` file. Now Apache will load the PHP module when needed. Copy the default `ini` file to `/usr/local/lib`, and then restart the Web server:

```
[root@winbook php-3.0.15]# cp php3.ini-dist /usr/local/lib/php3.ini
[root@winbook php-3.0.15]# /etc/rc.d/init.d/httpd restart
Shutting down http:                                    [  OK  ]
Starting httpd:                                        [  OK  ]
```

Now you must check to see if the Apache Web server is running. Use the `ps ax` command, pipe through `grep`, looking for `httpd`:

```
[root@winbook root]# ps ax | grep httpd
  514 ?        S      0:00 httpd
  518 ?        S      0:00 httpd
  519 ?        S      0:00 httpd
  520 ?        S      0:00 httpd
  521 ?        S      0:00 httpd
```

```
522 ?        S      0:00 httpd
523 ?        S      0:00 httpd
524 ?        S      0:00 httpd
525 ?        S      0:00 httpd
813 pts/1    S      0:00 grep httpd
```

You should see something like the previous printout. If you don't, read the "Troubleshooting the Installation" section in Chapter 4, "Apache Web Server."

You now have PHP correctly installed with the Apache Web server. You will want to read the section "Apache Web Server." That section describes a configuration file change to allow Apache to use PHP files as main index pages. Now would be a good time to skip back to Chapter 4, to the section titled "Testing the PHP and IMP Configuration."

Troubleshooting the Installation

The first time I installed PHP, everything appeared to go well. I started the Apache Web server, and it indicated it had started, using the following messages:

```
[root@winbook php-3.0.15]# /etc/rc.d/init.d/httpd restart
Shutting down http:                                    [  OK  ]
Starting httpd:                                        [  OK  ]
```

Unfortunately, when I looked for the Web server in the process list (using the ps ax command), it wasn't there. I looked in the error file /var/log/httpd/error_log, and all I found was this:

```
[Mon Apr  3 18:30:59 2000] [notice] Apache/1.3.9 (Unix)  (Red Hat/Linux)
➡PHP/3.0.15 configured -- resuming normal operations
[Mon Apr  3 20:13:15 2000] [notice] caught SIGTERM, shutting down
```

The first thing I did was reduce the PHP options to the minimum. I decided I only wanted to see the Web server run with PHP installed. I built PHP with the command line

```
./configure --with-apxs
```

and then I installed it and ran the Web server. No dice. I then read the instructions in the file in the PHP directory named INSTALL.REDHAT. It put a note in which said "--with-xml is required for Apache 1.3.6 or higher." Doh! After this occurred, the Web server loaded and ran with PHP.

Now I was ready to tackle the rest. I put in the --with-mysql option. Same problem as before. I looked at the INSTALL.REDHAT documentation. No dice. So then I went to the PHP Web page and looked around. There is a FAQ section on the Web site. I went to it and started looking for anything that had "mysql" in it. I found a note about some other problem that mentioned the MySQL option looking like this: "--with-mysql=/usr". I put that into the command-line option, and it worked!

The point of all of this is to read and reread the documentation carefully when things break. Also, go to the World Wide Web and search for information. If you have no luck, join a mailing list and ask questions. PHP has a very good mailing list that is very helpful. I have used it in the past. The creator of PHP himself pointed out a stupid mistake on my part, without browbeating. Information on how to join that list is at `http://www.php.net`.

PHP in a Nutshell

The PHP language is described as an "HTML embedded scripting language" in the online documentation. It strongly resembles the C language, so if you have experience in that language you are in great shape. You place PHP commands on a Web page and have the server interpret those Web pages before sending the results to the Web browser.

In any computer language, you have three main capabilities. These capabilities can vary in degree of implementation, but they exist. In every language you can make calculations, perform actions, and change the course of execution based on decisions.

PHP allows you to do all of this. For example, in PHP, you can use Perl-like syntax to add two numbers together:

```
$a = $b + 3;
```

You can also perform actions. With PHP, you can print information to the Web browser, operate on files, and run other programs. To print something to the screen with PHP, you could do this:

```
printf("This is a test\n");
```

You can also use `print()` or echo to print something on the screen. The `printf()` function works exactly like its C counterpart. The `print` statement has a similar counterpart in Perl.

With PHP you can decide to execute instructions based on results of previous answers. The two constructs are "if (test) A else B", and "switch(test)". For example, the following will print "B is less than 3" if the value of B is less than 3, and will print the "B is greater than…" statement in all other cases:

```
$b = $a+ 1;
if ( $b < 3 )
        printf("B is less than 3\n");
else
        printf("B is greater than or equal to 3\n");
```

The switch statement allows you to select from individual answers and execute code based on the answer. The following prints one, two, three, or none of the above, based on the value of $b:

```
switch ($b)
        {
        case 1:
        printf("one\n");
        break;
        case 2:
        printf("two\n");
        break;
        case 3:
        printf("three\n");
        break;
        default:
        printf("none of the above\n");
        break;
        }
```

PHP supports looping constructs. Loops are sections of code that continue executing until a condition is met. Instructions to exit from a loop early are also available, as shown in Table 5.1.

Table 5.1 PHP Looping Instructions

Statement	*Description*
while (condition) {statements}	Execute statements while condition evaluates to TRUE.
do { statements; } while (condition)	Execute the statements at least once, continuing to execute while condition evaluates to TRUE.
for (start; continue_execution ; statement) {statement}	Execute the statements while the continue_execution condition evaluates to TRUE.
continue	This immediately takes you to the conditional test of a statement, bypassing the execution of rest of the code in the loop for that pass.
break	When this is encountered, the loop is executed, bypassing the execution of the rest of the code in the loop, and ignoring the conditional test.

PHP also enables you to include code written in other files. You do this using the include or require statement with strings or variables as arguments. The require statement always reads the file in, even if the contents of the file will not be used. The include statement might not actually cause the file to be read if a conditional test causes PHP to skip execution of the line the include is in. The following includes code from another file. If you enter your code exactly as shown, the file will be included twice:

```
require "filename";
$a = "filename";
include $a;
```

PHP also enables you to create your very own functions, put them in files, and include them using the previously mentioned `include` or `require` statements. You can also create and use functions in the current Web page. You use your own functions in much the same way you would use built-in database functions. With this ability, PHP allows you to build up a comfortable set of personal tools that you can use to greatly speed up Web page development. For example, the following function will print "`this is my function`" and return a value of 3 to the caller:

```
function my_function()
{
    echo "this is my function";
    $returnvalue = 3;
    return $returnvalue;
}
```

A *function* is a subroutine that is "called." When you *call* a function, you place its name in the code and the PHP parser begins executing the code in the function when it encounters the function name. When a function returns a value, the PHP parser takes the value of the expression the function places in the `return` statement and treats the function call as if it were a variable. In the following code, `$a` will have a value of 5 when using the `my_function()` call defined previously:

```
$a = my_function() + 2;
```

For many people, functions are hard to understand because they are so simple. In PHP, a function's code will not be used until it is called. This enables you to carry functions in a page and not worry about their effect.

General Format

The PHP language has a few general rules to follow. The first rule is that almost every statement ends with a semicolon. If the end tag is encountered (?>), the semicolon is assumed to exist. You can stack multiple statements on a line by ending each one with a semicolon. For example

```
$a=$b+$c; $g=$d+$e ;  $f= $f+1; // starting at the '//' is a comment
```

The exception to using semicolons is a comment. Comments don't require semicolons. Comments are notes you make in the code that the compiler ignores completely. Comments can span several lines, or can be only part of a line. Multiline-capable

comments start with /* and end with */. Single-line or partial-line comments start
with // or #. The first comment below is a multiline comment. The rest are single-line
or partial-line comments. Even single-line comments only comment to the end of the
block, as indicated by the ?> tag.

```
/* This is a comment
   that spans several
   lines */
// this is a single line comment.  It ends at the end of the line.
$a=$b+$c;// this is a line comment.  It starts
➥at the // and ends here.
<?php a=3;// this comment ends at the tag ?> this is displayed
➥by the bowser
$b=$c+$a;# This is a shell style line comment.  It starts
➥at # and ends here.
```

All variables in PHP begin with a $ sign. There are a few types of variables in PHP.
The PHP parser automatically determines these types at run time, although you can
override this automatic determination. The types of variables will change depending
on use in a statement.

The types and modes of variables available in PHP are the following:

- **Integer number**—Can be represented in octal by beginning with the number
  0, or in hexadecimal by beginning with 0x. For example, 010 is an octal number
  with a value of 8. The number 0x10 is a hex number with a value of 16. The
  number 10 is a decimal number with a value of 10. For example, each of the
  following sets the variable a to a value of 16:

  ```
  $a = 16;
  $a = 020;
  $a = 0x10;
  ```

- **Floating-point number**—Floating-point numbers have decimal points. The
  value 123.45 is a floating-point number. The following sets the variable a to a
  value of 16.5:

  ```
  $a=16.5;
  ```

- **String**—A string is enclosed in quotation marks or single quotes.
- **Array**—Arrays can be of one or more dimensions. An array can be indexed by a
  value or by an association. By association, you can associate the name George
  with the value super, as in the following example:

  ```
  $a["super"]= "George";
  ```

If you use $a["super"] in an expression, it will return "George." You can also use numbers to index arrays:

```
$b[1] = "George";
$c[1] = 14.56;
$d[1][1] = 12;
```

- **Object**—An object is similar to a C++ object. You generate an object definition with a class statement, and set a variable to be an object using the new statement. For example:

```
class MyClass {
        function MyClassFunction()
                {
                echo "This is the MyClassFunction";
                }
        } // the end of class MyClass

$ACV = new MyClass;
// call the MyClassFunction in the new object $ACV
        $ACV->MyClassFunction();
```

- **Variable variables**—A variable that is a string can be used as a variable name by using two $ symbols in a row. (Note: Strictly speaking, this is not a type of variable. The result of the interpretation of the string is the resulting type of the variable.) For example, let's make a variable with a value of "test." Then let's create a variable named "test," and fill it with the value of "complete." After this, print the value of the $test variable.

```
$a = "test";
$$a = "complete";
echo " $a == $$a, the same as $test";
```

- **Type-cast variables**—You can change the type of a variable by casting. If a variable is an integer, you can force it to be a double. The types available to you for casting are the variable types already covered. You can also abbreviate int for integer, or use the terms real or float instead of double. To do this, you must put the type in parentheses:

```
$b = 3; // $b is an integer
$a = (real)1 +(float)$b;//forces everything to double,
åand $a now equals 4.0
```

- **Null**—A variable that is Null does not yet have a value assigned to it. It does not yet exist in memory space. This is new to PHP 4.

- **Boolean**—The Boolean value is either TRUE or FALSE. In PHP 3, TRUE is 1, FALSE is 0.

- **Resource**—An identifier that specifies a system resource, such as returned from a mysql_connect() call. This is new to PHP 4.

Strings and Parsing

PHP does some interesting things with strings. A string is a group of characters that is usually displayed verbatim. Under PHP, strings change their meaning. What you get might not be what you expect unless you are very careful.

For example, assuming $a has a value of 3, the statement

```
echo "This is a string. The value of \$a is $a."
```

will print

```
This is a string. The value of $a is 3.
```

The second occurrence $a variable was expanded to print out the string equivalent of its value. The first occurrence was not expanded because it was escaped by the use of the \character. The escape character tells PHP to use the next character literally, and not to try to interpret it before printing it.

To avoid printing the expanded value of the variable, put the string in single quotes. This line

```
echo 'This is also a string. The value of $a is $a.'
```

will print

```
This is also a string.  The value of $a is $a.
```

A string using quotation marks will have the internal value of all variables that are listed in them printed. For example, suppose the variable $a equals 3, and $b has the value of Hello. The following will print "3 brown cows," and "Hello, George."

```
echo "$a brown cows.  $b, George.";
```

Web Page Use

To use PHP, you must let the server know that it could possibly call the PHP interpreter for a Web page. You do this by encoding the Web page type in the extension. Most Web pages for Linux end in .html. It is typical practice to end the Web page in .php (or in .php3 if you are running the PHP version 3 interpreter) to indicate a PHP Web page.

PHP can change the contents of a Web page as delivered to the user. When you view a Web page on a browser, you will see the results of the PHP script. In very few cases, you will see the PHP code behind the script when you use the view page

5

source command that is available in most browsers. I recommend you do this when you test your PHP pages. You might discover information you want to hide.

The showing of source code is usually because of a mistake you have made in wrapping your code. If the PHP interpreter does not expect to see source code at certain places in your document, it will not remove that code.

Apache Web Server

Normally, the main page in a Web server directory is titled `index.html`. In our project, it is necessary to use an `index.php3` Web page as the main Web page. To enable this, edit the `/etc/httpd/conf/httpd.conf` file, and around line 448 (for Red Hat 6.1 Apache installation), change the `DirectoryIndex` line to look like this:

```
#
# DirectoryIndex: Name of the file or files to use as a pre-written HTML
# directory index.  Separate multiple entries with spaces.
#
DirectoryIndex index.php3 index.html index.htm index.shtml index.cgi
```

The standard for PHP version 3 is to use `.php3` as your extension. For PHP version 4, the standard is to use `.php`. This enables you to run both versions 3 and 4 simultaneously on a Web site. This version of IMP was written for PHP 3, and needs the `.php3` extension. You can also add `index.php` to the `DirectoryIndex` line, in addition to `index.php3`.

If you still have the `/home/httpd/html/test` directory you set up in Chapter 4, under "Testing the PHP and IMP Configuration," you can test this change. First, restart the server, and then load the test page by specifying only the test directory:

```
[root@winbook net]# /etc/rc.d/init.d/httpd restart
Shutting down http:                                      [  OK  ]
Starting httpd:                                          [  OK  ]
[root@winbook net]# lynx http://127.0.0.1/test
```

In this situation I used the command-line Web browser called lynx. It comes with every version of Red Hat, and is an easy and quick way to test a Web page. I use it whenever I want to see something very quickly. It loads quickly and usually does not hang for long periods of time. If it does, a Ctrl + C will exit it.

You should see the PHP info page that is generated by the `phpinfo()` function call. If it does not show, make sure you don't have an error in your changes to the

/etc/httpd/conf/httpd.conf file. Verify the server restarted properly by running ps ax | grep httpd. If it did not, refer to the "Troubleshooting" section of Chapter 4.

EXCURSION

Interaction of Web Server and Browser

One problem that occurred is very interesting. Whenever I entered a http://127.0.0.1/test line without the trailing slash, I was told the server was unavailable. I had temporarily changed the IP address on the computer, and the normal Web server-Web browser interaction threw a wrench into the works.

When your browser asks for a page, it does it exactly as you type it in. In our case, test is a directory, not a page. The browser is refused. This always happens, and is not a problem. The browser then requests the page with a trailing slash, to save you frustration. (In this case it turns /test into /test/) When it does that, it also substitutes the name of the server it received from the first contact in place of the IP address. If this name resolves differently from the original IP address, you might be told that it couldn't find the server!

If you enter the line with the trailing slash, it will find the page right away, because it does not do another lookup. Therefore, if you have problems finding a page, try entering the directory name with a trailing slash. It can lead you to the solution of a problem.

This happened because I had temporarily changed the IP address on my machine, and the Web server name was no longer resolvable back to my machine's IP address. The server name entry in the /etc/httpd/conf/httpd.conf file could have been changed to resolve to the new IP address. However, adding a / at the end of the line is the lazy way of solving a temporary problem.

PHP Use

The IMP project actively uses PHP. It takes information from the MySQL database for the current user to display the address book, and to set preferences. It also displays images and embeds PHP code in HTML pages.

In this section, I cover the concepts behind IMP's use of the MySQL database, the use of images, and the embedding of PHP within HTML pages. You will be given the opportunity to try out some of these concepts.

Database Interfacing

PHP provides database interface routines specific to the particular database you are using. Because you are using MySQL, I will cover only the MySQL API. The other databases have APIs similar in nature to MySQL, so the same concepts apply.

To use a database, you must first connect to it. When you connect to a database, you give the database your name and password. This validates you as a user and gives you privileges to particular tables which that database has.

Whenever the IMP user logs in to the system through the initial page, the database accesses are made based on the password you set in the PHP files. The IMP scripts have been carefully written to not allow the user to generically access the database.

> **Note**
>
> Because the database login and password is given in the PHP Web page, you must be careful to log in as a user that has very limited capabilities. If you log in to the database as a superuser, you invite trouble. An error in a PHP Web page can reveal your superuser login and password to any Web browser. This error might not occur except in extraordinary circumstances, and thus escape detection during initial testing.

When connected to a database, you look up data in the database and display that data on a Web page. You take input from a user in the form of Web page button clicks or fields that are filled out, and save that data into the database. This is exactly what IMP does with the address information the user enters.

Let's analyze an example Web page that connects to our MySQL database. We will use the IMP database tables that were previously set up. I will show you step by step how to connect to the database using PHP.

First, let's use the test directory because you already have a Web page there and have used it. To connect to a MySQL database, first connect to a server with the `mysql_connect()` function using a username and password. Change the `index.php3` Web page to the following:

```php
<?php
  printf("opening db....");
  $db = mysql_connect("localhost","impmgr", "impmgr");

  printf("closing db\n");
  mysql_close($db);

 ?>
```

Save it, and bring up the Web page. I used lynx on my computer,

```
[root@wmaxlaptop test]# lynx http://127.0.0.1/test/
```

and I got the following printout:

```
    opening db....closing db
```

I wondered about this, because it seemed too easy. So I deliberately entered the password incorrectly by putting the letter s in front of the password. The result was markedly different:

```
    opening db....
    Warning: MySQL Connection Failed: Access denied for user:
```

```
'impmgr@localhost' (Using password: YES) in
/home/httpd/html/test/index.php3 on line 3
closing db
Warning: 0 is not a MySQL link index in
/home/httpd/html/test/index.php3 on line 6
```

As you can see from the printout, PHP gives you the line number in error when it prints out error messages. This is not always the case, and depends in part on how well the included library code is written.

Now that you have a connection, let's put data into the database and retrieve that data. You can select the database with the `mysql_select_db()` function. Then you run a query on the database using `mysql_query()` and retrieve the results with `mysql_fetch_object()`, `mysql_fetch_row()`, or `mysql_fetch_array()`. Or, you can do both simultaneously with `mysql_db_query()`. Change the `index.php3` page you are working with to the following:

```php
<?php
  printf("opening db....<p>");
  $db = mysql_connect("localhost","impmgr", "impmgr");
  $result = mysql_select_db("imp",$db);
  $user = "me@test.com"; $nick = "meme";
  $result = mysql_query(
          "INSERT into imp_addr (user,nickname) values ('$user','$nick')",
          $db);

  $result = mysql_query("select user,nickname from imp_addr",$db);
  $rows = mysql_num_rows($result); //will be 1 in our case
  for ($index = 0 ; $index < $rows; $index++)
   {
   $data = mysql_fetch_object($result);
   printf("user = $data->user, nick=$data->nickname<p>\n");
   }
  printf("closing db\n");
  mysql_close($db);
 ?>
```

Look at the sequence of events in this PHP code before you load the Web page. I will walk you through each statement:

1. The `<?php` tag indicates to the Web server this is a PHP script. It calls the PHP parser to work on this Web page. Without this statement, you get the PHP code displayed on your Web page.

2. You print a line of code with the HTML tag `<p>`, which forces a line break. This is not necessary to connect to the database.

3. Connect to the `mysql` database engine with the `mysql_connect()` function. As you saw before, if you have an error here, you will get an error displayed on the Web page.

4. Select the database you want to use. This can be combined with the query function using the `mysql_db_select()` function.

5. Set up the variable values that will be inserted into the database. This might have been done well before this code was ever executed. You can create a function of your own to insert data, passing in the variables to the function.

6. Use the `mysql_query()` function call to send an SQL statement to the database, inserting data into the database. If the `$result` is `FALSE`, the call failed. For this demonstration, we did not check the return from the function call, but we should have. It can indicate an error with the data or database rather than the code.

7. Again, use the `mysql_query()` call to ask the database for the information just inserted.

8. Determine the number of rows returned by the SQL statement using `mysql_num_rows()`. You must feed this function the $result from the last query. You will typically use this with a counting variable that determines how many times you will go through a retrieval loop.

9. The `for` loop is a good loop construct to use to gather data. A `while` loop is also good. I chose a `for` loop, and counted from zero to one less than the number returned from `mysql_num_rows()`.

10. To retrieve the rows, you have several options. Because I knew the names of the fields in this example, I used the `msyql_fetch_object()` function.

11. Print the data returned from your query. I used the `printf()` function. It is my favorite because of being identical to the heavily used C library function of the same name.

12. A "closing db" line is printed. This is not necessary, but is an aid in debugging. If you use print statements to aid debugging, you would typically remove them before you put your code in production.

13. The database connection is closed using `mysql_close()`.

Every use of a database from a Web page involves the same basic steps previously explained. When using the data retrieved from an SQL query, you can use functions other than `mysql_fetch_object()`. You can also use one of the following:

```
mysql_fetch_array()
mysql_fetch_field()
mysql_fetch_lengths()
mysql_fetch_row()
mysql_field_name()
mysql_field_table()
mysql_field_types()
```

```
mysql_field_flags()
mysql_field_len()
```

All these are described in the appendix, "PHP Language Reference."

Graphics

You can use PHP to get the size of JPEG, GIF, and PNG images. If you have the GD library installed, which is standard with Red Hat 6.x, you can also create and manipulate images.

 Note

Version 1.6 or greater of the GD library will no longer manipulate GIF images. The holder of the patent for compressed GIF images has recently been fairly active in pursuing Web sites that use GIF manipulation programs that were created without paying patent fees.

Many people using the Internet have moved from the GIF format to the PNG format for that reason. If you need to use GIF images, you need to acquire licensed software that gives you the right to manipulate and display these images.

5

All the image manipulation functions provided by the GD library begin with "Image." You can draw arcs, boxes, lines, and rectangles. You can create polygons and fill them with colors. You can draw characters in various fonts. The following snippet of code draws a rectangle with a background and foreground color and places a string in it:

```
$image = ImageCreate(150,30);/* create blank image */
$bkgcolor = ImageColorAllocate($image,255,255,255);/* background color */
$fgccolor = ImageColorAllocate($image,0,0,0);/* foreground color */
ImageFilledRectangle($image,0,0,150,30,$bkgcolor);/* fill background */
ImageString($image,1,5,5,"This is an image",$fgccolor); /* display a msg */
```

Using PHP in HTML Documents

Two approaches exist to using PHP in HTML pages (Web pages). The first approach is to create a Web page with an editor such as Microsoft's FrontPage, embedding PHP script in the page at the appropriate spots. The second approach is to dynamically generate the entire page using PHP.

Every HTML document should begin with an HTML DOCTYPE tag and a <HTML> tag and end with a </HTML> tag. With today's browsers, this is not very important, unless you are trying to use some advanced HTML features. Our test pages were generated without any HTML tags whatsoever.

If you do need to use advanced features, proper opening tags are used to notify the browser what to expect. If you wanted to use HTML version 3.2, you would need a skeleton that looks like this:

```
<!DOCTYPE HTML PUBLIC "-//W3C//DTD HTML 3.2 Final//EN">
<HTML>
<HEAD>
<TITLE>Your Document's Descriptive Title Here</TITLE>
... document info /heading
</HEAD>
<BODY>
... html document body
</BODY>
</HTML>
```

> **Note**
>
> In actuality, the HTML, HEAD, and BODY tags are not needed in HTML version 3.2 because the browser can infer them. Adding these tags is a matter of taste. If you add them, some earlier browsers will be able to render the page more or less properly (except for tags it does not understand). The TITLE tag is required.

Assuming you are using a good Web page editor, these things will be taken care of for you. Your PHP code would typically be inserted in the HTML document body, after the `<BODY>` tag. Because the PHP code is typically stripped from the Web page before it is sent to the browser, you can insert PHP functions before the beginning of the HTML tags if you want.

If you want to create the entire Web page using PHP, you need to generate the HTML tags using `print` (or `echo` or `printf`) statements. The above skeleton Web page could be written in PHP as follows:

```
<?php
 print('<!DOCTYPE HTML PUBLIC \"-//W3C//DTD HTML 3.2//EN\">');
print('<HTML>');
print('<HEAD>');
print('... document info /heading');
print('</HEAD>');
print('<BODY>');
print('... html document body');
print('</BODY>');
print('</HTML>');
?>
```

It is generally much easier to generate your Web page using a good visual editor and spice it with PHP code. You do have to be careful with some editors because they might try to strip the PHP code from the Web page. If you use FrontPage, for example, it is usually best to turn on ASP style tags and use PHP that way. Otherwise you tend to have problems when re-editing the page.

Summary

In the business world, everything revolves around the manipulation of information and the exposition of that information in document form. Until the Web browser and Web server came along, it was very expensive and very difficult to generate well-crafted documents that were served to unlimited readers. That is now common place.

With the technology enhancement provided by PHP, you can generate customized documentation based on individual requirements. By combining database access, dynamic inclusion of images in HTML documents, and the ability to dynamically change the contents of a Web page, PHP provides you with the ability to create applications that were once the purview of large mainframe systems.

Our project is an Internet mail reader that reads a database and builds a dynamic Web page with images and on-the-fly–generated HTML delivered to your Web browser. You could also build a custom inventory-tracking program, a Web-based contact program, or a trouble-monitor program. You now have the tools. The possibilities are limitless.

5

Chapter 6

IMP

IMP provides a very good Web-based interface to your electronic mail. It is similar in effect to Microsoft's HotMail, or Netscape's WebMail (see Figure 6.1). With IMP, you can set up an intraoffice, interoffice, or Internet mail system that will work with almost any operating system. The only requirement is a Web browser that can handle JavaScript, tables, and cookies. The list of operating systems that have such Web browsers includes Microsoft Windows 3.1, Windows 95, Windows 98, Windows NT 3.5, Windows NT 4.0, Windows 2000, Macintosh (System 8 or later has Internet Explorer as its standard browser), Linux, Solaris, BSD, and more.

IMP is fun! The basic IMP package provides a very pleasant screen that is easy to use. The satisfaction of seeing it work the first time is hard to beat. Let's get started.

Figure 6.1

Typical IMP session.

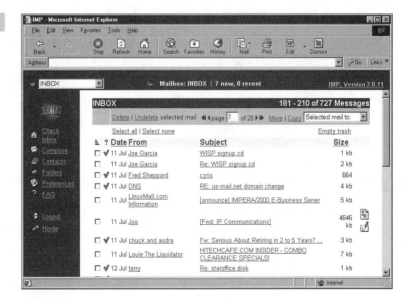

GPL and GNU Library General Public License

IMP is distributed under the GNU Public License (GPL), which I've described in Chapter 5, "PHP." The horde libraries that IMP uses are distributed under the GNU Library General Public License (LGPL). The LGPL is a variant of the GPL with an important restriction lifted. A copy of the LGPL library is included in this book.

Under the GPL, any code you write that links to code that is written under the GPL falls under the GPL. This can be undesirable in some cases. You might have a portion of your system that is a trade secret. In this case, linking with GPL code would force you to open up your code.

Under the LGPL, you can link your code with the code covered under the LGPL without causing your code to fall under the GPL or LGPL. This allows you to have trade-secret software that uses publicly available libraries. The customer has access to the source code of the libraries. Your source code can stay hidden.

Use of IMP Under the GNU Public License

You are free to sell media that contains IMP, but you must provide a way for the customer to get the source code. Any modifications you make to IMP must be passed to a customer at their request if you sell IMP on a disk to that customer. You can provide a for-fee service using IMP. You can provide a free service with IMP. You can put IMP on as many computers as you choose without paying royalties. You can sell computers that have IMP installed. You can modify IMP to suit your needs.

For example, suppose you were to modify IMP to add some very interesting feature. Let's assume this feature is rotating banner ads at the bottom of each message. You also packaged it so that it was a single-click install. You could sell the program at any retail store. You would have to either include the source code on the disks you sold or give the customer the ability to obtain the source code. After users buy the package, they could copy it, give it to anyone and install it on as many machines as they want. They can also copy and modify the features you added to IMP.

You could also start a Web-mail–based email service and charge users a nominal fee for use. Companies that provide Web-based email usually support themselves through advertising and offering extra services beyond a minimal level for a charge.

What Is IMP?

IMP is described as an "Imap Webmail program" on the main Web site (`http://www.horde.org`). IMP allows anyone with a JavaScript-capable Web browser to access email.

IMP Description

IMP is a collection of PHP scripts and JavaScript browser instructions. These scripts connect to an IMAP server on the target machine, which can be the machine that IMP is running on. It is possible to set up a set of IMP Web servers that connect to a central IMAP server.

IMP Installation

In this section, I will guide you through the installation and configuration of IMP. The following steps depend heavily on the previous chapters. If you haven't finished the previous chapters successfully, IMP installation and configuration will fail. If you do have problems, see the troubleshooting section near the end of this chapter.

Obtaining the Software

You can download IMP from the Web site at `http://www.horde.org`. When you do, get version 2.0.11 because that is the version I will be working with.

> As of the writing of this book, IMP 2.2 became available. However, it is not yet ready for prime time. When I gave it my mailbox, it immediately logged me out. I'm sure it will be ready for use soon. After you have gone through the process of installing IMP 2.0.11, you can upgrade to IMP 2.2 because the concepts are very similar.
>
> IMP version 2.2 includes session support, which requires PHP 4 (also newly released). This feature will make it a very nice upgrade.
>
> The philosophy of this project is to give you a verifiably working product, which is IMP 2.0.11. By the time the book is in circulation, the newer version of IMP will have matured, and should be ready for general use. However, software never pays attention to schedules!
>
> You can also check Macmillan's Web site for changes or corrections to this book. The Web site for updates to this book is
>
> `http://www.mcp.com/updates.cfm?item=0789724405`

IMP comes in two parts. The first part is the horde library. Copy the `horde-1.0.11.tar.gz` file into the imp directory you created in your home directory. Also copy the `imp-2.0.11.tar.gz` file. Untar both, as shown in the following code:

```
[root@winbook imp]# tar xvzf horde-1.0.11.tar.gz
```

Output

```
......(file list printed here)....
horde-1.0.11/templates/signup/signup.inc
horde-1.0.11/templates/status/
horde-1.0.11/templates/status/status.inc
```

Output

```
[root@winbook imp]# tar xvzf imp-2.0.11.tar.gz
.......(file list printed here).....
imp-2.0.11/templates/spelling/
imp-2.0.11/templates/spelling/footer.inc
imp-2.0.11/templates/status/
imp-2.0.11/templates/status/body.inc
[root@winbook imp]#
```

At this point, it is a good idea to look at the two directories that were created. Get a feel for the list of files and how the directory structure is arranged.

The next step is to copy the horde and IMP directories to the correct spot in the Web server directory structure. At the same time, we will rename them. The internal scripts expect to be in directories horde/ and horde/imp/:

```
[root@winbook imp]# cp -a horde-1.0.11 /home/httpd/html/horde
[root@winbook imp]# cp -a imp-2.0.11 /home/httpd/html/horde/imp
```

You now have the basic system installed. It does not yet work properly. A couple of options are available for making IMP work. I will walk you through the Web-based setup of IMP. After it is finished, you will need to tweak a few settings in PHP to use IMP.

 Note

IMP 2.0.11 does not work with PHP version 4. If you install PHP version 4 and try to run the IMP setup, you will get a `Parse Error` message on line 79 of the library file in the setup directory. The fix for this is to remove PHP 4 and install PHP 3.

PHP 4 is generally compatible with PHP 3, but some differences do exist. It will take some time for these differences to be well known.

IMP 2.2 has just been released. This new IMP requires PHP version 4 and requires the installation of a new PHP library. As of this writing, a new security hole has been found in it, and an update will be available almost immediately.

I have a philosophy about new releases. "Don't use version .0 (dot-zero) of any software package!" For example, PHP 4.0 is now at 4.01p2 (version .01, patch level 2) because of bugs found in release.0. I fully expect IMP 2.2 will go through similar revisions. My experience indicates that a release of .02 (IE: 4.02) is the first release anyone should install of any software package on a production server.

The versions of IMP and PHP we are using represent the most stable and most secure versions available. They are the best candidates for providing a good level of service with the least amount of trouble.

Configuring the Program

Strictly speaking, IMP is not compiled. The horde libraries are configured based on the type of database used, among other things. Three ways to install IMP are available. These are the totally manual way, the script way, and the Web page way.

The Web page way uses PHP to do the configuration and builds the libraries with changes. That is the way we will do it.

Installing IMP

Horde comes with a `setup.php3` Web page. This page is defaulted to not be readable so that no one can modify your IMP settings. The creator of the Web-based setup script has provided an easy way to get the ball rolling. From a command prompt, change to the horde directory, and run the `install.sh` script:

```
[root@wmaxlaptop horde]# cd /home/httpd/html/horde/
[root@wmaxlaptop horde]# sh ./install.sh
```

Output

```
Your blank configuration files have been created, please go to
the configuration utitlity at :

your install path url/setup.php3
```

This shell script sets up a default system that is mostly blank. No database support is provided. To finish setting up horde, you need to run the Web page setup script. You can run the setup script using lynx, Netscape, or Internet Explorer.

To use lynx in an xterm, enter the following

```
[root@wmaxlaptop net]# lynx http://lin/horde/setup.php3
```

(where `//lin` is the Web server name.)

I will show you the pages as we go. In many cases, only the relevant part of the screen will be printed. Lynx often gives helpful instructions at the bottom of the Web page it is displaying.

6

EXCURSION

IP Addresses and Traveling Computers

I move between networks on a daily basis. Each location provides me with different IP addresses for my machine and different machine names. Because of the problems associated with my IP address changing, I decided to give myself a private IP address that was not on any of the networks and did not share any characteristics with those networks.

To that end, I chose 192.168.1.66 for my machine. When I hook up a Windows machine on the same network, I have to give it a 192.168.1.x address to let it talk to my Linux machine. I chose 192.168.1.70 for that machine. I modified my `/etc/hosts` file to reflect the 192.168.1.x private addresses. If you take this approach, be sure to modify your Windows **hosts** file also. Speaking from experience, this can be a perplexing problem.

To make things easier for me during my network changes, I created a set of scripts. These scripts are placed in a directory named **net/**, in root's home directory. Only root can run these scripts. The basic script looks like the following:

```
#!/bin/bash
ifdown eth0
```

```
cp -f /root/net/clog/network /etc/sysconfig/network
cp -f /root/net/clog/ifcfg-eth0 /etc/sysconfig/network-scripts
cp -f /root/net/clog/resolv.conf /etc
ifup eth0
route add default gw 172.16.1.1
rm -f core
```

In the `clog/` directory, I have modified copies of the files that control network configuration. These files come from the `/etc/sysconfig/` directory. By executing the `ifdown` program, the ethernet card driver is turned off, and its IP address is removed. When the `ifup` program is executed, the new IP address is activated. The default gateway must be set up again, because it was typically removed during the process.

It is much faster running a script than rebooting. Linux shines in such areas.

If you are running the lynx browser, it will ask you to allow a cookie. Indicate yes:

```
lin cookie: chuckmIMPlang=en  Allow? (Y/N/Always/neVer)Y
```

The configuration Web page is brought up. It asks you for the default language (see Figure 6.2).

Figure 6.2

IMP Web-based setup, Step 1.

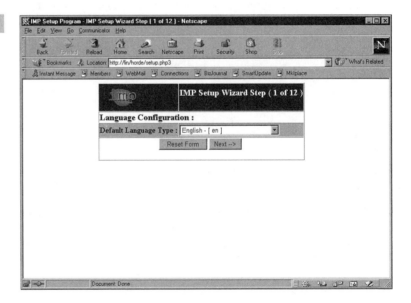

In my case, the default language is English. Currently, Brazilian Portuguese, German, French, Italian, and Slovak are supported through a drop-down menu. Choose your language and click the Next button.

Note

As you can tell, you have several languages to choose from. I recommend that you start with English because that is the de facto language of the Internet. The other languages are always available to the user, and the user can customize the language for his or her logon.

If you decide to leave the language as is, you can use the left arrow key to escape from this list. Use the down arrow key or tab key to move from one field to another.

On the next page, you are asked to enter the server name. It picks up the Web server name from the Server Name field in the /etc/httpd/httpd.conf file (see Figure 6.3).

Figure 6.3

IMP Web-based setup, Step 2.

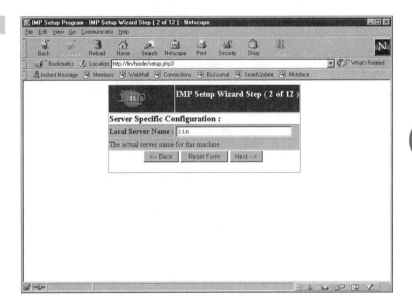

6

In my case, the server name is perfectly acceptable. This name will resolve back to the Web server with no problems on my test network. On the Internet, this should be the fully qualified domain name of your server. For example, assuming your machine name was mail, and your domain name was domain.com, the Local Server Name entry would be mail.domain.com. You can use the backspace key to erase the characters. Select the Next button. You will see the screen shown in Figure 6.4.

This part is very interesting. You are allowed to change the Root Base URL. However, I have found that if you do that, many things within the PHP scripts must be changed. My first attempt at doing this failed, and I did not have enough time to go through all the scripts and fix it. Keep the defaults in this screen for this installation. Click the Next button. You will see the screen shown in Figure 6.5.

Figure 6.4

IMP Web-based setup, Step 3.

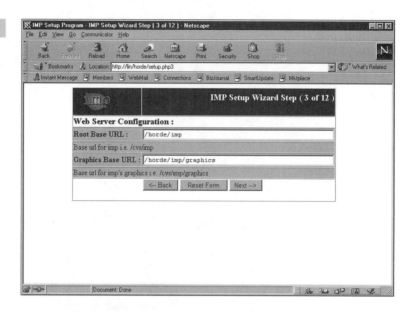

Figure 6.5

IMP Web-based setup, Step 4.

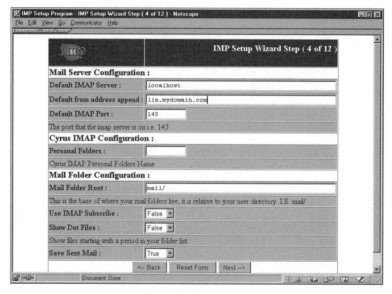

The first editable field is the default IMAP server. Because IMP will be running on our local machine, the `localhost` entry is acceptable. You can point it to some other server on your network. If you give the user the ability to change IMAP servers, this entry will show up in that field as the default choice.

The next field is the default from address that is appended to the user's name. In my case it is `lin`, and because the `hosts` files on all my machines understand `lin`, it works. For a machine on the Internet, it would be the Internet domain name. If your machine name is lin and your domain is mydomain.com, you enter lin.mydomain.com.

The default IMAP port is just fine as is. All requests for IMAP service are made to this port.

For this installation, the Cyrus IMAP server is not available. You will skip all of those fields.

The Mail Folder Configuration is acceptable. All mail will be stored in the user's home directory, under the directory named Mail. Within that folder, other folders or files will be created for the inbox, sent mail, saved mail, and so forth.

You should not allow IMAP to subscribe for now. You need to have full control over adding users to your system. You must, as root, add a user to the system before that user can access email through IMP.

EXCURSION
Adding a User to Red Hat Linux

For someone to log on to the IMP system, they must be entered as a user in your system. However, when you do that, you open up some possible security holes. In the following, I address adding users and small steps in securing your box to prevent the casual crack attempt from being successful.

The process for adding a user is simple. First, log on as root. Run the command **adduser** with the user's logon name. You can also use linuxconf to add the user.

For security reasons, you will want to do a modification to the standard add-user process under Red Hat. Whenever a user is created, that user's home directory is made. The files in the /etc/skel directory are copied into his home directory. By default, any user is allowed to telnet into your system if the network or IP addresses is allowed in /etc/hosts.allow or not denied in /etc/hosts.deny. You can circumvent this by setting the user's shell to be /dev/null, rather than the default /bin/bash. This is inconvenient, and might not protect you from a cracker.

I edit /etc/skel/.bash_profile and place the word exit at the end of the file. Whenever a user logs in, the shell is immediately exited. I have not found a way of bypassing this process, so it appears to be quite safe. To allow a user to telnet in, simply edit the .bash_profile in the user's directory and remove the exit line.

After you have added the user as root, change into the user's directory and run **chown root .bash*** to cause the bash profile files to be owned by the root user. This prevents a user with FTP access from overwriting that file and providing unwanted access.

This simple modification has saved me some grief. A few years ago a buffer overflow was in **bind** that allowed a cracker to execute arbitrary commands on my system. The cracker deleted /etc/hosts.deny. Then the cracker created user **rewt** using **adduser**, and gave that user superuser privileges. The cracker then used telnet to log on to the machine. The cracker was immediately logged out, and did not come back. I found the evidence in the logs the next day. I cleaned up and used the **chattr +i /etc/hosts.deny** command to make /etc/hosts.deny undeletable without the extra step of running **chattr** again.

6

> The point of this story is that crackers typically are running scripts that expect the system to be in a default condition. I would estimate about 90% of the newly installed systems are in that state. If you provide a few simple hurdles to cracking, you will protect your system from all but the most determined crackers.
>
> You should note that if a cracker really wants to own your system, he generally can. However, much greener pastures are out there with less expenditure of effort. Your job is to make things as inconvenient as possible for the cracker. This generally makes it inconvenient for you, too.

The show dot files is a switch that allows the user to see normally invisible files in a directory. For security purposes, this should be set to `False`.

Unless you have problems with disk storage space, allow the user to save sent mail. This provides a level of convenience similar to Microsoft Exchange.

The next screen configures cookies (see Figure 6.6).

Figure 6.6

IMP Web-based setup, Step 5.

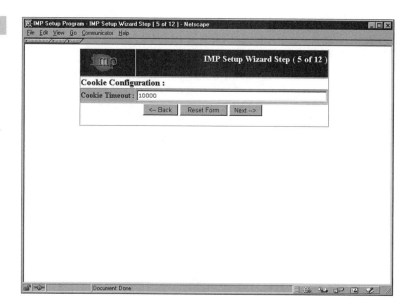

Web servers use cookies to give the user a contextually correct browsing session. From the Web server's point of view, every time a Web browser asks it for a page, it is the first time it has ever talked to that browser. Cookies were designed to allow the Web server to keep information about what the current user is doing, or has done in the past. All cookies have a timeout value. This value determines how long the information the cookie carries will be valid. It can make the cookie rather permanent. Generally, the timeout value is in seconds.

> **Note**
>
> Web browsers know what time it is based on the clock of the computer on which they are running. If the clock is too far off the clock on the Web server, cookies can expire early.
>
> Some problem users have with IMP can be traced to their computer's clock being too far off the Web server clock.
>
> The correct action to take is to correct the clock of the computer running the Web server. However, this is not always possible.
>
> You can make this less of a problem by increasing the cookie time out in the `Cookie Timeout` field. I recommend keeping this at 10,000 for now, but increase it to 100,000 (or more) if you have users who can't set their clock to the correct time of day.

The screen shown in Figure 6.7 allows you to point to helper programs.

Figure 6.7

IMP Web-based setup, Step 6.

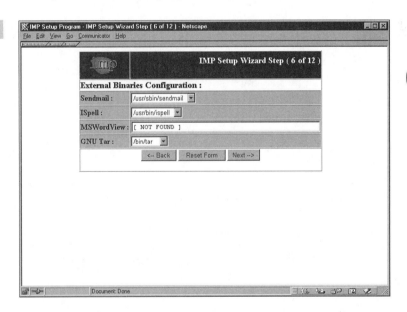

Screen 6 shows the external binaries that IMP needs to execute to do its job. The default Red Hat installs include `ispell`, `tar`, and `sendmail`. The IMP setup program does a very good job of locating these executables. You absolutely need `sendmail`. If you want to spell check the words in an outgoing email, you need `ispell`. `Tar` is used in some cases to package files for distribution. The `mswordview` package is not a necessity, but you should obtain it and install it if at all possible. It makes viewing email produced by Microsoft products a little easier.

The screen shown in Figure 6.8 gives you control over what the user can modify.

Figure 6.8

IMP Web-based setup, Step 7.

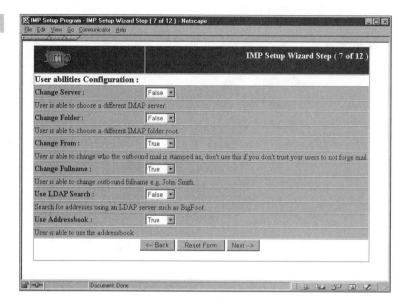

The Change Server entry allows the user to pick an IMAP server to log on to. That server can be anywhere on the Internet. You should set this to `False`. With the Change Folder entry, the user can pick a different directory in which to store the email. This should remain `False`.

Allowing the user to set the IMAP server can present a security risk if you are connected to the Internet. A user can try to log on to an IMAP server elsewhere on the Internet. This could be used illegally to gain access to other people's mail if a person guesses an account and password.

The probability of this is rather low. However, in today's environment, you must examine all security issues and determine if the risks are acceptable. I recommend you do not allow the user to enter the IMAP server.

If you can trust your users, you can allow them to indicate the email is from someone else. This is a security issue that you must carefully consider. It allows people to generate UCE or anonymous email that is difficult to trace to the individual that sent it. It should be set to `False` for most systems, which disallows this modification.

In some cases a user can be allowed to change their from address on their email. If they are using a temporary account, or it is a roving accessible mailbox, their mail might need to appear to be from their home box. This is a judgment call, and one bad apple spoils the entire barrel.

The Change Full Name entry, if `True`, allows users to hide their given name. This is usually safe to allow.

The Use LDAP Search can safely remain `False`. It allows people to search LDAP servers for addresses.

If you set the Use Address Book to `True`, the user can administer private address book entries. These entries are stored in the MySQL server IMP tables previously set up. This is a useful service.

Next comes the email notification screen shown in Figure 6.9.

Figure 6.9

IMP Web-based setup, Step 8.

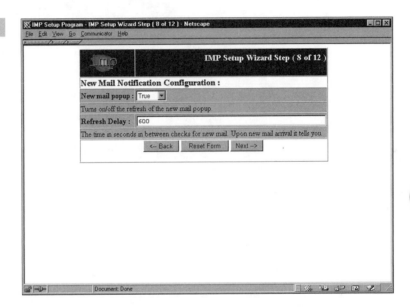

With this screen, you enable the ability to open a window telling the user new mail has arrived. The default is to check once every 10 minutes. The user is then able to keep a Web browser open and minimized, and not miss new mail. The default settings are generally acceptable.

The next screen, shown in Figure 6.10, allows some advertising features.

Using the features on this screen, you can include hidden and visible messages in each message sent from the system. The hidden parts are the X mailer directives, and go in the front of the message using the `header.txt` file. (You can put a visible header by not making it an X directive.) The visible message will go in the `trailer.txt` file. It is best to keep these options `False` for now. Feel free to experiment with them after you have the system working.

The MIME text view should be left `True`. It allows Internet Mail Extension text to be viewed in the email text display window in your Web browser. You can play with this setting later and see if the effects are to your liking.

Figure 6.10

IMP Web-based setup, Step 9.

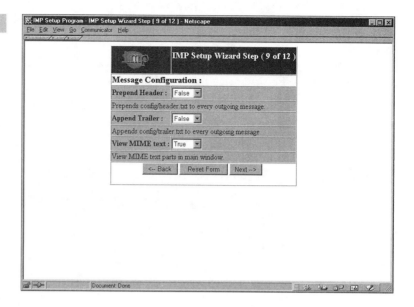

EXCURSION

Additional Security Setting

You can use the `header.txt` file to provide additional security features. The default entry in that file contains the following line:

```
X-Originating-IP: %REMOTE_ADDR%
```

This line will cause the PHP interpreter to put the IP address of the machine that is connecting to the Web server in the outgoing message as an X directive. This could allow you to cross check with your logs to determine which machine sent an email. For security reasons, this would be a good feature to enable. I recommend you wait until IMP is working, and then enable it.

Now we have the database screen shown in Figure 6.11.

The database screen connects IMP's PHP scripts to the correct database. Change the Use Database entry to True. Move to the Database Type field, and change it to Mysql. In Chapter 3, "MySQL," you set up the impmgr user with a password of impmgr. Enter these values in the User Name and Password. The default entries for the Server Name and tables are correct and can be left as is.

The PHP script then generates the setup file it will write and displays the file for your approval, as partly shown in Figure 6.12.

Figure 6.11

*IMP Web-based setup,
Step 10.*

Figure 6.12

*IMP Web-based setup,
Step 11.*

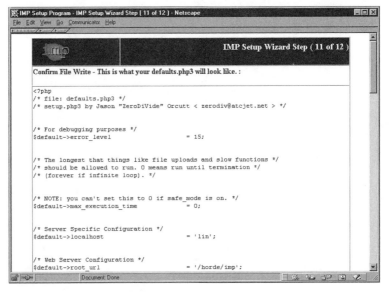

The entire contents of the file are listed following, as printed by the lynx browser:

Output

```
                         IMP Setup Program - IMP Setup Wizard Step ( 11 of 12 ) (p1 of
5)

     IMP

IMP Setup Wizard Step ( 11 of 12 )

Confirm File Write - This is what your defaults.php3 will look like. :

<?php
/* file: defaults.php3 */
/* setup.php3 by Jason "ZeroDiVide" Orcutt < zerodiv@atcjet.net > */


/* For debugging purposes */
$default->error_level                  = 15;


/* The longest that things like file uploads and slow functions */
/* should be allowed to run. 0 means run until termination */
/* (forever if infinite loop). */


/* NOTE: you can't set this to 0 if safe_mode is on. */
$default->max_execution_time           = 0;


/* Server Specific Configuration */
$default->localhost                    = 'lin';


/* Web Server Configuration */
$default->root_url                     = '/horde/imp';
$default->include_dir                  = './templates';
$default->graphics_url                 = '/horde/imp/graphics';


/* Default IMAP Server Configuration */
$default->server                       = 'localhost';
$default->from_server                  = 'lin';
$default->port                         = '143';


/* Default IMAP Folder Configuration */
$default->folders                      = 'mail/';
$default->use_imap_subscribe           = false;
$default->show_dotfiles                = false;
$default->save_sent_mail               = true;
$default->sent_mail                    = 'sent-mail';
$default->postponed                    = 'postponed';
```

```
/* Allow caching of the pages */
$default->cache_pages                = false;


/* Ldap searching */
$default->use_ldap_search            = false;


/* Server list : user is presented with a list */
/* of available imap servers */
$default->use_server_list            = false;


/* User changeable items */
$default->user_change_server         = false;
$default->user_change_folder         = false;
$default->user_change_from           = true;
$default->user_change_fullname       = true;
$default->user_use_addressbook       = true;


/* Check For New Mail Configuration */
$default->newmail_popup              = true;
$default->refresh_delay              = '600';


/* Cookie Configuration */
$default->cookie_timeout             = 10000;
$default->session_enabled            = 0;
$default->session_timeout            = '10000';


/* External Binaries Configuration */
$default->path_to_sendmail           = '/usr/sbin/sendmail';      /* Sendmai
l */
$default->path_to_ispell             = '/usr/bin/ispell';         /* ISpell
*
/
$default->path_to_mswordview         = '[ NOT FOUND ]';     /* M$WordView */
$default->path_to_tar                = '/bin/tar';         /* Tar */


/* SSL Configuration */
$default->secure                     = true;


/* Cyrus Configuration */
$default->personal_folders           = '';    /* i.e. INBOX. */


/* Default Language Configuration */
$default->language                   = 'en';


/* Message Configuration */
```

```
$default->append_header                = false;
$default->append_trailer               = false;


/* Text Viewing */
$default->text_parts_inline            = true;


/* Database Configuration */
$default->use_db                       = true;
$default->database_driver              = 'mysql';
$default->db_user_name                 = 'impmgr';
$default->db_password                  = 'impmgr';
$default->db_name                      = 'imp';
$default->db_server_name               = 'localhost';
$default->db_pref_table                = 'imp_pref';
$default->db_address_table             = 'imp_addr';
$default->db_connect_string            = '';
$default->db_server_port               = '';
$default->db_server_options            = '';
$default->db_server_tty                = '';


?>
```

<--- Back Write File--->

Check these settings carefully. If you like them, click the Write File button, which is at the bottom of the Web page. The screen shown in Figure 6.13 will appear.

Figure 6.13

IMP Web-based setup, Step 12.

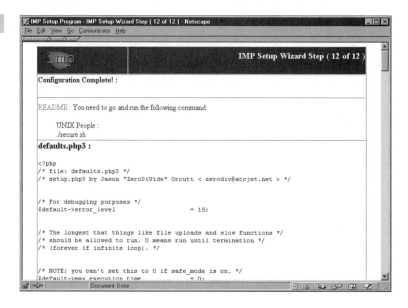

Now you must disable the setup script as instructed by the Web page. In an xterm window, change to the horde directory, and run the secure.sh script:

```
[root@wmaxlaptop root]# cd /home/httpd/html/horde/
[root@wmaxlaptop horde]# sh ./secure.sh
```

Output

```
I have made your configuration files, and libraries mode 0555
which is read / execute for everyone.

And the setup.php3 is mode 0000 which is no access period.
```

We need to do a couple of things to the configuration file to make the IMP installation complete. First, edit /usr/local/lib/php3.ini, and look for magic_quotes_gpc. Change the settings for all magic_quotes to Off. In the standard PHP installation, only magic_quotes_gpc is On, as shown by this listing:

Output

```
;;;;;;;;;;;;;;;;;;;
; Data Handling ;
;;;;;;;;;;;;;;;;;;;
magic_quotes_gpc       =       Off      \
➥ ; magic quotes for incoming GET/POST/Cookie data
magic_quotes_runtime   =       Off      \
➥ ; magic quotes for runtime-generated data, e.g. data from SQL, from exec(),
etc.
magic_quotes_sybase    =       Off      \
➥; Use Sybase-style magic quotes (escape ' with '' instead of \')
```

The last change is done for esthetic reasons. I don't really want people to have to remember to enter http://lin/horde/imp to get to their email. So I edited the /etc/httpd/conf/httpd.conf file, and found the aliases section by searching for Alias. I entered one line there:

```
Alias /webmail "/home/httpd/html/horde/imp"
```

I then restarted the httpd server, and logged in to http://lin/webmail. The IMP server screen shows up! The Webmail URL is much easier to remember.

The installation of IMP is complete. If you can't get the IMP Web page to show, skip to the troubleshooting section. Some of my trials and tribulations are documented there.

Testing IMP

To test IMP, you will need to set up some user accounts to send mail from and to. I will walk you through the process, and give you some additional things to consider as you think about the use of your IMP system.

Setting Up User Accounts

The Red Hat system provides several command-line programs for basic user maintenance. Whenever you add a user to the system, that user is automatically allowed to send and receive email. The user's password is the same password used to log on using IMP.

 Note   For the X Window environment, you can use the linuxconf program. It works well, but is not my personal favorite. It allows the root user to add a user to the system. However, you still must set the password using the command-line passwd utility in a terminal screen.

The adduser command adds a user to the system. No password is set for the user at that time. You must run the passwd command to do that. Only root can set the initial password for the user.

If you give the user shell logon ability, the user can change several identifying items by running one of several utilities. The user's real name is set using the chfn utility. The chsh utility allows the user to change the default logon shell. To execute these functions, a user must be logged in to your system. The root user can change these items for the user.

Here is an example where the user test is entered, with the password test. Note how the system complains about the password. It is never, ever, a good idea to give the user a password that is the same as the logon name. The user's real name is also changed by the root user:

```
[root@wmaxlaptop /root]# adduser test
[root@wmaxlaptop /root]# passwd test
```

Output

```
Changing password for user test
New UNIX password: test
BAD PASSWORD: it is too short
Retype new UNIX password: test
passwd: all authentication tokens updated successfully
[root@wmaxlaptop root]# chfn test
Changing finger information for test.
Name []: Test User
Office []:
Office Phone []:
Home Phone []:
[root@wmaxlaptop root]# tail /etc/passwd
......[various lines]...
test:x:503:503:Test User:/home/test:/bin/bash
[root@wmaxlaptop root]#
```

The information shown in italics at the `passwd` command is not echoed to the screen. If you look in the `/home` directory, you will see a test directory. In the `/etc/passwd` file, you will see an entry for user test. This file controls the login directory and user name. In the `/etc/groups` file you will find another entry for user test. This is the group that the user is in.

EXCURSION

User IDs, Group Numbers, and Security

Linux provides a standardized way of controlling access to files. The root user arbitrarily assigns all users to one or more groups. All users have a unique user ID. Each file is owned by a single user. With these three facts, a good security system has been created.

A file or directory has three basic attributes: read ability, write ability, and execute ability. The security system in Linux assigns these abilities to the owner of the file, the group the file is in, and anyone else, known as other.

Using `chmod` to change these settings, you can make a file readable or unreadable by the owner(!), users in the group the file belongs to, or others. You can also add or remove write and execute privileges from any of the above. Either the owner of a file or the root user is always allowed to restore any privileges to a file, unless the file has been made immutable using the `chattr` function.

Files can have their owner changed using `chown`. The group that files are in can be changed using `chgrp`. Only the owner of a file or the root user can successfully run these functions on files.

Tip

To find out more about commands listed in this book, use the `man` command. The `man` program prints out the manual pages for a command.

For example, to print out the manual page for `chown`, start an xterm in X windows, and enter the following:

```
man chown
```

The manual page for `chown` will be shown. It might take a little while to understand what the manual pages are telling you. After you get used to them, they are invaluable.

You can have a situation where parts of a mail folder become read-only for a user. If so, check to see that the root user does not own the user's mail directory or any files in the mail directory. This happened to me when I edited a file as the root user to fix a problem. The user could no longer save sent mail!

Connecting to IMP

IMP will normally be used over a network. You can set IMP up on your computer and run it locally. This is an easy way to initially test IMP.

In most cases, you will be connecting to your Web server using Windows machines. You can use any computer system that has network access and a Web browser that runs JavaScript. In the following sections, I will cover the most popular options for connecting to IMP.

Logging On from Your Red Hat Desktop

At the time of this writing, if you are using Netscape to connect to IMP, it must be Netscape browser version 4 or later. Earlier versions of Netscape don't support JavaScript.

 Note   If you are using Internet Explorer on a Windows machine, you must use version 3.02 or later. Most of the Web browser illustrations are taken while using Internet Explorer Version 4 under Windows to connect to IMP running on a Red Hat server.

A new commercial Web browser called Opera may work. It is currently in the beta test stage.

If the IMP you are testing resides on the same machine you are running the X Window System on, you can enter this URL: `http://127.0.0.1/horde/imp`. You will be taken to the logon screen.

Logging On from Another Machine on the Network

You have multiple choices when logging on from other machines. Depending on the operating system, you will be able to use Netscape, Internet Explorer, Opera (still in beta), or other Web browsers that support Java script. Many of the examples will be shown using Internet Explorer running under Windows. (After all, most of your customers will use Windows. They don't have to know what platform IMP is running on!)

You must be able to ping the computer that contains IMP by name or IP number from another machine on the network. To ping the IMP machine by name, the name must be correctly entered in a DNS server or in the `hosts` file in your computer.

For example, let's suppose the name of the IMP server is imp. If I can type `ping imp` from a command prompt, then I would be able to connect to the imp server by using this URL: `http://imp/horde/imp`.

If you are running Windows 98, you could also do the following from the command line:

```
C:\WINDOWS>ping imp
```

Output

```
Pinging imp [10.101.168.47] with 32 bytes of data:
```

```
Reply from 10.101.168.47: bytes=32 time=2ms TTL=254
Reply from 10.101.168.47: bytes=32 time=2ms TTL=254
Reply from 10.101.168.47: bytes=32 time=2ms TTL=254
Reply from 10.101.168.47: bytes=32 time=2ms TTL=254

Ping statistics for 10.101.168.47:
    Packets: Sent = 4, Received = 4, Lost = 0 (0% loss),
Approximate round trip times in milli-seconds:
    Minimum = 2ms, Maximum =  2ms, Average =  2ms


C:\WINDOWS>start http://imp/horde/imp
```

Using IMP

If you have the network connection set up, and IMP properly configured, you are presented with a logon screen as shown in Figure 6.14. Enter the username, the password, and click the logon button.

Figure 6.14

IMP logon screen.

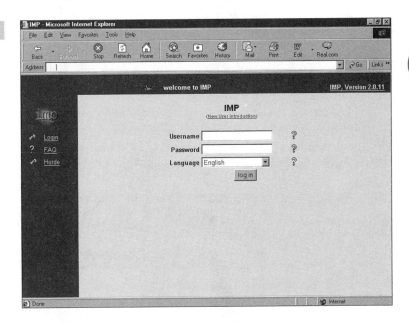

Reading Email

After you are logged on, the Inbox folder is shown (see Figure 6.15). All the messages available to the user are shown. Unread messages have an envelope icon beside them. To delete a message, click the check box beside the message and click the hyperlink Delete selected mail. A deleted message has a trash can symbol beside it. After a message has been deleted, it is not removed from the system until you click the Empty trash hyperlink.

Figure 6.15

IMP main email listing screen.

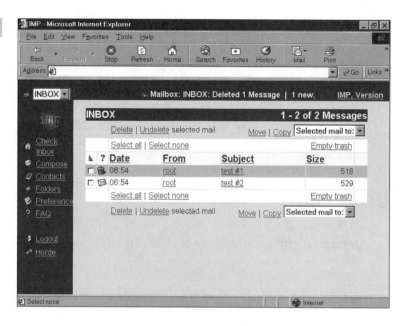

Figure 6.15

IMP main email listing screen.

To read a message, a user clicks the subject line hyperlink. The window changes as shown in Figure 6.16, opening the message in a scrolling frame.

The user is given new options while reading a message. The user can delete mail, reply to the sender of an email, reply to all addresses in a received email, forward mail, bounce a message back to the sender, save the mail message, or add an email address to the user's address book. The mail message can be moved or copied to a different folder.

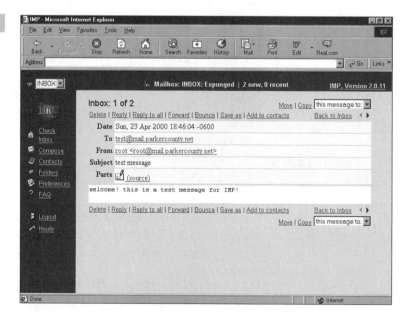

Figure 6.16

IMP message reading screen.

Replying to Messages

While reading a message, a user can choose to reply to the message. When the Reply hyperlink is clicked, the window shown in Figure 6.17 appears.

The reply address is listed in the To field. One or more addresses can be put in the CC field. Messages will be copied to these folks. The BCC field is for blind copies sent to people. Normally, email recipients do not see the other BCC recipients when they open a message.

Figure 6.17

IMP message reply screen.

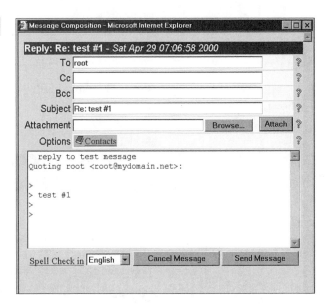

Composing Messages

When the user clicks the Compose hyperlink on the left side of the screen, the window shown in Figure 6.17 opens. In this case, the To address field is not filled in. The user can use the personal address book to enter an address in the To, CC or BCC fields. To do this, the user clicks the Contacts hyperlink. When this is done, the screen in Figure 6.18 is shown.

To add a new address to the address book, the user enters the email address in the Address field, such as phil@somewhere.com. A nickname for the user is entered in the Nickname field. The Nickname is used to look up an address when briefly entered in the To, CC, or BCC fields. The addressee's full name is entered in the Fullname field. The address is stored by clicking the Submit button.

To insert an address, the drop-down list of addresses is scrolled to the correct address. The address information for the selected contact appears in the fields (see Figure 6.18). The user clicks any of the Insert into To: buttons to insert the address into the email message. This window stays open until the user clicks the Close Window hyperlink.

Figure 6.18

IMP contact screen.

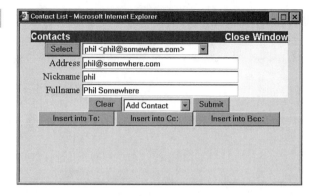

Attachments

Attaching files is a two-step process. First, you click the Browse button. The Choose file dialog shown in Figure 6.19 appears. Select your file and click Open. Repeat the process to add other files to the list.

Figure 6.19

IMP Choose file dialog.

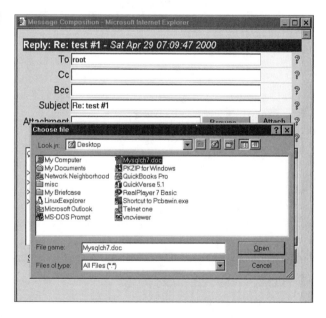

When you have the list of files, click the Attach button. This adds the contents of the files to the mail message. The file(s) will show in a list under the Attach button, with the size of each file, and the total number of bytes attached, as shown in Figure 6.20.

If you have added the wrong file, click the check box next to the filename(s) and click the Delete Attachments to remove the file(s).

Figure 6.20

IMP message with attached files.

When you are finished, click the Send Message button. This will cause the message with attached files to be sent. This can be a lengthy process, especially over a dial-up modem.

How IMP Works

Now that you have been given an overview of IMP, I will give you some details on how IMP works. This information is useful if you have problems later on. A good understanding of the fundamentals is invaluable when you have problems!

IMP presents a logon Web page to the customer. The user enters a logon name and password. This is the same logon name given to the user when the adduser command is executed in Linux. The password is the same password that is given to the user with the passwd command. This provides you with a good level of security and makes it harder to have your site hijacked.

EXCURSION

Password Security

If you installed Red Hat Linux, you were given the option of using shadow passwords. This feature creates a file named shadow in the /etc directory, alongside the always-present passwd file.

The passwd file is world readable. If your passwd file contains your passwords, it can be read by anyone who is logged in to a shell account. If you put a PHP script on your system that has a security flaw, the script could possibly be tricked into reading the passwd file. This security hole existed in IMP 2.0.10, and is fixed in version 2.0.11.

After a person has read your passwd file, he can then run a crack program against the file and recover some passwords. This is a security risk.

Only the root user can read the shadow file. This means a user cannot log on to the system and read the shadow file under most circumstances. This prevents most users from cracking your password list.

Another option you were given for passwords was MD5 encryption. In previous installations of Linux, you were given the standard Linux encryption of passwords. This encryption was very weak and easily broken. Using MD5 encryption makes it much harder to break passwords, and is much superior.

If you are running Linux and don't have shadow passwords, you need to enable shadow passwords. If the file /etc/shadow exists, you have shadow passwords enabled. If it does not, run either pwconv or pwconv5 from a command prompt.

If the program complains that it cannot convert the passwords, you are partially converted. Any new users will have their passwords entered into the /etc/shadow file. Old users still have their passwords in the /etc/passwd file. At this point, you can use removeuser to remove a user, and adduser to add the user back to the system. The user password then shows up in the shadow file.

If you are very skilled, you can move the passwords using a text editor. This is dangerous! However, it is the only way I have found to move the root password over to the shadow file when pwconv fails. However, I have also prevented the root user from logging back in after I have done this because of mistakes.

1. Log on as root.
2. Make backup copies of /etc/shadow and /etc/passwd.
3. Open the /etc/passwd file, cut the text between the first and second colons in the /etc/passwd file, and move them to the same location in the /etc/shadow file.
4. Save both files. Don't log out.
5. Switch to another console and attempt to log on as the root user.
6. If it allows you to log on, you were successful. If not, copy the backup files over the original files, and call in an expert.

The IMAP server is called with these parameters, and the mail in the user's inbox folder is scanned. All the from and subject lines are displayed. The user clicks the subject lines to read the mail. The current status of each message is shown on a line to the right. Various hyperlinks allow the user to delete mail, move mail between folders, and reply to, forward, bounce, or save mail. Addresses can be added to the user's address book.

To send a message, the user clicks the Compose hyperlink. A screen appears, and the message is entered. Attachments are done here. A click on the Send Message button sends the message on its way, using the IMAP server.

What IMP Does for You

The IMP system ties your Web server into your email system. Users are able to read and send email using any host that supports the IMAP protocol and allows IMP to connect.

With IMP, you can send and receive attachments from anywhere. If you have Microsoft Office installed along with Internet Explorer on Windows platforms, you can view Microsoft Word documents within the Web browser under Windows 95, 98, and NT. You are also able to save contact addresses in a personal address book.

IMP provides a good level of security through a logon and password requirement. You can restrict who is able to use IMP through the security features in your Web server. In the case of Apache, you can limit the viewing of the IMP pages to arbitrary IP address ranges.

Getting Online Help for IMP

The main Web site for IMP is `http://www.horde.org`. At that site you will find all the latest software, along with a Frequently Asked Questions (FAQ) list. A mailing list is available. To subscribe, send an email to `imp-request@lists.horde.org`, with the word subscribe in the *subject* of the message (not the body). More information about the available mailing lists is at `http://www.horde.org/mail/`.

Troubleshooting the Install

After IMP in installed, the first thing to do is to bring up the IMP logon page by pointing your Web browser to the IMP URL. In the following example, substitute your machine's name or its IP address:

```
http://www.yourmachinesname.com/horde/imp
```

The first time I did this, nothing happened. This section covers the problems I had during the install, and how these problems were resolved.

Problem 1—Nothing Happens

The first time I tried to connect using IMP, nothing happened. I looked in `/etc/hosts.allow`, and `/etc/hosts.deny`, and they were blank because of re-installing the imap server. This in itself would not prevent me from using IMP, because `/etc/hosts.deny` was empty. I entered the correct information in both files.

I tried IMP again. No go. I looked at `/etc/inetd.conf`, and the `imap` line was commented out. I enabled it by removing the `#` at the beginning of the line. I then restarted `inetd` with the `killall -HUP inetd` command.

I brought IMP up again and tried a logon. No luck! It was starting to get frustrating. I looked in my log files. Nothing of importance showed in /var/log/messages. I ran a `tail` command on /var/log/secure. Finally! It showed the following:

Output

```
[root@wmaxlaptop root]# tail /var/log/secure
.......
Apr 22 07:42:56 wmaxlaptop imapd[1026]: warning: /etc/hosts.allow, line 6: can't
verify hostname: gethostbyname(localhost.mydomain.net) failed
Apr 22 07:42:56 wmaxlaptop imapd[1026]: refused connect from 127.0.0.1
```

I had to make sure that /etc/hosts had the fully qualified domain name for my host for `imap` to run. So I edited the `hosts` file to put in the string that was fed into the `gethostbyname()` function.

The correct string was there. I was puzzled. I finally decided to edit the /etc/hosts.allow file and enter the word ALL to test it:

```
imapd : ALL
```

That worked! Encouraged, I changed ALL to the IP address of my localhost. Bingo! For some reason, either the forward or reverse lookup for `localhost` and `local-host.mydomain.net` is failing, causing `inetd` to reject IMP's imap connection. However, with `127.0.0.1` in the entry, it worked:

```
#
# hosts.allow   This file describes the names of the hosts which are
#               allowed to use the local INET services, as decided
#               by the '/usr/sbin/tcpd' server.
#
imapd : 127.0.0.1
```

At this point, I must note that I have successfully used machine names in /etc/hosts.allow whenever a DNS server provided the correct name resolution. I have also used IP network address ranges successfully. This problem appears to be an isolated case. Regardless, the IMP installation is now working. Onward to the next test.

Problem 2—Can't Delete Mail

I had IMP loaded and ready to go. I sent user test several test messages. I then went in to delete a message, and received the screen shown in Figure 6.21.

I was stunned! I *had* downloaded the latest software! I went back to the online site, http://www.horde.org, and went to their FAQ area. Searching for `imap`, I came across an error message that described the problem. The first part of the page I read online is shown in Figure 6.22.

Figure 6.21

My first test of IMP installation.

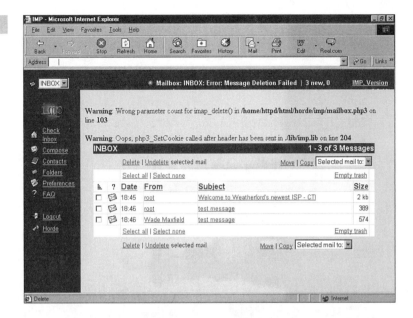

Figure 6.22

Horde.org *Web page explaining the problem.*

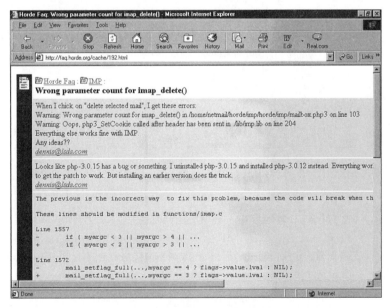

The latest and greatest PHP I had downloaded (version 3.0.15) contained an error! The horde Web page indicated this was fixed in PHP version 3.0.16. I went back to the PHP download page and downloaded the latest PHP. After compiling and installing, the problem was fixed.

Between the first download and the second, only 20 days had passed. This is a good example of Internet time. It usually takes much longer for a closed-source corporation to make fixes available.

Problem 3—Can't Send or Receive Mail

In Red Hat systems, the `sendmail` program is almost configured straight out of the box. If you are sending mail to yourself on the same machine and you have a DNS server configured, it can take 30 seconds or more for mail to complete delivery on your machine when not connected to the Internet. This is because the system waits for the DNS server to send a reply before continuing. Because the server is not available, the full amount of time will pass.

If you are on the Internet, you need a domain name to send and receive mail. You need to have a proper DNS entry set up for your mail machine based upon that domain.

You should also have an MX record set up for your mail machine if it accepts mail for your domain. Mail can be sent to specific machines without MX records, but mail addressed to a domain will probably not be delivered to your mail machine unless the MX record exists. If your domain name resolves to your mail machine, it might work.

Finally, in `/etc/sendmail.cw`, all the aliases your machine accepts mail for must be listed. If the mail arrives for `mydomain.com`, `foo.mydomain.com`, and `mail.mydomain.com`, all three of these must be listed in the d file like this:

```
mydomain.com
foo.mydomain.com
mail.mydomain.com
```

Remember to restart `sendmail` whenever you change any of its configuration files. The easiest way to do this is with the following command line:

```
/etc/rc.d/init.d/sendmail restart
```

Everyday Use of IMP

Now that you have IMP working, you need to consider how to use it. You might wish to customize IMP to some degree. You might be wondering what to do next to deploy it in your office, or on the Internet. Let's explore these possibilities.

Customizing IMP

The quickest and easiest way to customize IMP is to change the images `horde/imp/graphics` directory. These are gif images that provide embellishments to the IMP Web page.

You can replace any of these images with your own. The IMP logo can be replaced with your business logo. This is permitted under the GPL license. Changing these images is very easy to do, and very low risk. In other words, it will be hard to break IMP by changing a gif image. Feel free to experiment!

To change the operation of IMP, go to the `horde` and `horde/imp` directories and edit the files in those directories. All the files in these directories that end with `.php3` are editable with a text editor. You can make changes to these files once you understand the PHP language.

If you are businessman, you will want to hire PHP professionals. You can join the PHP mailing lists at `http://www.php.net`, and probably find someone to help you there. An excellent place to look for help would be on mailing lists hosted by `http://www.horde.org`. These folks are actively involved in IMP and PHP, and would be able to make modifications.

The best course of action in modifying IMP is to set up a server that won't be in production. You can then change the code and operation of this server to your heart's content. After you like your changes, you can migrate them to the server used by your customers, the one that is in production.

Email Inside an Office

The most common use of IMP in a small office will be to provide an intra-office email system. If so, you are ready to go. If you already have a network, all you have to do is put your server on a battery-backed UPS, and plug it into the network. Assign unique IP addresses to all the machines on the network.

If you don't know how to set up a network, find a friend who knows. Even if she don't want to set it up for you, she will be invaluable to you as a resource to check the work of someone you hire.

After you have the server on the network, with all of your office machines able to ping each other, you are ready to set up users. Set up a user account for everyone who will be logging in to IMP. Assign passwords that are hard to guess. Test getting into users' user's accounts from each computer. Send messages between users, and verify they were received.

Next, have a training session. You will find that the interface is very intuitive. In my experience, any secretary who can use a word processor can use IMP without formal training.

That's it! You now have a very useful email system. You should have about 10 megabytes of disk storage for each user you place on the system in this environment. This level of storage will allow for years of typical email message storage. You can support as many as 1000 users on a 300MHz Pentium-based system, with a 10GB hard drive, and 64MB of memory.

Email on the Internet

To place your computer on the Internet, serving customers at large, you should hire professional help. Many options and possibilities are available. I will cover the outline of what you need to do to use IMP to serve your business employees or customers in this fashion.

Step 1: Obtain a Domain Name

To do business on the Internet, you need a domain name. You can register your domain at many locations. The first registrar that handled all the registrations on the Internet was `http://www.internic.net`.

Competing companies now offer registration. It is best to get help to get this step done. The main problem you will run into is that most of the good names are already spoken for.

Step 2: Get an Internet Connection and IP Address Set

This next step requires a lot of consideration and communication with an ISP. Because I own an ISP, I have definite opinions, and they are presented here.

You can choose to leave your server at the ISP's office. This is called co-location. You typically get one Internet IP address, and a very fast connection to the net. This can sometimes be the least expensive choice, and can range from as little as $50 a month to several thousand a month. However, physical access to your machine is limited.

You can choose to get a DSL link to your office. For businesses, this can be an inexpensive choice. You will find that business DSL rates are about 10 times the consumer access price. Expect to pay about $300 a month for acceptable access speeds. The connection is brought to your office, if you are close enough to a telephone company's central office. Generally, all non-phone company DSL installations for business are done incorrectly, and require a lot of complaining to the DSL provider to get the bandwidth that you are paying for.

You can choose to get an ISDN link to your office. This is typically the least amount of trouble, and with DSL competition driving costs down for alternative services, it can provide you with a very reasonable cost-to-speed ratio. You can get full-time ISDN connectivity for as little $45 a month per line.

Finally, you can get a T1 or better connection. The costs range from about $1000 a month on up to $28000 a month, depending on the speed required.

I recommend either the DSL or ISDN connection. Within the next few years, DSL will dominate and prices will come down. Also, the installation and service problems will be worked out, leading to a very reliable service.

Step 3: Set Up Your Server

This step most definitely requires professional help. Even if you have some experience, you will have to coordinate with technicians on the other side of your connection. It is best to pay to have this done because the problems involved can be very difficult to solve. Most ISP's are running on shoestring budgets, with minimal help. If you don't know what you are doing, you can have trouble explaining the problem to the support person on the other end. This always delays a proper turn up.

During the setup and installation of your server, be sure to have a security expert look over your system. You do not want to hang a "Welcome to Crackers" sign on your computer! If you have ever been cracked, you understand what I am saying. If you haven't been cracked, think of it as someone who comes along and drives your car while you are asleep, and leaves it parked in the driveway in the morning. This is not a good experience.

Step 4: Go Live!

At this point, you are ready to add users and go on the air! If your business model depends on providing this service, you need to hire someone to set up customers. They will have to be trained to set up users on your server.

You should also work with someone who can create software to automate your customer sign up so you don't have to it all by hand. In the meantime, written procedures can be used to train your staff.

Appendix A

PHP Language Reference in this Appendix

PHP is a general-purpose language. Almost all functionality is because of using function calls provided by libraries. You can extend PHP with functions you write. PHP supports algebraic form arithmetic expressions using variables, subroutine calls, general purpose I/O, and the capability to execute other programs.

PHP is very fast. In comparable projects on identical equipment, I have seen the PHP/MySQL/Linux combination outperform the ASP/SQL Server/NT 4 combination by a large margin.

EXCURSION

Speed and Data Integrity

When comparing MySQL/PHP/Linux to other server-side scripting languages in conjunction with databases, the MySQL/PHP/Linux combination will almost always be faster.

Some of this speed is because of operating system architecture. Linux can outperform NT in many areas. In some areas, NT will outperform Linux. This can be because of how each OS handles resource constraints. It is my experience that Linux handles overload more gracefully than NT.

From my experience in real-world situations, PHP is faster than ASP. When processing raw pages with commands, PHP appears to do much better in the situations I have worked with. However, feelings are not quantifiable.

I searched and found a benchmark at `http://www.caucho.com/articles/benchmark.xtp`. That site is attempting to show that the newer Java Server Pages can be as fast or faster than anything else available. As part of the testing, the benchmark shows that PHP is roughly nine times faster than ASP at executing script on a page. Although IIS with ASP is faster at delivering static Web pages with no scripts, the performance difference between PHP and ASP when interpreting the script is dramatic.

Some of the speed that you get from the PHP/MySQL combination is because of MySQL. This is most likely because MySQL does not support database transactions. In a database that supports transactions, the database will not be updated until the final piece of the data is in place and the transaction is committed.

A good article comparing MySQL and PostgreSQL can be found at `http://www.phpbuilder.com/columns/tim20000705.php3`. It shows how fast MySQL is, and gives other insightful information on its use.

The real-world implication of transactions is that if a power failure occurs in the middle of an update, the entire transaction is lost and the data in the database retains referential integrity. With MySQL, you can have pieces of the data in the database, and pieces of the data lying on the floor. In some cases, you would not know what state the database is in, and your referential integrity would be compromised.

If you carefully think through the implications of such situations, you can take steps to avoid data integrity breakdown. I have read estimates that indicated as many as 95% of the database systems installed *do not need transaction technology.* This is because most data is monotonic. Much of the data is not mission critical. Monotonic data enters the database as one entry in one table. Noncritical data can usually be re-entered later. A transaction is not needed in these situations.

Starting with MySQL 3.23.15, support for transactions has been added.

Our IMP application is a prime example. If the address book entry is being updated during a crash, the user can easily re-enter it after the system is up. Multiple tables are not involved, so the data can't get partially into the system.

The database could have been designed to require transactions, even for such a simple table as the address book. However, the design does not need such technology. The key here is that the system design and table design cooperate to minimize data loss in emergencies.

The bottom line is that if you need transaction technology, use a sophisticated DBMS (Data Base Management System) that can provide it. Sybase, Oracle, Informix, and Microsoft's SQL Server are among those that can provide transaction support. The price you pay is in speed and cost. You will pay thousands to support multiple users with transaction technology. However, that price can pale in comparison to the cost of recovering a damaged database.

When doing math, most of the standard algebraic formula notation is allowed. You can add ($a+$b), subtract ($a-$b), multiply ($a*$b), and divide ($a/$b). You can also take the remainder of a division. This operation is called *modulus* ($a%$b). To raise a number to a power or take the root of a number, you must use a library function. (For example, to raise a number to a power, use the pow() function. To find the square root, use the sqrt() function.)

In addition to the mathematical expressions, PHP allows you to do bitwise manipulation on the binary (base 2) values. You can bitwise or ($a|$b), and ($a&$b), exclusive or ($a^$b), and, not, also called one's complement (~$a).

Basic Syntax

PHP generally follows the C syntax, with a little flavor of Perl shown during string handling. All statements end with a semicolon. Algebraic-style formulas are used for mathematical operations. You have the standard C-like printf function. However, under PHP, strings delimited with " are expanded on-the-fly.

For example, to write the formula E=MC^2 (E equals M times C squared) in PHP:

```
$E = $M * ($C * $C);
```

The next statement shows available math functions, including a function call which works just like its C counterpart:

```
$result = ($a * $b) / $c + bcpow(($d - ($e % 5)),3,2);
```

This function multiplies a by b, and then divides the result by c. It then takes the remainder of e divided by 5, and subtracts that from d. That result is given to the bcpow() function, which raises the result to the third power and returns that value. That value is then added to the result of the multiply and divide part of the equation and the answer is assigned to the variable $result.

Comparisons are done with special operators. All comparison operators consist of two characters side by side from this list: =, <, !. You can test for equal to (==), greater than (>), less than, less than or equal to, greater than or equal to, not equal to (!=), identical to (both in value and type) (===) or not identical to (!===).

In PHP 4, you can compare arrays using the equality operator (==) or the identity operator (===):

```
$myArray = array ( 4, 2, 1, 3, 5);
$myArray2 = array ( 1, 2, 3, 4, 5);
$myArray3 = array ( 4, 2, 1, 3, 5);
if ($myArray == $myArray3)
   echo "\$myArray is equal to \$myArray3<BR>";

if ($myArray === $myArray3)
   echo "\$myArray is identical to \$myArray3<BR>";
if ($myArray == $myArray2)
   echo "\$myArray is equal to \$myArray2 <BR>";
```

The previous code displays:

```
$myArray is equal to $myArray3
$myArray is identical to $myArray3
```

A

The PHP parser will take a string and expand any variables within that string before it uses the string. If a string is delimited with single quotes, the PHP parser will leave the string alone. Strings are put together with the concatenation operator, which is a period, (.).

You are allowed to put commonly used code in subroutines. These subroutines are called *functions*. You can define your own functions or use functions included in the PHP library. The function calls follow the C syntax.

Variables and Types

The concept of a variable is borrowed from algebraic notation. A variable always begins with a $, and what the variable represents (or contains) can be changed at any time during execution of the program. Variables are case sensitive. The variable $Path is different from $path. Under certain conditions, variables exist before your program is executed. All other variables are named and created by you.

Variables take on characteristics known as *types*. These types include arrays, objects, strings, integers, real (also known as floating point), and resources. PHP will change the types of variables on-the-fly. Numbers become strings at will. Strings become numbers. Integers are changed to floating point. These changes are done behind the scenes, without any direct intervention on your part.

The following sections will give you a brief overview of the basic PHP types.

Arrays

When strings are used as subscripts in arrays, the result of an array lookup might not be obvious. If you have a two-dimensional array, it becomes even more of a problem.

Suppose you have an array that is describing dog types and names in two dimensions. The types are hound and lab. We have two hound dogs. The brown one is named Bill and the red one is named Hillary. We have two labs. The red one is named Lee and the black one is named Gore. There are two ways of setting up the arrays. The first is easiest to understand:

```
$dog["hound"]["brown"]="Bill";
$dog["hound"]["red"]="Hillary";
$dog["lab"]["red"]="Lee";
$dog["lab"]["black"]="Gore";
```

The second way is equivalent, and is a bit faster to write:

```
$dog = array (
    "hound" => array (
            "brown" => "Bill",
            "red" => "Hillary"
            ),
```

```
    "lab" => array (
            "red" = "Lee",
            "black" = "Gore"
            )
    );
```

Either way of initializing the array works. In both cases, using the variable `$dog["lab"]["red"]` will give you Lee. This can be a very powerful feature of PHP. It is very difficult to use unless you are using it with values that are placed in the PHP script directly. For example, you can't control how the word *color* is spelled. A British user will most likely spell it *colour*. This would cause an associative lookup based on the index "color" to fail.

Integers

In all computer languages I know of, and by definition in mathematics, an integer is a number without a decimal point. Integers can represent only whole numbers. An integer is assigned to a variable by using the equal sign:

```
$a = 3;
```

Floating Point

A number that has a fractional amount represented by numbers after a decimal point is called a *floating point number*. Floating point numbers can result from division or assignments. To assign a floating point number to a variable, use a decimal point in the number:

```
$a = 1.345;
```

Objects

You can use objects to group items together that are aspects of an idea or item. To illustrate this point, let's use a dog object. Nearly every dog has hair, most have tails, and all have ears. All dogs have a color. A dog will usually be able to bark. A dog can whine. All dogs eat. All dogs weigh a certain amount and can increase that weight by eating. They can lose weight by not eating.

To create this dog object, we will first describe a dog class. A class is simply an empty outline. When we use the class, we fill in the details, as shown in the following class:

 Note　When you define variables in a class, you use the $ character with the variable name. When you use variables from a class, you do not use the $ character with the variable name. For example, if you have the variable `$Color` in a `Dog` object, to reference it you would use the following syntax:

```
$Dog->Color = "Brown";
```

```
class DogClass {
    var $color;
    var $hair; // 1 (yes) or 0 (no)
    var $bark; // 1 (yes) or 0 (no)
    var $whine; //1 (yes) or 0 (no)
    var $weight;
    function eat() { $this->$weight = $this->$weight + 1; }
    function dont_eat() { this->$weight = $this->$weight - 1; }
    function bark() {
        if ( $this->$bark )
            return 1;
        else
            return 0;
    }
    function whine() {
        if ( $this->$whine )
            return 1;
        else
            return 0;
    }
};

$Hairless = new DogClass;
$No = 0; $Yes = 1;
$Hairless->Hair = $No;
$Hairless->Bark = $Yes;
if ($Hairless->bark())
    printf("Dog barked!\n");
else
    printf("Dog is silent.\n");
if ($Hairless->Hair == $Yes)
    print ("Dog has hair\n");
else
    print ("Dog does not have hair\n");
```

Resource

A resource is a new type introduced in PHP 4. It is the identifier returned from calls that use system resources, such as a call to `mysql_connect()`. The variable is automatically assigned this type. This type has no affect on your PHP programming practices.

Strings

To put separate strings together, use a period (.). This process is called *concatenation*. Suppose you have "Old MacDonald" and "had a farm." To put these two strings together and print the result, you could do either one of the following:

```
echo "Old MacDonald" . " " . "had a farm."
$a = "Old MacDonald";
$a = $a . " " . "had a farm";
print($a);
```

Note that I had to insert a space between the two strings to make them acceptable when concatenated. Otherwise it would have printed MacDonaldhad as opposed to MacDonald had...

Also note that the concatenation operator works with variables as well as with strings.

You can also embed special characters in strings to force line breaks, tabs, and other special characters. To embed a character in a string, precede the character with a backslash (\). The backslash alerts PHP's parser to treat the next character as a representation of what you want done. The most-used list of embeddable characters is shown in the following table:

Escape Sequence	Meaning
\\	backslash
\n	newline
\"	double quote
\'	single quote
\r	return
\$	dollar sign
\t	tab

You can use the backslash for any character. If you do this, a warning will be put out at the highest warning level.

When PHP encounters a string with an arithmetic expression, it tries to convert the string to a value. For example, in the following, $a is a string and then changes into a number.

```
$a = "3"; // $a is a string
$b = $a +5; //$a is now the number 3, making $b equal to 8
$c = $a + 2 + "3 little pigs"; // $c is now equal to 8
```

In the above statements, the Unix library function strtod() is used. To find out more about how the conversion of strings to numbers works, run man strtod in a terminal window.

Basically, any number in the beginning of a string is converted and the rest of the string is ignored. If the number in the string contains a . or the letters e or E it will become a double. If the string does not begin with a number, it will translate to a 0. You can use exponent notation to produce a number. This is sometimes known as *scientific notation*. The string 1e2 evaluates to 100 (1 followed by 2 zeros).

You must be careful when you use variables in PHP to avoid unexpected results. When the type conversions bite you, it is generally funny, unless the deadline is too close for comfort!

Type Casting and Conversion

You can force variables to be different types. This is called *casting*, and is useful for clarity. If you don't cast variables, they are automatically converted from one type to another on-the-fly.

Strings will be converted to numeric values. The conversion is based on the rules explained in the preceding section, strings.

You can change the type of a variable with `settype()`. To get the type of a variable, you can use `gettype()`. You can also use the functions `is_array()`, `is_double()`, `is_long()`, `is_object()`, and `is_string()`.

To temporarily change the type of a variable, use a cast. In the following examples, the number 12 is changed to a floating point number, and the floating point number 33.45 is changed to an integer:

```
$double = (float) 10; // $double now is 10.0
$smallint = (int) 33.45; // $smallint is now 33
```

The type casts allowed are shown in the following table. Alternative casts that have the same effect are shown separated by a comma:

Cast	Effect on Variable
(array)	changes to an array
(double), (float), (real)	changes to a floating point number
(int), (integer)	changes to an integer
(object)	changes to an object
(string)	changes to a string

Predefined Variables

Some variables are in existence before your PHP code is executed. These variables are environment variables, GET and POST variables, and cookies. These variables are used like any other PHP variables.

Cookies are sent from the client (the Web browser) and are available as PHP variables. The variable name is the same name as the cookie, with a $ prepended. Cookies that you have set using `setcookie()` will be returned by the browser in all following page requests.

Variable Scoping

The concept of variable scoping can be confusing at first. Basically, it answers the question "When is the variable available for me to use?" The availability of a variable is further complicated by the fact that you are allowed to create PHP variables as needed.

The basic rule is this: Variables defined outside of functions are not visible within functions unless the variable is preceded by the word *global* anywhere before use of the variable.

In the following example, the variables $one and $two are visible in the function. The variable $three is a new variable within the function, and changes to it do not affect the $three variable outside the function:

```php
<?php
$one = 1;
$two = 2;
$three = 3;
function foo() {
  global $one, $two;
  static $three;
  $three = $one *2 + $two * 2;
}
?>
```

The reverse concept is also true: Variables defined within a function are not visible to the rest of the program. Variables defined within a function also cease to exist when the function is exited, in most cases. If you put the word *static* in front of a function variable, it will continue to exist when you leave the function. When you call the function again, the variable can be used, and will have the last value put into it.

Variable Variables

A variable that is a string can be used as a variable name by using two $ symbols in a row. The content of the variable is matched against an existing variable if one exists. If one does not exist, a new variable is created. To illustrate, the following code

```php
$me = "me, you dummie!";
$who = "me";
printf ("who? $me \n<p>");
$$who = "george!";
printf ("who? $me \n");
```

will print the following:

```
who? me, you dummie!
who? George!
```

When using arrays as variable variables, you must use brackets to avoid ambiguity. Please note that you are not limited to using brackets for arrays. You can use them for all variable variables.

To use the contents of $a[1] as the variable name, you would write ${$a[1]}. To use the contents of $a as the array name, with an index of 1, you would write ${$a}[1].

You can also use the PHP defined $GLOBALS array for accessing variable variables. It is an associative array, with the name of the variable being the key. To access the contents of `$a[1]` using the `$GLOBALS` array, you would write `$GLOBALS[$a[1]]`, and to access the `$who` variable, you would write `$GLOBALS["who"]`.

External Variables

You can create or modify external environment variables by using the `putenv()` function. To create or modify cookies, use the `setcookie()` function. You can modify variables passed to you from HTML forms or the environment using a direct assignment. However, this only modifies the variable during execution of your PHP script.

HTML Form-Provided Variables

When your PHP Web page is called using a POST or GET method, the variable name is specified using `name=`. The variable contents are entered by the user. In the following example, a variable called `$item` is handed to the PHP script on the Web page. The `$item` variable can be used like any other variable.

```
<form action="postexample.hp3" method="post">
Item:<input type="text" name="item"><p>
<input type="submit">
</form>
```

In this case, you can change the value of `$item` during the execution of your script. If you do, you will not be able to get the original value of `$item` back. Be careful!

> In PHP 4, you can turn off this behavior by turning off `register_globals` in the `php.ini` file. If you do this, turn on access to external variables using the `track_vars` configuration directive in the `php.ini` file. If you do this, you then use `$HTTP_POST_VARS["varname"]`, `$HTTP_GET_VARS["varname"]`, `$HTTP_COOKIE_VARS["varname"]`, `$HTTP_ENV_VARS["varname"]`, or `$HTTP_SERVER_VARS["varname"]` to retrieve the variables.

Environment Variables

Environment variables were discussed in part in the section "Predefined Variables" and the introduction to this section, "External Variables." These variables are immediately usable within a PHP script.

Direct modification of environment variables within the PHP code might not give you the results you are after. If other variables have the same name as environment variables, they will override the environment variable's current setting. For that reason, it is best to use `getenv()` function to get the value of an environment variable. Changes to environment variables with the `putenv()` function might or might not carry forward to other PHP scripts that are executed. It is best to assume that changes to environment variables are temporary, unless you do a lot of testing to prove otherwise.

Constants and Expressions

Certain constants are defined for use in your PHP program. Several of these constants are very useful for debugging your scripts. For a list of pre-defined constants, see the defined constants in the Data Manipulation section in this appendix.

> **Note**
>
> In the following functions and discussions, you will see `true` (or TRUE), and `false` (or FALSE). In PHP `true` is actually a 1, and `false` is actually a 0. When a function is described as returning TRUE, it returns the value 1. When it is described as returning FALSE, it is returning the value 0.

You can also define constants yourself. These constants are created using the `define()` function. The following creates the constant `MY_NAME` and gives it the value of `"George Smith"`:

```
define("MY_NAME","George Smith");
```

PHP differs from C in that constants cannot contain macros. Constants can only contain scalar values. Constants can be used wherever variables or strings or numbers would be used. The following places `"George Smith"` in the variable `$name`:

```
$name = MY_NAME;
```

Operators

The types of operators are arithmetic, comparison, logical, execution, and string. Operators are typically defined by special characters.

If you don't use parentheses PHP will evaluate expressions left to right, unless operator precedence dictates a different evaluation order. Multiplication has a higher precedence than addition, and will be evaluated first. (In other words, a multiplication will precede an addition.) For example, 3 + 4 * 5 is equal to 23, not 35. If you use parentheses, the innermost set of parentheses is evaluated first, then the next innermost, and so forth, and then the normal order of precedence is used.

The following table gives the operator's precedence, with the highest priority item listed first in the table, left to right. The evaluation direction shows you where the parser first looks when evaluating, with neither indicating the statement is taken as a whole:

Operator	Evaluation Direction
new	neither
[	right
! ~ ++ -- (int) (double) (string) (array) (object) @	right
* / %	left

Operator	Evaluation Direction
+ - .	left
< <= > >= == !=	neither
& ^ | && || ?:	neither
= += -= *= /= .= %= &= != ~= <<= >>=	right
print	right
and xor or ,	left

Arithmetic Operators

Arithmetic operators are the operators used in algebraic expressions. These are the standard operators learned in math class, with slightly different symbols used. They are listed here:

- +—Addition
- -—Subtraction
- *—Multiplication
- /—Division
- %—Modulo (this returns the remainder of a division operation)
- ++—Increment by one. This can show before or after a variable. If before a variable (++$a),the variable is incremented before it is used in an arithmetic expression. If after a variable ($a++), the variable is used in the arithmetic expression, and then its value is incremented.
- -- —Decrement by one. This can show before or after a variable. If before a variable (--$a),the variable is decremented before it is used in an arithmetic expression. If after a variable ($a--), the variable is used in the arithmetic expression, and then its value is decremented.

Comparison Operators

All comparison operators return a true or false answer to the code and are used in statements to control code execution. When used with the if statement, a true will cause the code immediately after the if to be executed; a false will cause the code after the else to be executed. The following table shows the groupings. If a result is not true, it is false:

Operator	Name	Result
$1 == $r	is equal to (=)	true if $l is equal to $r
$1 < $r	is less than	true if $l is less than $r
$1 <= $r	is less than or equal to	true if $l is less than or equal to $r
$1 != $r	is not equal to	true if $l is not equal to $r

Operator	Name	Result
$l > $r	is greater than	true if $l is greater than $r
$l >= $r	is greater than or equal to	true if $l is greater than or equal to $r

Execution Operators

Some operators that I classify as *execution operators* modify normal execution of code. In other words, they can cause PHP to execute script differently depending on current conditions.

- @—Suppresses function error or warning. If a warning would have been printed by PHP, this will suppress the warning. The error_reporting() function can also be used.

- ?:—This is a logic comparison similar in effect to if (a) /*then*/ b else c; In the following statement, if $a is 5, then $b is set to 6, otherwise it is set to 7:

  ```
  $a == 5 ? $b = 6 : $b = 7 ;
  ```

- $funcName()—Dynamic function call. If the value of $funcName evaluates to an existing function, that function is called. In the following code, the function write() is called:

  ```
  function write() { echo "hello"; }
  $miscFunc = "write";
  $a = 3;
  if ($a == 3)
      $miscFunc(); // write() is called and prints hello
  ```

Assignment Operators

Assignment operators borrow heavily from the C language syntax. They can perform operations as the assignment occurs. The assignment operators are as follows:

Operator	Operation
=	Set left side to value of right side expression
+=	Add right side to left side, set left to result
-=	Subtract right side from left, set left to result
*=	Multiply right side by left, set left to result
/=	Divide left side by right, set left to result
%=	Get remainder of left side divided by right, set left to result
&=	Bitwise AND left and right, set left to result
|=	Bitwise OR left and right, set left to result
^=	Bitwise XOR left and right, set left to result
.=	Concatenate string on right to string on left
=>	Assign Array Element Index values. (see Arrays section in this Appendix).

A

Logic Operators

Logic operators exist in two different forms. One form deals with bitwise operators. The other form deals with logical truth statements.

When you use bitwise operators, you convert the number you are dealing with to binary and whenever the 1 or 0 is in the exact same position in the two numbers, the bitwise operator has an effect.

For example, if you bitwise OR two the numbers 8 and 4, you get an answer in this fashion:

```
1000 | 0100 = 1100
```

If you do the math conversion you will find that the answer is 12. In many cases, adding numbers together appears to give you the result of an OR. But this is not quite true. The OR function does not carry binary numbers across, so 1 OR 1 is still one, not two. Each number column in binary is called a *bit*.

When using logical operators, always use the binary system to determine what will happen. The results of the logical operators are always calculated one bit at a time.

EXCURSION

A Quick Lesson on Number Systems

We count from 0–9, with 10 being ten. That is why our number system is called a base ten system. In base eight (octal), you count from 0–7, with 10 being eight. For base 2, you count from 0–1, with 10 being 2. In base 16, it is 0–F (15), with 10 being 16.

In each base, the first column on the left is ones. For example, in base 10, it is one, two, three, ...nine. In base 8, it is one, two, three, ...seven.

In each base, the numbers in the next column to the left have a value equal to that base times the column value to the right. For example, in base ten, 1 is equal to one, 10 is equal to ten times one, 100 is equal to ten times ten, 1000 is equal to ten times one hundred. In base eight (octal), 1 is one, 10 is eight times one, 100 is eight times eight, 1000 is eight times sixty four. In base 2 (binary), 1 is one, 10 is two times one, 100 is two times two, 1000 is two times four.

To convert a number from one base to another, divide by the largest number in the base you are going to that results in an integer answer greater than 0. Then take the remainder and repeat.

To convert 19 to binary, divide it by the largest power of two you can. I start by counting by the base: 1, 2, 4, 8, 16, 32. Okay, 16 is the largest number. 19–16 = 3. That puts a 1 in the 16 spot. Now, for 8 and 4, we have zeros, because 3 is less than both. 3–2 = 1. There is a 1 in the 2 spot, and a 1 in the 1 spot. Now we have the information needed to convert to binary. Let's put it together in a binary number: 10011. To put it together backwards, it is 1 times 1 plus 1 times 2 plus zero times 4 plus zero times 8 plus 1 times 16 equals 19.

The truth table for bitwise operations is shown in the following table. In the table, X means any value of 1 or 0 (we don't care). The -- indicates that only one side is used in the operation. The operator used is in parentheses:

Bit	Operation	Bit	Result
1	OR (|)	X	1
0	OR (|)	0	0
1	AND (&)	1	1
0	AND (&)	X	0
1	XOR (^)	1	0
1	XOR (^)	0	1
0	XOR (^)	0	0
1	NOT (~)	--	0
0	NOT (~)	--	1

Logical truth operators deal with the logical answer from an expression. Generally, if an expression evaluates to zero, it is `false`. If it evaluates to any other number, it is `true`. The following table gives examples and results of the logical truth operations. In all cases the result is `false` unless the conditions described are met:

Operation	Description
`$a and $b`	Returns `true` if both $a and $b are `true`
`$a or $b`	Returns `true` if either $a or $b are `true`
`$a xor $b`	Returns `true` if either $a or $b is `true`, but `false` if both $a and $b are `true`.
`!$a`	Returns `true` if $a is `false`
`$a && $b`	Returns `true` if both $a and $b are `true`
`$a || $b`	Returns `true` if either $a or $b are `true`

Note that the precedence of `and` and `or` is different from the precedence of `&&` and `||`.

Reference Operators

Reference operators are used by the programmer to make PHP look further before determining what to do. They are usually used on objects to reference the function or method within that object. The reference operator for objects is `->`.

Assume you have an object named `mydog` with an attribute called `color`, and a method called `wag_tail()`. To set the color to red, and call the `wag_tail()` function within the object, you would write code like this:

```
$mydog->color = "red";
$mydog->wag_tail();
```

The reference operator & is also used on variables within function calls. Normally, PHP makes a copy of a variable and gives the copy to the function call. Changes to that variable change only the copy. If you use the & operator, the variable is not copied. Any changes you make to the variable in the function are made to the variable that was listed in the function call. This is called passing arguments by reference. For example:

```
$a = 4;
$b = 3;
function foo($c, $d) {
  $c = 5;
  $d = 6;
}
 foo($a,&$b);
printf("a is %d\n", $a); // will print a is  4
printf("b is %d\n", $b)_; // will print b is 6
```

> PHP 4 introduced assignment references. You can make a variable essentially become another name for another variable. The statement
>
> `$a = &$b;`
>
> causes $a and $b to point to the same variable. If you change $a, $b is changed, and vice versa. The variables $a and $b are identical in all respects.

String Operator

There is only one operator for a string. It is the concatenation operator. This operator is a period (.). Two strings are joined together with no intervening spaces when this operator is used:

```
$a = "This is a test";
$b = "of joining two strings";
echo $a.$b; // this prints "This is a testof joining two strings"
```

Program Flow Control Statements

The order of execution is changed using program flow control statements. These statements are borrowed from everyday logical argumentative speech. I'm sure you have said something like "If I get this then I will do that, else I will have to wait." The PHP parser supports this form of logical decision, and executes code based on the result.

The main program flow statements are for, if, while, and switch. The for and while statements execute code for as long as a condition is true. The if statement executes certain code if a statement is true, or other code if the statement is false. The switch statement takes a look at an expression and executes the code in the group that matches the value of the expression.

The `if` Statement

When the condition is met, execute the code directly after the condition test. For example, if $a has a value of 3, assign a value of 5 to $b. If not, do nothing, leaving $b equal to 4:

```
$b = 4;
if ($a ==3)
    $b = 5;
```

The `else` Statement

When the condition fails, execute the code directly after the `else`. In the following, if $a is not equal to 3, $b is set to a value of 6:

```
if ($a == 3)
    $b = 4;
else
    $b = 6;
```

The `elseif` Statement

When the first condition fails, try the second condition and make a decision based on it. In the following, if $a is equal to 3, then $b is set to 4. Otherwise, if $c is equal to 7, the $b is set to 8; if c is not equal to 7, then $b is set to 9:

```
if ($a == 3)
    $b = 4;
elseif ($c == 7)
    $b = 8;
else
    $b = 9;
```

The `while` Statement

Execute the code between the brackets while the condition in the parentheses evaluates to `true`. If the condition in parentheses evaluates to `false`, the code in the loop is not executed. In the following example, the $c will keep incrementing until $b is equal to zero (ten times). The variable $b is decremented once through the loop:

```
$b = 10;
while ($b > 0 ) {
  $c = $c +1;
  $b--;
}
```

The `do`/`while` Statement

Execute the code in the loop, and then test the condition in parentheses. If the condition is `true`, the code is executed again. The code will always execute at least once:

```
$b = 10;
do{
```

A

```
    $c = $c +1;
    $b--;
}while ($b > 0);
```

The for Statement

This is a three-part statement, with the parts separated by semicolons. The first part is an expression that is executed only once, and before the conditional test in the middle part is evaluated, the conditional test is made. If the test returns true, the code after the closing parentheses is executed. If the code after the closing parentheses is enclosed in brackets, all the code between the brackets is executed. If the test returns false, the bracketed code is not executed. At the end of the execution of the code between brackets, the expression in the third part is executed. At this point, the conditional test is made again, and the cycle repeats.

In the following example, $a is set to 0, the test is made, $b is incremented by 5, and then $a is incremented by one. When $a reaches the value of 6, program flow picks up with the statement after the for loop, causing $c to be set to 8:

```
for ($a = 0 ; $a < 6 ; $a++  ) {
    $b += 5;
    /* more statements can follow */
    }
$c = 8;
```

Each of the three parts can be empty. If the conditional test portion is empty, PHP always determines the result of the test is true, and will execute the code between the brackets until the loop is exited using a break or the script is ended with an exit:

```
for ( $a = 0 ; ; $a++) {
  $b++;
  if ($a > 10 )
    break;
  if ($c == 15 )
    exit;
 }
```

The switch Statement

A switch evaluates the expression in parentheses and executes the code under the case that has the same value. If none of the cases match the evaluation, the default code is evaluated. If no evaluation matches, and the default code does not exist, no code is evaluated.

In the following code, if $a is equal to 1, "One" will be printed. If $a is equal to 12, "Twelve" will be printed. If $a is equal to 99, then "Nine" will be printed. If $a is equal to 9, then "Nine" will be printed. In all other cases, "who knows" will be printed:

```
switch($a)
  {
  case 1:
```

```
  echo "One";
 break;
 case 12:
  echo "Twelve";
 break;
 case 99:
  echo "Nine ";
  /* it falls through the next statement*/
 case 9:
  echo "Nine";
 break;
 default:
  echo "who knows";
 break;
 }
```

The break Statement

This statement terminates execution of a loop or switch statement. Refer to the `for` and `switch` explanations for examples of its use.

The continue Statement

This statement causes the loop to immediately jump to the conditional test. If the conditional test evaluates to `true`, the loop is executed again. In the following example, $c is not incremented until $a is greater than 9. When $a is greater than 9, the $c is incremented, and the loop is exited:

```
$a = 0;
while (1)
  {
  $a++;
  if($a < 10)
    continue;

    $c ++;
    break;
    }
```

The require and include Statements

The `require` statement is replaced with the specified file. This happens only once. If you want to replace the statement with different files when executed in a loop, you must use the `include` statement. In the following example, the contents of `'include.inc'` are placed in the file, and the file `'loop1.inc'` is include the first time through the loop, and 'loop2.inc' is included the second time through the loop:

```
<?php
require 'include.inc';
$in = 'loop2.inc';

for ( $a = 0 ; $a < 2 ; $a ++)
```

```
{
if ($a < 1 )
   include 'loop1.inc';
else
   include $in;
}
```

include and require statements can appear anywhere in the code. You must be careful with opening and closing quotes, parentheses, semicolons, and brackets. It might not be obvious why a program fails when you include a file. Sometimes you have to merge the different files using a text editor to see the error.

User-Defined Functions

You can define a function to be called later. You can put the function in a file to be included in different Web pages. Functions you define are used just like library functions. You must define a function before you call it.

Functions can return values. If you use a return statement, the value after the return replaces the function call in a statement. For example:

```
function myfunc(){
   return 4;
}
$a = 1 + myfunc();
printf("a = %d\n",$a);//prints a = 5
```

Functions can be called with arguments. Arguments are lists of variables that can be used by the code within the function. Arguments can be passed by value or by reference. (For a detailed description of by reference/by value, see the Reference section under Operators in this Appendix.) You can define default values for function arguments. The following code assigns a default value to the argument in the function get_color():

```
function get_color($coat_length = "short") {
    if ($coat_length == "short")
        return "brown";
    else
        return "white";
    }

printf ("the short coat color is %s\n",get_color());
                        /* prints "the short coat color is brown */
printf("the long coat color is %s\n",get_color("long"));
                        /* prints the long coat color is white */
```

You must put default arguments on the right side of non-default arguments. The following shows the correct way and the incorrect way to assign default arguments:

```
function foo($arg1, $arg2 = "defaulted") {} // the right way
function foobad ($arg1 = "defaulted", $arg2 {} // the wrong way
```

In the preceding code, if foo is called with one argument; foo("hello"), then PHP is happy. If foobad is called with one argument; foobad("hello"), then you will get a warning similar to this:

```
Warning: Missing argument 2 in call to foobad() in
➥/home/httpd/html/test/test.php3 on line 4
```

Some of PHP's library functions require a user-written callback function as one of the parameters. For example, the usort() function sorts an array. It requires you to give it the name of a comparison function, as shown:

```
Function cmp($a,$b)
{
if ($a>$b)
   return 1;
 if ($a<$b)
   return -1;
 return 0; // must be equal
}
$arr[0]=5;
$arr[1]=2;
$arr[3]=4;
$arr[4]=1;

  usort($arr,"cmp");
```

In the current version of PHP 4, you can also pass an array containing an object and a method, as shown:

```
Class sort {
  Var $misc;
  Function compare($a,$b)
    {
    if ($a>$b)
        return 1;
     if ($a<$b)
       return -1;
    return 0; // must be equal
    }
 }
 $MySort = new sort;
$arr[0]=5;
$arr[1]=2;
$arr[3]=4;
$arr[4]=1;

  usort($arr,array($MySort,"compare"));
```

An old_func keyword has been deprecated. It should not be used. It allows you to define functions using the old PHP/FI2 syntax. If you do this, PHP3 has difficulty using the function thus defined, and the function should never be used in PHP 4. There is no reason to use that function. If you need to use old PHP2 code, use the PHP/FI2 -> PHP3 convertor.

Classes

The basic definition of a class has been discussed in the Types section in this appendix. In formal class definition, a function is known as a method, and a variable is known as an attribute. When referencing variables in a class, you use the reference operator (->), and you leave off the $ in front of variables.

As in other object-oriented languages, you can use other classes when creating new classes. In formal class terminology, you derive the new class from the former class. All the methods and attributes of the former class are available to you. This is called *inheritance*. The new class inherits the attributes and functions from the base class. The new ones are added to the list. To do this you use the keyword extends when defining the class.

Suppose you have a dog class. This dog class has ears, eyes, and a nose. You want to use this base class because it is so useful, but you need to add a tail and a function to set the length of the tail. The code might look something like this:

```
class BaseDogClass {
    var $eyes;
    var $ears;
    var $nose;
    function SetEyeColor($color)
        {
        $this->eyes = $color;
        }
    function SetEarSize($size) {
        $this->ears = $size; }
    function SetNoseTemperature($temperature) {
        $this->nose = $temperature;
        }
    }
$HisDog = new BaseDogClass;

class DogWithTailClass extends BaseDogClass {
    var $tail;
    function SetTailLength($length) {
        $this->tail = $length;
        }
    }
$MyDog = new DogWithTailClass;
```

In the previous code, $HisDog is an object and can be used. $MyDog is an object with all the methods and attributes of $HisDog. However, $MyDog has a $tail and $HisDog does not!

Note the use of $this. The variable $this is a reference to the attributes and methods of the object the code is currently in, and must be used to reference those methods or attributes. The $this variable is automatically defined by PHP when an object is created.

In formal class design, classes have functions that are called when the object is created using new. These functions are called *constructors*. Whenever a function exists that has the same name as the class, it becomes the constructor for that class. For example:

```
class MyNewDogClass extends BaseDog {
    var $tail;
    function MyNewDogClass() {  // this is the constructor for this class
        $this->tail = 3; // the size of the tail is 3 inches by default
        $this->eyes = "brown";
        $this->ears = "short";
        $this->nose = "cold";
        }
    }
$MyNewDog = new MyNewDogClass;//3 inch tail, brown eyes, short ears, cold nose
```

The $MyNewDog just created has brown eyes and a cold nose among other things. This is a very powerful concept to be used with objects. It can make your life much easier.

 When you have derived a class from another class, the constructor in the base class is not called automatically in PHP 3. (In PHP 4, if there is no constructor for the derived class, the constructor for the parent class is called.) You must call the base class constructor yourself. Let's assume BaseDog class has a constructor. To call it, you must put the BaseDog call in your derived class. For example, the following calls the BaseDog class constructor when the object is created:

```
class ExampleDog extends BaseDog {
    var $MyVar;
    function ExampleDog() {
        $this->BaseDog(); // call base class constructor
        $this->MyVar = 1;
        }
    }
```

You can also have an array that contains objects. You might be able to call the object directly from the array, if you are using PHP 3. PHP 4 handles this situation properly. If you have problems, the following code can be of some help:

```
$myArray[10] = new BaseDog;

$myArray[10]->SetEyeColor("red"); // this may fail in PHP 3
```

```
$tempObj = $MyArray[10]; // make a copy of the object
$tempObj->SetEyeColor("red"); // this will work instead, but updates the copy
```

The $tempObj variable is a copy of the object in $myArray. The variable being set is in the $tempObj object, not in the $myArray object. In PHP 4, the $myArray[10]->SetEyeColor() call would work.

Built-In Functions

PHP has very few built-in functions. When you use the configuration script and the compiler to build PHP, you cause functions to become visible to PHP. For all intents and purposes, they are "built in."

Some functions become available when you build PHP on a system that has a particular library. Other functions must be compiled in by specifying the functionality required on the configure command line. The sheer number of libraries available to PHP precludes listing all of them in this book. You will find a comprehensive list at http://www.php.net.

Arrays

One of the strengths of PHP is its strong suite of array manipulation functions. Arrays are covered in more depth in the chapter on PHP. The following section covers a useful subset of the array functions. (A complete PHP manual is online at http://www.php.net/manual.)

array

Description array is a construct, which creates and fills an array in one step.

Usage:

```
<?php
    $myArray = array ( 1, 2, 3, 4, 5);
?>
```

array array_count_values(array CheckedArray)

Description: Returns an associative array that contains the number of times each element occurred, with the key to that value being the element in the input array. In other words, if "hello" is in the CheckedArray three times, an array is returned that, when indexed by "hello", returns 3.

See Also: array, array_diff

Usage:

```
<?php
    $myArray = array ( 1, 1, 3, 3, 3, 4, 5);
    $Frequency = array_count_values($myArray);
    // the following prints "Frequency of 1 is 2"
```

```
    echo "Frequency of 1 is ".$Frequency["1"]."<BR>";
    //$Frequency["1"]=2,$Frequency["3"]=3,$Frequency["4"]=1,$Frequency["5"]=1
?>
```

array array_diff(array CheckedArray, array TestArray1, [array TestArray2],...)

Description: Returns an array that consists of all the members in CheckedArray that don't exist in any of the TestArrays.

See Also: array, array_count_values

Usage:

```
<?php
    $myArray = array ( 1, 2, 3, 4, 5);
    $myArray2 = array (4, 5, 6);
    $MyArray3 = array (3, 4, 5);
    $DifferenceArray = array_diff($myArray,$myArray2,$myArray3);
    // $DifferenceArray has in it the values 1,2
?>
```

array array_intersect(array FirstArray, array SecondArray, [array ThirdArray],...)

Description: Returns an array containing values that are present in all of the arrays. This is the logical reverse of the array_diff() function.

See Also: array_diff

Usage:

```
<?php
    $myArray = array ( 1, 2, 3, 4, 5);
    $myArray2 = array (4, 5, 6);
    $MyArray3 = array (3, 4, 5);
    $Intersect = array_intersect($myArray,$myArray2,$myArray3);
    // $Intersect now contains the values 4,5
?>
```

array array_keys(array CheckedArray, [mixed LookForThisValue])

Description: Returns an array containing the keys in the CheckedArray. If LookForThisValue is specified, only the key for that value is returned.

See Also: array_count_values

Usage:

```
<?php
    $myArray = array ( 1, 2, 3, 4, 5);
    $Frequency = array_count_values($myArray);
    //$Frequency["1"]=2,$Frequency["3"]=3,$Frequency["4"]=1,$Frequency["5"]=1
    $FreqKey = array_keys($Frequency);
    //$FreqKey now contains "1","3","4","5"
?>
```

A

array array_merge(array StartArray, MergeArray2, [MergeArray3],...)

Description: Appends MergeArray1, MergeArray2, and so forth to StartArray. If one of the MergeArrayx arrays has a string key (for example, "color") that is duplicated in StartArray, the last new value for that key will overwrite the value in StartArray. Simple numeric keys (normal indexes) are not overwritten, but the values are appended and placed in the new array.

See Also: array_diff

Usage:

```php
<?php
    $myArray = array ( "brown"=>1, "red"=>2);
    $myArray2 = array ("brown"=>12, "orange"=>5);
    $MergedArray = array_merge($myArray,$myArray2);
    // The new array is $MergedArray[]
    // $MergedArray["brown"] == 12, $MergedArray["red"] == 2
    // $MergedArray["orange"] == 5
?>
```

mixed array_pad(array WorkArray,int PadToThisSize,mixed ValueToPadWith)

Description: Pads a copy of the WorkArray with the ValueToPadWith so the array is the size of PadToThisSize. If PadToThisSize is the same size as or smaller than the array is already, no padding occurs. It returns the padded array.

See Also: array_pop

Usage:

```php
<?php
    $myArray = array ( 1, 2, 3);
    $paddedArray = array_pad($myArray,6,99);
    // $paddedArray now has 1,2,3,99,99,99
?>
```

mixed array_pop(array WorkArray)

Description: Removes the last element in WorkArray, and returns the value removed from the array.

See Also: array_push

Usage:

```php
<?php
    $myArray = array ( 1, 2, 3, 4, 5);
    $n = array_pop($myArray);
    echo "Value removed is $n<BR>";// $n is 5
    // $myArray now has 1,2,3,4
?>
```

int array_push(array WorkArray,mixed Value1, [mixed Value2],...)

Description: Adds Value1, Value2, and so forth onto the end of WorkArray, and returns the size of the new array. Adding one element is the same as doing $array[ ] = $newValue;

See Also: array_pop

Usage:

```php
<?php
    $myArray = array ( 1, 2, 3, 4, 5);
    $n = array_push($myArray,6,7);
    echo "There are now $n elements in \$myArray<BR>";
    // prints "There are now 7 elements in $myArray
?>
```

array array_reverse(array WorkArray)

Description: Returns an array that has the order of the elements in WorkArray reversed.

Usage:

```php
<?php
    $myArray = array ( 1, 2, 3 );
    $myArray2 = array_reverse($WorkArray);
    echo "Reversed Array element ";
    for ($index = 0 ; $index < count($myArray2); $index++)
        echo "$index = ".$myArray2[$index].", ";
    echo "<br>";
    // prints Reversed Array element 0 = 3, 1 = 2, 3 = 1
?>
```

mixed array_shift(array WorkArray)

Description: Removes the first element in WorkArray, and returns the value removed from the array. All remaining elements are moved down one.

See Also: array_pop

Usage:

```php
<?php
    $myArray = array ( 1, 2, 3, 4, 5);
    $n = array_shift($myArray);
    echo "Value removed is $n<BR>";// $n is a 1
    // $myArray now has 2,3,4,5
?>
```

array array_splice(array WorkArray, int OffsetIndex, [int Length], [array ReplacementArray])

Description: Removes elements from WorkArray, starting at OffsetIndex for Length elements. If ReplacementArray is provided, the elements removed in WorkArray are

A

replaced by the elements in ReplacementArray. If there are more elements in ReplacementArray than cut, the extra elements will be inserted.

If OffsetIndex is negative, the offset is calculated from the end of the array. If OffsetIndex is positive, the offset is calculated from the beginning of the array. Items are removed starting at the OffsetIndex value.

If Length is omitted, the rest of the array from OffsetIndex is used. If Length is positive, it specifies the number of elements to cut. If Length is negative, then it specifies the number of elements to leave on the end of the array from the end of the cut. For an example, see the usage section.

If OffsetIndex and Length have values that would cause no elements to be removed from the array, and ReplacementArray is specified, then elements from ReplacementArray are added into WorkArray starting at OffsetIndex.

Array_splice returns the removed elements in an array.

See Also: array_push, array_pop, array_shift

Usage:

```php
<?php
    $myArray = array ( 1, 2, 3, 4, 5);
    $myArray2 = array ( 6 , 7 , 8);
    $myArray3 = array ( 9, 10, 11);
    $RemovedItems = array_splice($myArray,3,1,$myArray2);
    echo "myArray=<BR>";
    for ($index = 0 ; $index < count($myArray); $index++)
        echo "item $index = ".$myArray[$index]."<br>";
    echo "<BR>RemovedItems=<BR>";
    for ($index = 0 ; $index < count($RemovedItems); $index++)
        echo  "item $index = ".$RemovedItems[$index]."<br>";
    echo "<BR>myArray2=<BR>";
    $RemovedItems = array_splice($myArray2,2,0,$myArray3);
    for ($index = 0 ; $index < count($myArray2); $index++)
        echo "item $index = ".$myArray2[$index]."<br>";
/* The following is printed:
myArray=
item 0 = 1
item 1 = 2
item 2 = 3
item 3 = 6
item 4 = 7
item 5 = 8
item 6 = 5

RemovedItems=
item 0 = 4

myArray2=
item 0 = 6
item 1 = 7
```

```
item 2 = 9
item 3 = 10
item 4 = 11
item 5 = 8
*/
    $myArray = array ( 1, 2, 3, 4, 5);
    $myArray2 = array ( 6 , 7 , 8);
    $RemovedItems = array_splice($myArray,2,-1,$myArray2);
    echo "myArray=<BR>";
    for ($index = 0 ; $index < count($myArray); $index++)
        echo "item $index = ".$myArray[$index]."<br>";
    echo "<BR>RemovedItems=<BR>";
    for ($index = 0 ; $index < count($RemovedItems); $index++)
        echo  "item $index = ".$RemovedItems[$index]."<br>";
/* The following is printed:
myArray=
item 0 = 1
item 1 = 2
item 2 = 6
item 3 = 7
item 4 = 8
item 5 = 5

RemovedItems=
item 0 = 3
item 1 = 4
*/
?>
```

A

int array_unshift(array WorkArray,mixed Value1, [mixed Value2],...)

Description: Puts Value1, Value2, and so on onto the front of the WorkArray, and returns the final number of elements in the array.

See Also: array_shift

Usage:

```php
<?php
    $myArray = array ( 1, 2, 3, 4, 5);
    $n = array_unshift($myArray, 10, 11, 12);// $n is 8
    // $myArray is now 10,11,12,1,2,3,4,5
?>
```

array array_values(array WorkArray)

Description: Returns the values in an array. This is best used with an associative array. It effectively turns the associative indexes into numerical indexes.

Usage:

```php
<?php
    $myArray = array ( "brown"=>1, "red"=>2);
    $newArray = array_values($myArray);
```

```
    // $newArray is now (1, 2), and
    // $newArray[0] = 1, $newArray[1]=2
?>
```

int array_walk(array WorkArray,string FunctionName,[mixed UserSuppliedData])

Description: Calls FunctionName for each and every element in WorkArray, handing the function the array value, the array key, and UserSuppliedData. If the user-defined function defines the value to be passed by reference, the value in the array can be changed directly. If you do not want to provide the UserSuppliedData, or if your function takes more than three parameters, call the walk function with an @ prepended to squelch warnings from PHP: @array_walk($array,"func");

Usage:

```
<?php
// this function defines the value to be passed by reference
// to allow it to change the array value directly
// and doubles each array value without checking to see
// if it is actually a number!
Function DoubleArrayValues(&$ArrayValue, $ArrayKey, $UserSuppliedData)
{/*function work here */
  echo "array value *2 == ".($ArrayValue*2)."<BR>";
  // now double the value in the array
  $ArrayValue = $ArrayValue * 2;
}
    $myArray = array ( 1, 2, 3, 4, 5);
    @array_walk($myArray,"DoubleArrayValues");
    for ($index = 0 ; $index < count($myArray); $index++)
        echo "array value is now ".$myArray[$index]."<br>";
    reset($myArray); // rest the array cursor
?>
```

void arsort(array WorkArray,[int SortFlags])

Description: Sorts an array in reverse order, per SortFlags. This function only affects associative arrays. The associative index still works, but the natural order in the array is affected. The reset() function must be called after using arsort() to reset the array cursor. The SortFlags can be one of the following:

- SORT_REGULAR—Compare each element in the array normally, as their type would dictate.
- SORT_NUMERIC—Compare each element in the array as numbers only.
- SORT_STRING—Compare each element in the array as strings only.

See Also: asort, sort, reset, array_values, each

Usage:

```
<?php
    $myArray = array( "first"=>"brown","second"=> "red", "third"=>"blue",
```

```
                      "fourth"=>"green", "fifth"=>"pink" );
  $myArray2 = array_values($myArray);
  echo "<BR>natural order =<BR>";
  for ($index = 0 ; $index < count($myArray2); $index++)
   echo "item $index = ".$myArray2[$index]."<br>";
  arsort($myArray);
  reset($myArray);
  echo "<BR>reverse sorted=<BR>";
  $myArray2 = array_values($myArray);
  for ($index = 0 ; $index < count($myArray2); $index++)
   echo "item $index = ".$myArray2[$index]."<br>";
  echo "note that 'first' is still ".$myArray["first"]."<BR>";
/* the following is printed:
natural order =
item 0 = brown
item 1 = red
item 2 = blue
item 3 = green
item 4 = pink

reverse sorted=
item 0 = red
item 1 = pink
item 2 = green
item 3 = brown
item 4 = blue
note that 'first' is still brown
*/
?>
```

void asort(array WorkArray, [int SortFlags])

Description: Sorts an array in order, per SortFlags. This function only affects associative arrays. The associative index still works, but the natural order in the array is affected. The reset() function must be called after using asort() to reset the array cursor. See arsort() for SortFlags definition.

See Also: arsort, reset, array_values, each

Usage:

```
<?php
  $myArray = array( "first"=>"brown","second"=> "red", "third"=>"blue",
                    "fourth"=>"green", "fifth"=>"pink" );
  $myArray2 = array_values($myArray);
  echo "<BR>natural order =<BR>";
  for ($index = 0 ; $index < count($myArray2); $index++)
   echo "item $index = ".$myArray2[$index]."<br>";
  asort($myArray);
  reset($myArray);
  echo "<BR> sorted=<BR>";
  $myArray2 = array_values($myArray);
  for ($index = 0 ; $index < count($myArray2); $index++)
   echo "item $index = ".$myArray2[$index]."<br>";
```

```
    echo "note that 'first' is still ".$myArray["first"]."<BR>";
/* prints this:
natural order =
item 0 = brown
item 1 = red
item 2 = blue
item 3 = green
item 4 = pink

sorted=
item 0 = blue
item 1 = brown
item 2 = green
item 3 = pink
item 4 = red
note that 'first' is still brown
*/
?>
```

int count(array WorkArray)

Description: Returns the number of elements in WorkArray. If the variable is not an array, but has been set, it returns 1. If the variable is not set, or if the variable has been initialized with an empty array, it returns 0.

See Also: array, array_values, each

Usage:

```
<?php
    $myArray = array ( 1, 2, 3, 4, 5);
    for ($index = 0 ; $index < count($myArray); $index++)
        echo "array index $index is now ".$myArray[$index]."<br>";
/* prints this:
array index 0 is now 1
array index 1 is now 2
array index 2 is now 3
array index 3 is now 4
array index 4 is now 5
*/
?>
```

mixed current(array WorkArray)

Description: Returns the value that the array cursor points to.

See Also: key, each, next

 Note

In PHP, an invisible array cursor exists for each array. This array cursor is used by several functions to allow PHP to "walk" through arrays one element at a time. You should call the reset() function before you start using any array function that manipulates this cursor, to guarantee you will start at the beginning of the array.

Usage:

```php
<?php
    $myArray = array ( 1, 2, 3, 4, 5);
    reset($myArray);
    $value = current($myArray);// $value is now == 1
?>
```

array each(array WorkArray)

Description: Returns a four-element array (from the WorkArray array cursor position) consisting of the key and value from an array indexed by 0 and 1, as well as by "key" and "value", respectively. If the WorkArray cursor points past the end of WorkArray, each returns FALSE. The each function advances the array cursor, unless it is already past the end of the array.

See Also: reset

Usage:

```php
<?php
  $myArray = array( "first"=>"brown","second"=> "red", "third"=>"blue",
                    "fourth"=>"green", "fifth"=>"pink");
  reset($myArray);// reset the array cursor (not needed in this case)
  while ($snoop = each($myArray))
    {
    echo "key ".$snoop["key"]." has a value of ".$snoop["value"]."<BR>";
    echo "key [index 0] ".$snoop[0]." has a value [index 1] of
".$snoop[1]."<BR>";
    }
/* prints this :
key first has a value of brown
key [index 0] first has a value [index 1] of brown
key second has a value of red
key [index 0] second has a value [index 1] of red
key third has a value of blue
key [index 0] third has a value [index 1] of blue
key fourth has a value of green
key [index 0] fourth has a value [index 1] of green
key fifth has a value of pink
key [index 0] fifth has a value [index 1] of pink
*/
?>
```

array end(array WorkArray)

Description: Sets the array cursor to the last element in the array.

See Also: prev, next, current, each, end, reset

Usage:

```php
<?php
    $myArray = array ( 1, 2, 3, 4, 5);
    end($myArray);
```

A

```
    $value = current($myArray);// $value is now == 5
?>
```

int in_array(mixed SearchFor, array SearchedArray)

Description: Returns TRUE if value SearchFor is found in SearchedArray. It returns FALSE if the variable is not found.

See Also: array

Usage:

```
<?php
    $myArray = array( "first"=>"brown","second"=> "red", "third"=>"blue",
                      "fourth"=>"green", "fifth"=>"pink");
    if (in_array("pink",$myArray))
        echo "found pink in myArray<BR>";// prints this message
?>
```

array key(array WorkArray)

Description: Returns the key for the current array cursor position.

See Also: prev, next, current, each, end, reset

Usage:

```
<?php
  $myArray = array( "first"=>"brown","second"=> "red", "third"=>"blue",
                    "fourth"=>"green", "fifth"=>"pink");
  reset($myArray);// reset the array cursor (not needed in this case)
  $key = key($myArray); // $key now == "first"
?>
```

array krsort(array WorkArray, [int SortFlags])

Description: Description: Sorts an array's keys in reverse order, per SortFlags. This function only affects associative arrays. The associative index still works, but the natural order of the values in the array is affected. The reset() function must be called after using krsort() to reset the array cursor. See arsort() for SortFlags definition.

See Also: arsort, assort, reset, array_values, each

Usage:

```
<?php
  $myArray = array( "first"=>"brown","second"=> "red", "third"=>"blue",
                    "fourth"=>"green", "fifth"=>"pink");
  $myArray2 = array_values($myArray);
  echo "<BR>natural order =<BR>";
  for ($index = 0 ; $index < count($myArray2); $index++)
   echo "item $index = ".$myArray2[$index]."<br>";
  krsort($myArray);
  reset($myArray);
  echo "<BR> sorted=<BR>";
  $myArray2 = array_values($myArray);
```

```
    reset($myArray);
    while(list($key,$value) = each($myArray))
        print "The sorted key is $key, and its value is $value<BR>";
    echo "<br>";
    for ($index = 0 ; $index < count($myArray2); $index++)
      echo "Natural order item $index = ".$myArray2[$index]."<br>";
    echo "note that 'first' is still ".$myArray["first"]."<BR>";
/* prints this:
natural order =
item 0 = brown
item 1 = red
item 2 = blue
item 3 = green
item 4 = pink

sorted=
The sorted key is third, and its value is blue
The sorted key is second, and its value is red
The sorted key is fourth, and its value is green
The sorted key is first, and its value is brown
The sorted key is fifth, and its value is pink

Natural order item 0 = blue
Natural order item 1 = red
Natural order item 2 = green
Natural order item 3 = brown
Natural order item 4 = pink
note that 'first' is still brown
*/
?>
```

array ksort(array WorkArray, [int SortFlags])

Description: Sorts an array's keys in order, per SortFlags. This function only affects associative arrays. The associative index still works, but the natural order of the values in the array is affected. The reset() function must be called after using ksort() to reset the array cursor. See arsort() for SortFlags definition.

See Also: arsort, assort, reset, array_values, each

Usage:

```
<?php
  $myArray = array( "first"=>"brown","second"=> "red", "third"=>"blue",
                    "fourth"=>"green", "fifth"=>"pink");
  $myArray2 = array_values($myArray);
  echo "<BR>natural order =<BR>";
  for ($index = 0 ; $index < count($myArray2); $index++)
    echo "item $index = ".$myArray2[$index]."<br>";
  ksort($myArray);
  reset($myArray);
  echo "<BR> sorted=<BR>";
  $myArray2 = array_values($myArray);
  reset($myArray);
```

```
    while(list($key,$value) = each($myArray))
        print "The sorted key is $key, and its value is $value<BR>";
    echo "<br>";
    for ($index = 0 ; $index < count($myArray2); $index++)
      echo "Natural order item $index = ".$myArray2[$index]."<br>";
    echo "note that 'first' is still ".$myArray["first"]."<BR>";
/* prints this:
natural order =
item 0 = brown
item 1 = red
item 2 = blue
item 3 = green
item 4 = pink

sorted=
The sorted key is fifth, and its value is pink
The sorted key is first, and its value is brown
The sorted key is fourth, and its value is green
The sorted key is second, and its value is red
The sorted key is third, and its value is blue

Natural order item 0 = pink
Natural order item 1 = brown
Natural order item 2 = green
Natural order item 3 = red
Natural order item 4 = blue
note that 'first' is still brown
*/
?>
```

void list(mixed Var1, [mixed Var2],...)

Description: list is a PHP construct that assigns variables values as if they were array elements. You can use this with any function that returns a list of items, such as mysql_fetch_row() or each().

See Also: prev, current, each, end, reset

Usage:

```
<?php
  $myArray = array( "first"=>"brown","second"=> "red", "third"=>"blue",
                    "fourth"=>"green", "fifth"=>"pink");
  while(list($key,$value) = each($myArray))
      print "The key is $key, and its value is $value<BR>";
  echo "<br>";
/* prints this
The key is first, and its value is brown
The key is second, and its value is red
The key is third, and its value is blue
The key is fourth, and its value is green
The key is fifth, and its value is pink
*/
?>
```

mixed next(array WorkArray)

Description: Advances the array cursor, and then returns the value that the array cursor points to, or FALSE if at the end of the array. It also returns FALSE if the array element at that location is empty.

See Also: prev, current, each, end, reset

Usage:

```php
<?php
    $myArray = array ( 1, 2, 3, 4, 5);
    reset($myArray);
    $value = next($myArray);// $value is now == 2
?>
```

mixed prev(array WorkArray)

Description: array is a construct, which creates and fills an array in one step.

See Also: next, current, each, end, reset

Usage:

```php
<?php
    $myArray = array ( 1, 2, 3, 4, 5);
    end($myArray);
    $value = prev($myArray);// $value is now == 4
?>
```

array rsort(array WorkArray, [int SortFlags])

Description: Sorts an array in reverse order, per SortFlags. The associative index is destroyed. The reset() function must be called after using sort() to reset the array cursor. See arsort() for SortFlags definition.

See Also: arsort, assort, reset, array_values, each

Usage:

```php
<?php
    $myArray = array ( 4, 2, 1, 3, 5);
    for ($index = 0 ; $index < count($myArray); $index++)
        echo "array index $index is now ".$myArray[$index]."<br>";

    rsort($myArray);
    echo "<BR>reverse sorted =<BR>";

    for ($index = 0 ; $index < count($myArray); $index++)
        echo "array index $index is now ".$myArray[$index]."<br>";
/* prints this:
array index 0 is now 4
array index 1 is now 2
array index 2 is now 1
array index 3 is now 3
array index 4 is now 5
```

A

```
reverse sorted =
array index 0 is now 5
array index 1 is now 4
array index 2 is now 3
array index 3 is now 2
array index 4 is now 1
*/
?>
```

array sort(array WorkArray, [int SortFlags])

Description: Sorts an array in order, per `SortFlags`. The associative index is destroyed. The `reset()` function must be called after using `sort()` to reset the array cursor. See `arsort()` for `SortFlags` definition.

See Also: arsort, assort, reset, array_values, each

Usage:

```
<?php
    $myArray = array ( 4, 2, 1, 3, 5);
    for ($index = 0 ; $index < count($myArray); $index++)
        echo "array index $index is now ".$myArray[$index]."<br>";

    rsort($myArray);
    echo "<BR>reverse sorted =<BR>";

    for ($index = 0 ; $index < count($myArray); $index++)
        echo "array index $index is now ".$myArray[$index]."<br>";
/* prints this:
array index 0 is now 4
array index 1 is now 2
array index 2 is now 1
array index 3 is now 3
array index 4 is now 5

reverse sorted =
array index 0 is now 1
array index 1 is now 2
array index 2 is now 3
array index 3 is now 4
array index 4 is now 5
*/
?>
```

void usort(array WorkArray, string CompareFunction | array(Object, string CompareMethodInObject))

Description: Sorts an array by calling a user-supplied function which return 0 when elements are equal, -1 when the first element is less than the second element, and 1 when the first element is greater than the second element. The user function can be a standalone function or a method within an object. To call it as a function within an object, pass the object and the name of the method as an array to usort.

See Also: asort

Usage:

```php
<?php
    $myArray = array ( 1, 3, 2, 5, 4);
Function cmp($a,$b)
{
if ($a>$b)
   return 1;
 if ($a<$b)
   return -1;
 return 0; // must be equal
}
  usort($arr,"cmp");// $myArray now = 1,2,3,4,5
/* an alternative method */
    $myArray = array ( 1, 3, 2, 5, 4);
Class sort {
  Var $misc;
  Function compare($a,$b)
    {
    if ($a>$b)
        return 1;
     if ($a<$b)
        return -1;
    return 0; // must be equal
    }
 }
 $MySort = new sort;
  usort($arr,array($MySort,"compare"));
?>
```

void usort(array WorkArray, string CompareFunction | array(Object, string CompareMethodInObject))

Description: Sorts an array by calling a user-supplied function which return 0 when elements are equal, -1 when the first element is less than the second element, and 1 when the first element is greater than the second element. The user function can be a standalone function, or a method within an object. To call it as a function within an object, pass the object and the name of the method as an array to usort. This should not be used on an associative array. You must call reset() after using usort() to reset the array cursor.

See Also: asort, arsort, reset, array_values, each

Usage:

```php
<?php
    $myArray = array ( 1, 3, 2, 5, 4);
Function cmp($a,$b)
{
if ($a>$b)
   return 1;
 if ($a<$b)
```

```
    return -1;
  return 0; // must be equal
}
  usort($arr,"cmp");// $myArray now = 1,2,3,4,5
/* an alternative method */
    $myArray = array ( 1, 3, 2, 5, 4);
Class sort {
  Var $misc;
  Function compare($a,$b)
    {
    if ($a>$b)
        return 1;
      if ($a<$b)
        return -1;
    return 0; // must be equal
    }
  }
  $MySort = new sort;
    usort($arr,array($MySort,"compare"));
?>
```

void uasort(array WorkArray, string CompareFunction | array(Object, string CompareMethodInObject))

Description: Sorts an associative array by calling a user-supplied function which return 0 when elements are equal, -1 when the first element is less than the second element, and 1 when the first element is greater than the second element. The user function can be a standalone function or a method within an object. To call it as a function within an object, pass the object and the name of the method as an array to usort. You must call reset() after using uasort() to reset the array cursor.

See Also: asort, usort, arsort, reset, array_values, each

Usage:

```php
<?php
Function cmp($a,$b)
{
if ($a>$b)
   return 1;
 if ($a<$b)
   return -1;
 return 0; // must be equal
}
Class sort
{
  Var $misc;
  Function compare($a,$b)
    {
    if ($a>$b)
        return 1;
      if ($a<$b)
        return -1;
    return 0; // must be equal
```

```
    }
  }
$myArray = array( "first"=>"brown","second"=> "red", "third"=>"blue",
                    "fourth"=>"green", "fifth"=>"pink");
  while(list($key,$value) = each($myArray))
    print "The key is $key, and its value is $value<BR>";
  echo "<br>";
  uasort($myArray,"cmp");// $myArray now = 1,2,3,4,5
  reset($myArray);
  echo "Sorted array =<BR>";
  while(list($key,$value) = each($myArray))
    print "The key is $key, and its value is $value<BR>";
  echo "<br>";

/* an alternative method */
 $myArray = array( "first"=>"brown","second"=> "red", "third"=>"blue",
                    "fourth"=>"green", "fifth"=>"pink");
 $MySort = new sort;
  uasort($myArray,array($MySort,"compare"));
  echo "<BR>alternative sort method<BR>";
  while(list($key,$value) = each($myArray))
    print "The key is $key, and its value is $value<BR>";
  echo "<br>";
/* prints this:
The key is first, and its value is brown
The key is second, and its value is red
The key is third, and its value is blue
The key is fourth, and its value is green
The key is fifth, and its value is pink

Sorted array =
The key is third, and its value is blue
The key is first, and its value is brown
The key is fourth, and its value is green
The key is fifth, and its value is pink
The key is second, and its value is red


alternative sort method
The key is third, and its value is blue
The key is first, and its value is brown
The key is fourth, and its value is green
The key is fifth, and its value is pink
The key is second, and its value is red
*/
?>
```

void uksort(array WorkArray, string CompareFunction | array(Object, string CompareMethodInObject))

Description: Sorts an associative array's keys by calling a user-supplied function which return 0 when elements are equal, -1 when the first element is less than the second element, and 1 when the first element is greater than the second element. The user function can be a standalone function or a method within an object. To call it as a function within an object, pass the object and the name of the method as an array to usort. You must call reset() after using uksort() to reset the array cursor.

See Also: asort, usort, uasort, arsort, reset, array_values, each

Usage:

```php
<?php
Function cmp($a,$b)
{
if ($a>$b)
   return 1;
 if ($a<$b)
   return -1;
 return 0; // must be equal
}
Class sort
{
  Var $misc;
  Function compare($a,$b)
    {
    if ($a>$b)
        return 1;
     if ($a<$b)
        return -1;
    return 0; // must be equal
    }
}

$myArray = array( "first"=>"brown","second"=> "red", "third"=>"blue",
                  "fourth"=>"green", "fifth"=>"pink");
 while(list($key,$value) = each($myArray))
    print "The key is $key, and its value is $value<BR>";
 echo "<br>";
 uksort($myArray,"cmp");// $myArray now = 1,2,3,4,5
 reset($myArray);
 echo "Sorted array =<BR>";
 while(list($key,$value) = each($myArray))
    print "The key is $key, and its value is $value<BR>";
 echo "<br>";

/* an alternative method */
 $myArray = array( "first"=>"brown","second"=> "red", "third"=>"blue",
                   "fourth"=>"green", "fifth"=>"pink");
 $MySort = new sort;
 uksort($myArray,array($MySort,"compare"));
 echo "<BR>alternative sort method<BR>";
 while(list($key,$value) = each($myArray))
    print "The key is $key, and its value is $value<BR>";
 echo "<br>";

$myArray = array( "first"=>"brown","second"=> "red", "third"=>"blue",
                  "fourth"=>"green", "fifth"=>"pink");
/* prints this:
The key is first, and its value is brown
```

```
The key is second, and its value is red
The key is third, and its value is blue
The key is fourth, and its value is green
The key is fifth, and its value is pink

Sorted array =
The key is fifth, and its value is pink
The key is first, and its value is brown
The key is fourth, and its value is green
The key is second, and its value is red
The key is third, and its value is blue


alternative sort method
The key is fifth, and its value is pink
The key is first, and its value is brown
The key is fourth, and its value is green
The key is second, and its value is red
The key is third, and its value is blue
*/
?>
```

I/O

Input and Output, also known as I/O, falls into two categories: sending or receiving text to and from a Web browser, and reading and writing data to a data storage device.

Getting text from Web browsers has already been covered in the Variables section in this appendix. The special case of file upload will be covered later in the File I/O section.

When sending text to a Web browser, you can use echo(), print(), printf(), flush(), and die(). Text that is placed outside of PHP tags is sent unmodified to the Web browser.

You can read data from a file and print it to the Web browser. You can also print data that is derived from databases or calculations. A few debugging functions are available to PHP that send text to a Web browser. These functions include phpinfo(), phpversion(), and show_source().

General I/O

This section covers general I/O functions available to the programmer. Some of these functions perform other tasks at the same time.

void die(string ExitMessage)

Description: Outputs a string and quit executing the current script. You can use the Perl-like syntax:

```
function_call() or die ('string');
```

This syntax can be used with any function that can return false when it has failed.

See Also: exit

Usage:

```php
<?php
    $a = 2; $b = 3;
    if ($a == 3 )
      die ("A is a bad value, exiting<p>\n");
    if ($b == 3 )
        die;  // exit without printing a message
    $file = fopen("filename","r") or die ("file did not open<p>");
?>
```

int dl(string LibraryName)

Description: Loads a PHP extension at runtime. The extension_dir configuration directive must be set in php.ini.

> **Note**   PHP 3 uses php3.ini as its configuration file. PHP190 4 changed the configuration file to php4.ini. On the Windows platform, if you try to use any php3_*.dll extensions under PHP 4, it will fail.

Usage: This is mainly useful under the Windows operating system. You must uncomment the extension=php_*.dll lines in php.ini under Windows to enable loading of the extension automatically. If you are doing it under Unix and Apache, change the .dll to .so in the php.ini file.

```php
dl('php_myextension.dll')
or die ('Extension myextension failed to load');
```

To do the same thing under Linux or Unix, you would use the following type of command:

```php
dl('calendar.so');
```

echo string str1,…string str2,...String str3,...;

Description: Outputs a string to the Web browser. If you use only one string in the output list, you can enclose it in parentheses.

See Also: print, printf, flush

Usage:

```php
echo 'Hello George',' how are you doing?';  echo ("Hello World");
```

void exit(void);

Description: Halts parsing of the script at that point. The function does not return.

See Also: die

Usage:

```
<?php
    if ( $a == 3 )
        exit; // stop! Don't return!
?>
```

void flush(void);

Description: Clears the output buffer by pushing all text to the Web browser, including text in whatever program or CGI scrip PHP is currently using.

Usage:

```
<?php
    print("hello"); // this may not yet show on the web browser
    flush; // it is now printed for sure
?>
```

void print(string str);

Description: Outputs a string. The print statement is not an actual function, but a PHP construct. You can see some unwanted side effects of using it. If you find you have problems, use `printf()` or echo instead.

Usage:

```
<?php
    print "Hello World<BR>";
    print ("Hello Again!<BR>");
?>
```

A

int printf(string format, [arg1], [arg2],[arg3],...);

Description: Outputs a string based on format. The number of arguments is variable. The format statement is a string. If it contains an escape character, the % character, the information following that character tells the printf code what to do. All other characters in the format string are copied verbatim to the output.

When the printf code encounters a %, it looks past the % for directives. These directives tell printf how to print the values represented by the arguments following the format string, in order. If no directives are in the format string, the arguments are ignored. If too few directives are in the format string, the additional arguments are ignored. If too many directives are in the format string, the resulting output is undetermined. The following list describes the characters following the escape character. These descriptions are in the same basic order of possible occurrence in the format string:

- 0—Specifies zero padding. Zeros will be filled in on the left until the spacing requirements are met.
- '<c>—Specifies padding using the character specified by <c>. The specified character will be filled in on the left until the spacing requirements are met.

- —The negative field with flag tells PHP to left-justify the answer. The answer is right-padded with blanks.•

- 8888—An optional decimal digit string of arbitrary length that specifies a minimum field width. If the converted value has fewer spaces than the field width, it will be padded with spaces on the left. If the negative flag is used, the padding will be on the right.

- 8888—An optional precision, consisting of a period ('.') followed by an optional decimal digit string of arbitrary length. This is the minimum number of digits to display after the decimal point. No digits present indicates to display 6 digits after the decimal point. This value has no effect on the display of numbers, which are not doubles.

- b—Use the argument as an integer and print it as a binary number.

- c—Use the argument as a integer and print it as an ASCII character of that value.

- d—Use the argument as an integer and print as an integer number.

- f—Use the argument as a floating point number and print accordingly.

- o—Use the argument as an integer and print as an octal (base 8) number.

- s—Use the argument as a string and print it accordingly.

- x—Use the argument as an integer number and print as a lower case hexadecimal number.

- X—Use the argument as an integer number and print as an upper case hexadecimal number.

- %—Print this character literally. No conversion is done.

A non-existing or small field width will be expanded to hold the result of the conversion. No characters will be truncated.

See Also: `print`, `echo`, `flush`

Usage:

```php
<?php
    // the following prints "Hello, My Name Is George, a=3"
    printf("%s, %s, a=%d","Hello","My Name Is George",3);
    // the following prints "The value of pi is 3.14159"
    printf("The value of pi is %.5f", 4 * atan(1.0));
?>
```

HTTP I/O

int connection_aborted(void)

Description: Returns TRUE if the client is disconnected. This can be used in conjunction with `ignore_user_abort()` or `register_shutdown_function()`, and with `connection_timeout()` or `connection_status()`. You can't send anything to a Web browser when the connection has been aborted.

See Also: connection_timeout, connection_status, register_shutdown_function, ignore_user_abort

Usage:

```php
<?php
function shutdown()
    {
    if ( connection_aborted())
      {
      /* handle an abort by the user here*/
      }
    else
      {
      /* handle a normal shutdown here */
      }
    }
  register_shutdown_function("shutdown");
?>
```

int connection_status(void)

Description: Returns a bitfield containing Web browser connection status. A 0 is Normal Status, 1 is Aborted Status, 2 is Timeout Status, 3 is both. You can't send anything to a Web browser when the connection has been aborted or timed out.

See Also: connection_timeout, connection_aborted, register_shutdown_function, ignore_user_abort

A

Usage:

```php
<?php
function shutdown()
    {
    if ( connection_status() != 0)
      {
      /* handle a timeout or an abort by the user here*/
      }
    else
      {
      /* handle a normal shutdown here */
      }
    }
  register_shutdown_function("shutdown");
?>
```

int connection_timeout(void)

Description: Returns a TRUE if the connection with the Web browser has timed out.

See Also: connection_status, connection_aborted, register_shutdown_function, ignore_user_abort

Usage:

```php
<?php
function shutdown()
    {
    if ( connection_status() != 0)
        {
        /* handle a timeout here*/
        }
    else
        {
        /* handle a normal shutdown here */
        }
    }
  register_shutdown_function("shutdown");
?>
```

array getallheaders(void)

Description: Returns an associative array containing all the headers in the current HTTP request. You must be using PHP as an Apache module to use this function.

Usage:

```php
<?php
$SessionHeaders = getallheaders();
while (list($OneHeader, $HeaderValue) = each($SessionHeaders)) {
    echo "$OneHeader: $HeaderValue<br>\n";
}
?>
```

object get_browser(string Agent)

Description: This function requires browscap.ini, which is installed on Windows systems, and under PHP 3, get_browser() does not appear to work under Red Hat 6.1. Later versions of PHP might fix the problem. The browscap.ini file provided with Windows is a proprietary file and should not be copied to any other system. You can get a browscap.ini file from http://www.cyscape.com/asp/browscap/, after answering a questionnaire.

Usage:

```php
<?php
    $browser = get_browser();
     echo "browser name ".$browser->browser;
?>
```

int header(string str)

Description: Sends the string as a raw header to the browser. More information on raw headers is available at http://www.w3.org/Protocols/rfc2068/rfc2068. This function must be called before any other output is done to work properly.

See Also: getallheaders

Usage:

```php
<?php
header("Location: http://www.new.net");  /*Redirect browser to another site*/
?>
```

int ignore_user_abort(int [abort_setting])

Description: Changes abort setting only if abort_setting is given. Always returns previous setting. In the abort_setting, 0 is Normal Status, 1 is Abort setting, 2 is Timeout setting, 3 is both.

See Also: connection_status, connection_aborted, register_shutdown_function, connection_timeout

Usage:

```php
<?php
/* read the status without changing */
$CurrentAbortSetting = ignore_user_abort();
/* set the status */
 ignore_user_abort(3); /* ignore both timeout and abort */
?>
```

array iptcparse(string iptcblock)

Description: Parses a binary IPTC block into single tags. For more information, see http://www.xe.net/iptc/. The array returned has the tag marker as the index, and the value in the array is the value of the tag. A false is returned if it is not a valid IPTC block. Note that although most image functions require the GD library, this one does not.

Usage:

```php
<?php
$ImageSize = GetImageSize("myimage.jpg",&$ImageInfo);
if (isset($ImageInfo["APP13"])) {
$iptcData = iptcparse($ImageInfo["APP13"]);
        var_dump($iptcData);
    }
?>
```

int setcookie(string CookieName, string [CookieValue], int [CookieExpiration],string [CookiePath],string [CookieDomain], int [CookieSecure])

Description: Sends a cookie to a browser. You must send a cookie before any other headers are sent. If you send a cookie with PHP, place the code before the <HTML> or <HEAD> tags in the Web page.

You must have a CookieName. All other arguments are optional. If you only have a CookieName, the cookie of that name at the Web browser is deleted. To skip an argument, use an empty string ("") for the string arguments, and 0 for the CookieExpiration and CookieSecurity arguments.

- CookieName is an arbitrary name.
- CookieValue is an arbitrary value, and can be any text string.
- CookieExpiration is in seconds. CookieExpiration is most easily built using the time() function, and adding an arbitrary number of seconds to it.
- CookiePath is a subdirectory to store a cookie in. Internet Explorer 4, service pack 1, does not appear to handle the path properly.
- CookieDomain is a string that specifies the domain name for the cookie, such as .mydomain.com.
- CookieSecure is a flag that tells PHP to send the cookie over an https (secure) connection.

Note that Internet Explorer 3.x and Netscape Navigator 4.05 don't appear to handle cookies properly if path and time aren't set.

Usage:

```php
<?php
setcookie("MyTestCookie","First Cookie!");
setcookie("MySecondCookie","Expires soon!",time()+7200);
                                // this cookie expires in 2 hours
$value = "yes!";
//the following cookie is sent secure,
//will expire in 3 hours, and is sent over
// a secure link.  It will be placed in directory "mycookies"
setcookie("MyThirdCookie",$value,time()+7200+3600,
                    "/mycookies/",".mydomain.com",1);
// You can't access these cookies now, until the page is refreshed
// Once they reload the page, the cookies are available the following ways:
echo $MyTestCookie;
echo $HTTP_COOKIE_VARS["MyTestCookie"];
echo $MySecondCookie;
?>
```

File I/O

string basename(string *filepath*)

Description: Strips the path information away and returns the filename.

See Also: dirname, chdir

Usage:

```php
<?php
$filepath = "/home/httpd/html/test/index.php3";
$file = basename($filepath); // $file now equals "index.php3"
?>
```

int chdir(string DirectoryPath)

Description: Changes the current working directory to be the directory in `DirectoryPath`. You must have permission to enter this directory. It returns FALSE if it failed, TRUE if it succeeded.

See Also: basename, dirname

Usage:

```php
<?php
 chdir ("/home/html/httpd/test/mydata")
    or die ("Could not change into directory");
?>
```

int chgrp(string *FileName*, mixed group)

Description: Changes the group the filename is in. You must own the file, or be the superuser, and must be in the group you want to change the file to. Returns TRUE (1) if successful, FALSE (0) if failed. Under Windows this does nothing. This command, along with chown and chmod, is useful for system administration and power users.

See Also: chown, chmod

Usage:

```php
<?php
    if (chgrp("/home/httpd/html/test/new.dat","nobody"))
        echo "Change group succeeded.";
    else
        echo "Change group failed.";
?>
```

int chmod(string *FileName*, int Mode)

Description: Changes the read, write, and execute characteristics for this file. The format is best given in octal, using a leading 0. When given in octal, three numbers are used to specify the owner of the file, the group the file is in, and all others, in order.

> **Note**
>
> In binary, the bits for each number are in the order of read (100), write (010), and execute (001). In octal, these values would be 4 (read), 2 (write), 1 (execute). To set a file to be readable, writeable, and executable (rwx) by everyone, the Mode would be 0777. To only let the owner have rwx privileges, the value would be 0700. To let everyone read the file, and only the owner write and execute the file, the value would be 0744. To let everyone, including the owner, read and execute but not write the file, the Mode would be 0555.

Only the owner, the superuser, or someone with write privileges to the file can change its mode. Even if the file can't be written by the owner, the owner can change its mode and make it writeable.

Returns TRUE on success, FALSE on fail.

See Also: chown, chgrp

Usage:

```php
<?php
  if (chmod("myfile",0777))
    echo "success!";
  else
    echo "could not change file mode";
?>
```

int chown(string *FileName*, mixed user)

Description: Changes the owner of the filename. You must own the file or be the superuser. Returns TRUE if successful, FALSE if failed. Under Windows this does nothing and returns TRUE.

See Also: chmod, chgrp

Usage:

```php
<?php
  if (chown("myfile","brucelee"))
    echo "success!";
  else
    echo "could not change file owner";
?>
```

void clearstatcache(void)

Description: Clears the file status cache. The results of the following calls are cached from the first call, so subsequent calls are faster: stat, lstat, file_exists, is_writeable, is_readable, is_executable, is_file, is_dir, is_link, filectime, fileatime, filemtime, fileinode, filegroup, fileowner, filesize, filetype, and fileperms.

This call clears that cache. It will make the next call much slower, but will force an update of the cache. This update will reflect the current state of the file at the time of the update. The newly cached information will be used in subsequent calls.

See Also: lstat, file_exists, is_writeable, is_readable, is_executable, is_file, is_dir, is_link, filectime, fileatime, filemtime, fileinode, filegroup, fileowner, filesize, filetype, and fileperms.

Usage:

```php
<?php
  $status = stat("myfilename");
 /* information used */
  clearstatcache();
?>
```

void closedir(int DirectoryHandle)

Description: Closes the directory opened by opendir.

See Also: opendir, readdir, rewinddir, dir

Usage:

```php
<?php
    $dirH = opendir("/home/httpd/html/test");
    closedir($dirH);
?>
```

int copy(string SourceFile, string DestinationFile)

Description: Makes a copy of SourceFile and names it DestinationFile. Returns TRUE for success, FALSE for failure. You must have read privilege to the source file and write privilege to the destination directory.

See Also: rename, chmod

Usage:

```php
<?php
    copy("/home/httpd/html/test/index.php3","/home/httpd/html/test/index.bak")
    or die ("Unable to copy index.php3");
?>
```

delete—does not exist

Description: This function is listed in the PHP documentation, and explained as being a dummy manual entry. You must create it yourself if you want to use it.

See Also: unlink, unset

Usage:

```php
<?php
 function delete($filename){
    return (unlink($filename));
    }
 delete("/home/httpd/html/test/index.bak") or
    die("unable to delete this filename");
?>
```

dir(string DirectoryName)

Description: An internal pseudo-object. DirectoryName is opened. The dir object's path and handle attributes are set to represent the open directory's information.

The skeleton of the user visible class definition of the dir object is as follows:

```php
class DirClass {
    var $handle;
    var $path;
    function read(){}
```

```
function rewind(){}
function close(){}
}
```

See Also: opendir, readdir, rewinddir

Usage:

```php
<?php
    $DirObj = dir("/etc/httpd/conf");
    printf ("Directory handle is %d<p>",$DirObj->handle);
    printf ("Directory path is %s<p>",$DirObj->path);

    while ($DirectoryEntry = $DirObj->read())

        {
        printf("Item: %s<p>",$DirectoryEntry);
        }
    rewinddir($DirObj->handle);
    $DirObj->Close();
?>
```

string dirname(string *FullPath*)

Description: Returns the directory portion of the FullPath.

See Also: basename

Usage:

```php
<?php
    $DirName = dirname("/home/test/index");
    echo $DirName; // prints "/home/test"
?>
```

float diskfreespace(string DirectoryName)

Description: Returns the number of bytes free on the disk containing DirectoryName.

See Also: dirname

Usage:

```php
<?php
    $FreeSpace = diskfreespace("/home");
    echo "Number of bytes available on /home is ".$FreeSpace;
?>
```

int fclose(int FilePointer)

Description: Closes file represented by FilePointer. Returns TRUE on success, FALSE on failure.

See Also: fopen, feof, fgetc, fgetcsv, fgetss, flock, fpassthru, fputs, fread, fsockopen, fseek, ftell, fwrite, pclose, popen, rewind, set_file_buffer

Usage:

```php
<?php
    $FilePointer = fopen ("/home/httpd/html/test/data.dat","r");

    fclose($FilePointer) or die ("could not close data.dat");
?>
```

int feof(int FilePointer)

Description: Returns TRUE if at the end of the file represented by FilePointer, FALSE otherwise.

See Also: fclose, fopen, fgetc, fgetcsv, fgetss, flock, fopen, fpassthru, fputs, fread, fsockopen, fseek, ftell, fwrite, pclose, popen, rewind, set_file_buffer

Usage:

```php
<?php
    $fp = fopen("test.dat","r");
    while (!feof($fp))
        $data =fread($fp,100);
    fclose($fp);
?>
```

string fgetc(int FilePointer)

Description: Returns a single character string from file pointed to by FilePointer. Returns FALSE upon failure.

See Also: fopen, popen, fread, fgets, fsockopen

Usage:

```php
<?php
    $file = fopen("test.dat","r") or die ("failed to open test.dat");
    if ( $str = fgetc($file))
      echo "got character ".$str;
?>
```

array fgetcsv(int FilePointer, int Length, string [Delimiter])

Description: Reads a CSV file and return an array of the fields read from the file. FilePointer is the result of an fopen. Length must be longer than the longest field in the CSV file. The Delimiter defaults to be a comma (,) unless you specify it.

See Also: fopen, fgets

Usage:

```php
<?php
 $numrows = 1;
  $csvFile = fopen("myfile.csv","r")
        or die ("open of myfile.csv failed<BR>");
  for (;;)
    {
```

```
    if ($csvData =fgetcsv($csvFile,1000))
        {
        $number = count($csvData);
        echo "<p> $number fields in row $numrows";
        $numrows++;
        for ($k = 0 ; $k < $number ; $k++)
            echo $csvData[$k]."<p>";
        }
    fclose($csvFile);
    }

?>
```

string fgets(int FilePointer, int Length)

Description: Returns a string from file pointed to by FilePointer, of maximum length dictated by argument Length. The string stops being read from the file at the newline character, at Length-1 bytes, or at end of file. Returns FALSE at a failure, usually caused by being at end of file when requesting a string.

See Also: fopen, fread

Usage:

```
<?php
    $fp = fopen("test.dat","r");
    while ($line = fgets($fp,81))
     echo "retrieved line ".$line."<p>";
    fclose(fp);
?>
```

string fgetss(int FilePointer, int Length)

Description: Reads a string from a file, and strip HTML and PHP tags from the string. It is identical to fgets in all other respects.

See Also: fopen, fgets

Usage:

```
<?php
    $fp = fopen("test.php3","r");
    while ($line = fgets($fp,81))
     echo "retrieved line ".$line."<p>";
    fclose(fp);
?>
```

array file(string *FileName*)

Description: Reads an entire file into an array. It works identically to readfile in all other respects.

See Also: readfile, count

Usage:

```php
<?php
  $FileArray = file("test.dat");
  for ($k = 0 ; $k < count($FileArray); $k++)
    echo "line #".$k." ".$FileArray[$k]."<p>";
?>
```

int file_exists(string *FileName*)

Description: Returns TRUE if file exists, FALSE otherwise.

See Also: clearstatcache, fopen

Usage:

```php
<?php
    if (file_exists("test.dat"))
        echo "test.dat exists";
    else
        echo "test.dat does not exist";
?>
```

int fileatime(string *FileName*)

Description: Returns the time that the file was last accessed. It returns FALSE if an error occurs, which is usually an indication the file does not exist.

See Also: clearstatcache, fopen

Usage:

```php
<?php
 $ftime = fileatime("test.dat") or die ("could not get info on test.dat");
?>
```

int filectime(string *FileName*)

Description: Returns the time the file was last changed. It returns FALSE if an error occurs, which is usually an indication the file does not exist.

See Also: fileatime, clearstatcache, fopen

Usage:

```php
<?php
 $ftime = filectime("test.dat") or die ("could not get info on test.dat");
?>
```

int filegroup(string *FileName*)

Description: Returns the group ID number of the group the file is in. It returns FALSE if an error occurs, which is usually an indication the file does not exist.

See Also: clearstatcache, fopen

A

Usage:

```
<?php
 $fgroup = filegroup("test.dat");
 if ($fgroup == False )
     echo "no information on test.dat";
?>
```

`int fileinode(string FileName)`

Description: Returns the file system inode of the file. It returns FALSE if an error occurs, which is usually an indication the file does not exist.

See Also: clearstatcache, fopen

Usage:

```
<?php
 $finode = fileinode("test.dat");
 if ($finode == False )
     echo "no information on test.dat";
?>
```

`int filemtime(string FileName)`

Description: Returns the time the file was last modified. It returns FALSE if an error occurs, which is usually an indication the file does not exist.

See Also: clearstatcache, fopen

Usage:

```
<?php
 $ftime = filemtime("test.dat");
?>
```

`int fileowner(string FileName)`

Description: Returns the ID number of the owner of the file. It returns FALSE if an error occurs, which is usually an indication the file does not exist.

See Also: clearstatcache, fopen

Usage:

```
<?php
    $fowner = fileowner("test.dat"):
    if (!$fowner)
        echo "file owner not obtained";
?>
```

`int fileperms(string FileName)`

Description: Returns a number representing the file permissions. It returns FALSE if an error occurs, which is usually an indication the file does not exist. See the permissions explanation under chmod.

See Also: `chmod, clearstatcache, fopen`

Usage:

```php
<?php
    $fperms = fileperms("test.dat");
    if (!$fperms)
        echo "could not get file permissions";
?>
```

int filesize(string *FileName*)

Description: Returns the size of a file in bytes. It returns FALSE if an error occurs, which is usually an indication the file does not exist.

See Also: `clearstatcache, fopen`

Usage:

```php
<?php
    $fsize = filesize("test.dat")
        or die ("could not get file size for test.dat");
?>
```

string filetype(string *FileName*)

Description: Returns a string indicating type of file. It returns FALSE if an error occurs, which is usually an indication the file does not exist. The possible returns are `block`, `char`, `dir`, `fifo`, `file`, `link`, and `unknown`.

See Also: `clearstatcache, fopen`

Usage:

```php
<?php
  $ftype =  filetype("test.dat");
?>
```

bool flock(int FilePointer, int LockRequested)

Description: Locks a file using a portable advisory method. This method of file locking works across most operating systems, including Windows. Returns FALSE on failure, TRUE on success. You must first open the file using `fopen()`. The type of lock requested is one of the following:

- 1—A shared lock for reading.
- 2—An exclusive lock for writing.
- 3—Release a lock (either 1 or 2).
- 4—Added to the previous numbers to prevent a block on this file while requesting a lock. If a block occurs, your program will hang until the lock is granted.

See Also: `fopen`

Usage:

```php
<?php
    $fp = fopen("test.dat","a+");
    if (flock($fp,2+4))
        echo "locked";
    else
        echo "could not get a lock";
?>
```

int fopen(string *FileName*, string Mode)

Description: If a normal filename is given, a file will be opened for reading or writing or both as specified by mode. In all cases, a FALSE is returned for a failure.

If the filename argument begins with http:// (not case sensitive), an HTTP 1.0 connection is made with the Web server containing the page, and the internal file pointer is positioned at the beginning of the response. You must include a trailing slash (/) after a directory name. The file is opened for reading only.

If the filename argument begins with ftp:// (not case sensitive), a passive FTP connection is made with the server, and the internal file pointer is positioned at the beginning of the response. The FTP session can be opened for reading or writing, but not both at the same time. If a passive connection is not supported by the FTP server, this will fail.

The Mode a file is opened for can include one or more of the following character sets:

- r—Open for reading only. The internal file position pointer is placed at the beginning of the file.

- r+—Open for reading and writing. The internal file position pointer is placed at the beginning of the file.

- w—Open for writing only. The internal file position pointer is placed at the beginning of the file. The file is shortened to zero bytes in length. If the file does not exist, it will be created. If permissions for the directory do not allow for creating the file, or if the creation fails for other reasons, an error is returned.

- w+—Open for reading and writing. The internal file position pointer is placed at the beginning of the file. If the file does not exist, it will be created. If permissions for the directory do not allow for creating the file, or the creation fails for other reasons, an error is returned.

- a—Open for writing only. The internal file position pointer is placed at the end of the file. If the file does not exist, it will be created. If permissions for the directory do not allow for creating the file, or the creation fails for other reasons, an error is returned.

- a+—Open for reading and writing. The internal file position pointer is placed at the end of the file. If the file does not exist, it will be created. If permissions for the directory do not allow for creating the file, or the creation fails for other reasons, an error is returned.

- b—This letter can follow the r, the w, or the a. On non-Unix systems, it can be used to tell the OS that the file is a binary file rather than a text file. If it is not needed, it is ignored.

See Also: `feof, fgetc, fgetcsv, fgetss, flock, fclose, fpassthru, fputs, fread, fsockopen, fseek, ftell, fwrite, pclose, popen, rewind, set_file_buffer`

Usage:

```php
<?php
    $fp = fopen("/home/httpd/html/test/test.php3","a+")
            or die ("could not open test.php3");
    $fp = fopen("http://www.php.net","r")
            or die ("web page not available");

    $fp = fopen("ftp://ftp.redhat.com/pub/linux/dosutils/fips.com","r") or
        die ("ftp file not available");
?>
```

int fpassthru(int FilePointer)

Description: Sends all data left in a file to the standard output. If an error occurs, returns FALSE. The file must have been opened by `fopen` or `popen` or `fsockopen`. When `fpassthru` is finished, the file is closed, and `FilePointer` can no longer be used.

See Also: `fopen, popen, fsockopen, fclose, readfile`

Usage:

```php
<?php
    $fp = fopen("test.dat","r");
    if (!fpassthru($fp))
        echo ("error dumping file");
?>
```

int fputs(int FilePointer, string String, int Length)

Description: `fputs` is identical to `fwrite`. If `Length` is not specified, the entire string is written.

See Also: `fwrite, fopen`

Usage:

```php
<?php
    $fp = fopen("test.dat","w+");
    if (!fwrite($fp, "This is a test\n"))
        echo ("Could not write to test.dat");
    fclose($fp);
?>
```

```
string fread(int FilePointer, int Length)
```

Description: Reads up to Length bytes from FilePointer, or when EOF is reached.

See Also: fopen, fgets, fgetss, fpassthru

Usage:

```php
<?php
    $fp = fopen("test.dat","r");
    $Data = fread($fp, 1000);
    fclose($fp);
?>
```

```
int fseek(int FilePointer, int Offset)
```

Description: Sets the internal file position pointer referenced by FilePointer to the byte count indicated by Offset. Returns 0 on success, -1 on failure. You can seek past EOF without an error. This function cannot be used on http:// or ftp:// files.

See Also: fopen, ftell, rewind

Usage:

```php
<?php
    $fp = fopen("test.dat","r");
    /* seek 10 bytes into the file */
    fseek($fp, 10);
    $Data = fread($fp,20); // read 20 bytes starting at location 10
    fclose($fp);
?>
```

```
int ftell(int FilePointer)
```

Description: Returns the current offset into the file opened with fopen, unless the file is an http:// or ftp:// file. Returns FALSE if an error occurs.

See Also: fseek, fopen

Usage:

```php
<?php
    $fp = fopen("test.dat","r");
    fseek($fp,10);
    $Offset = ftell($fp);// $Offset is now 10
    fclose($fp)
?>
```

```
int fwrite(int FilePointer, string String, int [Length])
```

Description: Writes a maximum Length bytes from argument String to the file pointed to by FilePointer. Length is optional, and if used, will cause the configuration option magic_quotes_runtime to be ignored. When that configuration option is ignored, slashes will not be stripped from string. If Length is not given, the entire string will be written to the file.

See Also: `fopen, fsockopen, popen, fputs, set_file_buffer`

Usage:

```php
<?php
    $fp = fopen("test.dat","w");
    $Str = "This is a test";
    fwrite($fp,$Str,5) ;
    fclose($fp);
?>
```

int is_dir(string Name)

Description: Returns TRUE if Name exists and is a directory, FALSE otherwise.

See Also: `clearstatcache, is_file, is_link, is_executable, is_writeable, is_readable`

Usage:

```php
<?php
    if(is_dir("/home"))
        echo("/home is a directory");
    else
        echo("/home is not a directory");
?>
```

bool is_executable(string FileName)

Description: Returns TRUE if *FileName* exists and is executable, FALSE otherwise. The test made is for the user the Web browser runs as. This is usually the user 'nobody'. That user has limited privileges.

See Also: `clearstatcache, is_dir, is_file, is_link, is_readable, is_writeable`

Usage:

```php
<?php
    if(is_executable("/bin/ls"))
        echo("/bin/ls is executable");
    else
        echo("/bin/ls is not executable");
?>
```

bool is_file(string FileName)

Description: Returns TRUE if *FileName* exists and is a file (as opposed to a pipe, device, or directory), FALSE otherwise.

See Also: `clearstatcache, is_link, is_executable, is_dir, is_readable, is_writeable`

Usage:

```php
<?php
    if(is_file("/bin/ls"))
        echo("/bin/ls is a file");
```

```
    else
        echo("/bin/ls is not a file");
?>
```

bool is_link(string *FileName*)

Description: Returns TRUE if *FileName* exists and is a symbolic link, FALSE otherwise.

See Also: clearstatcache, is_file, is_dir, is_executable, is_readable, is_writeable

Usage:

```
<?php
    if(is_link("/bin/ls"))
        echo("/bin/ls is a symbolic link");
    else
        echo("/bin/ls is not a symbolic link");
?>
```

bool is_readable(string *FileName*)

Description: Returns TRUE if *FileName* exists and is a readable file, FALSE otherwise. The test made is for the user the Web browser runs as. This is usually the user 'nobody'. That user has limited privileges.

See Also: clearstatcache, is_file, is_dir, is_executable, is_writeable

Usage:

```
<?php
    if(is_readable("/bin/ls"))
        echo("/bin/ls is a readable file");
    else
        echo("/bin/ls is not a readable file");
?>
```

bool is_writeable(string *FileName*)

Description: Returns TRUE if *FileName* exists and is a writeable file, FALSE otherwise. The test made is for the user the Web browser runs as. This is usually the user 'nobody'. That user has limited privileges.

See Also: clearstatcache, is_file, is_dir, is_executable, is_readable

Usage:

```
<?php
    if(is_writeable("/bin/ls"))
        echo("/bin/ls is a writeable file");
    else
        echo("/bin/ls is not a writeable file");
?>
```

```
array lstat(string FileName)
```

Description: This function is identical to stat, except that if FileName is a symbolic link, the status of the symbolic link is returned instead of the status of the file pointed to by the symbolic link. An array is returned. The array elements are as follows, with item 1 being index 1 into the array (for example, $a[1] == item 1):

1. Device.
2. Inode.
3. Number of links.
4. User ID of owner.
5. Group ID the file or dir or device is in.
6. Device type if inode device. This is only valid on systems that support the st_blksize type. Under Windows, it returns -1.
7. Size in bytes.
8. Time of last access.
9. Time of last modification.
10. Time of last change.
11. Block size for file system I/O. This is only valid on systems that support the st_blksize type. Under Windows, it returns \1.
12. Number of blocks allocated.

See Also: clearstatcache, stat

Usage:

```php
<?php
    $Stats = lstat("/home/httpd/html/test/test.php3");
    for ( $k = 0 ; $k < count($Stats) ; $k++)
        echo "Statistic number $k =".$Stats[$k]."<p>";

?>
```

```
int link(string Target FileName, string LinkName)
```

Description: Creates a hard link of LinkName to TargetFileName. For soft links, see symlink.

See Also: symlink, readlink, linkinfo

Usage:

```php
<?php
   link("/home/httpd/html/test/test.php3","/home/httpd/html/test/test.test");
?>
```

```
int linkinfo(string PathToLink)
```

Description: Returns the st_dev field from the Unix C library stat structure, as obtained by the lstat system call. Returns FALSE in case of error. This is used to verify that a link really exists.

See Also: link

Usage:

```
<?php
    if (linkinfo("/home/httpd/html/test/test.lnk"))
        echo "link exists.";

?>
```

int mkdir(string DirPathAndName,int Mode)

Description: Creates the directory DirPathAndName with permissions defined by Mode. For more information on permissions, see the note under chmod.

See Also: chmod, fopen

Usage:

```
<?php
    if (mkdir("/home/httpd/html/test/test.dir",0700))
        echo "directory created";
?>
```

int opendir(string DirPathAndName)

Description: Opens a directory specified by DirPathAndName and return a handle to it. The handle is used in readdir, rewinddir, and closedir.

See Also: readdir, rewinddir, closedir

Usage:

```
<?php
    $dirHandle = opendir("/home/httpd/html/test");
    closedir($dirHandle);
?>
```

int pclose(int $PipePointer)

Description: Close the pipe opened with popen.

See Also: popen

Usage:

```
<?php
    $pp = popen("/bin/ls -l","r");
    pclose($pp);
?>
```

int popen(string Command, string Mode)

Description: Executes a program specified by Command, and return a file pointer to be used by fgets, fgetss, fputs. The Mode can be "r" or "w" but not both. You must close the file pointer using pclose.

See Also: pclose, fgets

Usage:

```php
<?php
    $pp = popen("/bin/ls -l","r");
    while ($line = fgets($pp,256))

    {
    echo "line received was ".$line."<p>";
    }
    pclose($pp);
?>
```

string readdir(int DirectoryHandle)

Description: Returns the filename of the next file in directory opened by opendir. Returns FALSE at end of list. The filenames are not returned in any particular order.

See Also: opendir, closedir, rewinddir

Usage:

```php
<?php
    $dp = opendir(".");
    while ($fileName = readdir($dp))
        echo $fileName."<p>";
    closedir($dp);
?>
```

int readfile(string *FileName*)

Description: Reads a file and puts it to standard output. Returns the number of bytes written to standard output. If an error occurs, returns FALSE, and prints an error message unless it is called with an @ sign in front (@readfile()). The readfile function follows the same rules for http:// and ftp:// files as described under the fopen function. For an alternate method of reading an entire file, see the file function.

See Also: fopen, file

Usage:

```php
<?php
    @readfile("/home/httpd/html/test/test.php3");
?>
```

A

string readlink(string *Path*)

Description: If the file is a symbolic link, it returns the name of the file it links to, or FALSE in case of an error.

See Also: linkinfo, symlink

Usage:

```php
<?php
    echo "/dev/cdrom links to ".readlink("/dev/cdrom");
?>
```

int rename(string OldName, string NewName)

Description: Renames a file or directory from OldName to NewName. Returns TRUE on success, FALSE on failure.

See Also: fopen

Usage:

```php
<?php
    rename("test.php3", "test.old");
?>
```

int rewind(int FilePointer)

Description: Resets the file position pointer, as reported by ftell, to the beginning of the file.

See Also: fopen, fseek

Usage:

```php
<?php
    $fp = fopen("test.txt","r");
    $line = fgets($fp,80);
    rewind($fp); // set pointer back to beginning
    $line2 = fgets($fp,80); // $line2 and $line are the same
    fclose($fp);
?>
```

void rewinddir(int DirHandle)

Description: Resets the directory pointer to the beginning.

See Also: opendir, dir

Usage:

```php
<?php
    $dh = opendir("/home");
    while ($name = readdir($dh))
    {
    //processing of directory names here
    }
```

```
    rewinddir($dh); // point back to beginning
    while($name2 = readdir($dh))
    {
    // do processing of same name list
    }
    closedir($dh);
?>
```

int rmdir(string PathAndDirName)

Description: Attempts to remove directory specified by `PathAndDirName`. You must have permission to do this, and the directory must be empty. Returns `FALSE` upon error.

See Also: `opendir`, `chmod`, `fopen`, `mkdir`

Usage:

```
<?php
    rmdir("/home/httpd/html/test/test.dir")

        or die ("test.dir was not removed");
?>
```

int set_file_buffer(int FilePointer, int BufferSize)

Description: Sets the size of the buffer used for input and output to `BufferSize` bytes. If `BufferSize` is `0`, then writes are not buffered. This setting would provide the most safety, and the slowest speed. It returns `0` on success, `EOF` upon failure.

See Also: `fopen`

Usage:

```
<?php
    $fp = fopen("test.dat","r")
        or die("could not open test.dat<BR>");

    if( set_file_buffer($fp,16384) != 0 )

        echo("file buffer set failed!");
    fclose($fp);
?>
```

array stat(string *FileName*)

Description: This function is identical to `lstat`, except that the file pointed to by the symbolic link is queried. Refer to the `lstat` function description.

See Also: `lstat`, `fopen`

Usage:

```
<?php
```

```
    $statArray = stat("test.dat");
    echo "owner id =".$statArray[4]."<P>";
?>
```

int symlink(string TargetName, string *LinkName*)

Description: Creates a soft link *LinkName* that points to TargetName.

See Also: readlink, linkinfo, link

Usage:

```
<?php
    symlink("test.dat", "test.lnk");
        // test.lnk is now a link pointing to test.dat
?>
```

string tempnam(string DirName, string Prefix)

Description: Creates a unique filename in the specified directory DirName, using Prefix as the beginning of the filename. On Windows, the TMP environment variable overrides the DirName parameter. Under Linux, the TMPDIR environment variable overrides the DirName parameter. Other Unix systems behave differently. Use man to look up the tempnam(3) system function to determine how this function will work on your system. Returns the temporary filename upon success, a null string on failure.

See Also: fopen

Usage:

```
<?php
    $tn = tempnam("/tmp","boo");
    if ($tn == "")
        echo "tempnam failed.";
?>
```

int touch(string *FileName*, int [Time])

Description: Changes the *FileName* modification time to the Time argument. If Time is not present, current system time is used. The file is created if it does not exist. Returns TRUE on success, FALSE on failure.

See Also: stat

Usage:

```
<?php
    touch("/tmp/test.foo");// create test.foo,
                           // or set it to current modification time
    $sA = stat("/tmp/test.foo");
    echo "modification time is ".$sA[9]."<P>";
?>
```

```
int umask(int [Mask])
```

Description: Sets the umask to Mask & 0777. When being used as a server module, the umask is returned to previous state after each run is finished. A umask specifies bits to be turned off when a function is executed to create a file. To turn off the write bits on a file for 'group' and 'others', you would set the umask to 022. For more information on modes, see chmod. The old umask is returned. To get the current umask, call umask with no argument.

See Also: chmod, fopen, touch

Usage:

```php
<?php
    oldmask =umask(022);
?>
```

```
int unlink(string FileName)
```

Description: Deletes Filename. See rmdir to remove a directory. Returns FALSE on error. You must have permission to delete the file.

See Also: rmdir, fopen, chmod

Usage:

```php
<?php
    unlink("test.dat");
?>
```

Network I/O

```
int checkdnsrr(string Host,string [Type])
```

Description: Searches DNS records, looking for Type of entry corresponding to Host. Returns TRUE if Host found, FALSE otherwise. Host can be the name in the form of name.domain.com, or an IP address in the form of 172.16.1.1. The Type can be A (Address), MX (Mail Exchange), NS (Name Server), SOA (Authority), PTR (IP Address Pointer to Name), CNAME (Alias), or ANY (Any record whatsoever).

See Also: getmxrr, gethostbyaddr, gethostbyname

Usage:

```php
<?php
    if (checkdnsrr("foo.mydomain.com","ANY"))

        echo ("Host DNS entry exists!");
    else
        echo ("could not locate host DNS entry");
?>
```

A

```
int closelog(void)
```

Description: Closes the connection to the system logger. The use of this call is optional because the connection will be closed when PHP exits.

See Also: openlog, syslog

Usage:

```php
<?php
    closelog();
?>
```

```
int debugger_on(string IPAddress)
```

Description: Enables the internal PHP debugger and connects it to IPAddress, in the form of 172.16.1.1.

See Also: debugger_off

Usage:

```php
<?php
    debugger_on("172.16.1.1");

?>
```

```
int debugger_off(void)
```

Description: Turns off the internal PHP debugger.

See Also: debugger_on

Usage:

```php
<?php
    debugger_off();
?>
```

```
int fsockopen(string HostName,int PortNumber,int [&ErrorNumber], string
[&ErrorString], double TimeOut)
```

Description: Either set up a TCP stream connection to a HostName on PortNumber or a Unix connection to a socket specified by Hostname. For the Unix connection, the PortNumber must be 0. If the TimeOut argument exits, it is the number of seconds before timing out and giving up on a connection. The TimeOut argument is passed to the connect system call.

If an error occurs, the function returns FALSE, otherwise it returns a file pointer. If the function returns FALSE, and if ErrorNumber and ErrorString are included in the call, they are filled in with the cause of the error.

The socket will be opened in the blocking mode unless you use the set_socket_blocking function call.

See Also: `fclose, set_socket_blocking, pfsockopen`

Usage:

```php
<?php
    // try connecting to the web server at php HQ
    $fp = fsockopen("www.php.net", 80, &$ErrorNumber, &$ErrorString, 30);
    if (!$fp)// if an error occurred, print it
        {
        printf("Error number %d, %s<p>\n",$ErrorNumber, $ErrorString);
        exit;
        }

    fputs($fp,"GET / HTTP/1.0\n\n");// ask the web server for data
    while (!feof($fp))// print each line from the web page
        printf("%s",fgets($fp,255));
    fclose($fp);

?>
```

string gethostbyaddr(string IPAddress)

Description: Returns the hostname specified by `IPAddress`. If an error occurs, it returns the `IPAddress` string.

See Also: `gethostbyname`

Usage:

```php
<?php
    $Name = gethostbyaddr("172.16.1.1");
    if ($Name == "172.16.1.1")
        echo "Host name not found!";
?>
```

string gethostbyname(string HostName)

Description: Returns the `IPAddress` string of the Internet host specified by `HostName`.

See Also: `gethostbyaddr, gethostbyname1`

Usage:

```php
<?php
    echo "Ip Address of mydomain.com is ".gethostbyname("mydomain.com")."<P>";

?>
```

array gethostbynamel(string HostName)

Description: Returns a list of addresses that resolve to `HostName`.

See Also: `gethostbyname, checkdnsrr, getmxrr`

Usage:

```php
<?php
    $HostArray = gethostbynamel("foo.com");
    while( list($key,$value) = each($HostArray))
        echo "$key : $value <P>";
?>
```

int getmxrr(string HostName, array MXHosts, array [MXHostWeight])

Description: Searches DNS for MX (Mail Exchange) records corresponding to HostName. Returns TRUE if any records are found, FALSE otherwise. MXHosts contains the list of MX records found. If MXHostWeight exists, it will have the weight of the MXHosts. The MXHost with the smallest MXHostWeight is the preferred mail server for the domain the host belongs to.

See Also: checkdnsrr, gethostbyname, gethostbyaddr

Usage:

```php
<?php
    if (!getmxrr("foo.com",$MXHosts,$MXHostWeight))
        echo "no mail exchange records found!";
?>
```

int openlog(string Ident,int Option, int Facility)

Description: Opens a connection to the system logger for the program. The string Ident is added to each entry in the log file, and is customarily set to the program or script name. The Option is an OR of any of the following values:

- 1—LOG_PID—Log the pid with each message
- 2—LOG_CONS—Log to the console if errors in sending to the syslog facility
- 4—LOG_ODELAY—Delay opening connection until first syslog(). This is the default behavior.
- 8—LOG_NDELAY—Don't delay opening connection
- 32—LOG_PERROR—Log to stderr as well

The Facility should be set to one of the following values:

- 0x8—LOG_USER (which is 1<<3)—User level logging messages
- 0x50—LOG_AUTHPRIV(which is 10<<3)—Authorization error.

More information can be found in the syslog(3) man pages, and in the /usr/include/src/syslog.h header file.

This call is optional, as syslog will call it if necessary, setting Ident to FALSE.

See Also: closelog, syslog, /usr/include/sys/syslog.h

Usage:

```php
<?php
    if (!openlog("MyPHP Program:",4,8))
        echo("openlog failed");
?>
```

int pfsockopen(string HostName,int Port,int [&ErrorNumber],string [&ErrorString], int [Timeout])

Description: Opens a persistent Internet or Unix socket. This function works exactly like fsockopen, except that the connection remains alive after the script finishes running.

See Also: fsockopen

Usage:

```php
<?php
    $fp = pfsockopen("www.php.net", 80, &$ErrorNumber, &$ErrorString, 30);
?>
```

int set_socket_blocking(int SocketDescriptor,int Mode)

Description: If Mode is FALSE, the socket is switched to non-blocking mode. If TRUE, it is switched to blocking mode. In blocking mode, calls like fgets() will wait until data is received. In non-blocking mode, those calls will return immediately, without transferring data, if the socket is hung waiting for an event.

See Also: fsockopen

Usage:

```php
<?php
    $fp = fsockopen("www.php.net", 80, &$ErrorNumber, &$ErrorString, 30);
    set_socket_blocking($fp,FALSE);// set non-blocking.
?>
```

int syslog(int Priority,string LogMessage)

Description: syslog opens a connection to the system logging facility and sends it LogMessage. LogMessage is a string that follows the printf formatting rules and argument list, with one exception. If the LogMessage string contains %m, then it will be replaced by the error message string that is produced by strerror().

The Priority argument must be one of the following values:

- 0—LOG_EMERG—System is unusable
- 1—LOG_ALERT—Action must be taken immediately
- 2—LOG_CRIT—Critical error
- 3—LOG_ERR—Error indicator

- 4—`LOG_WARNING`—A warning indicator
- 5—`LOG_NOTICE`—Send a notification to the logs
- 6—`LOG_INFO`—An FYI message
- 7—`LOG_DEBUG`—Debug-level information

See Also: `openlog`, `/usr/include/sys/syslog.h`

Usage:

```php
<?php
  $LOG_ERR = 3;
  syslog($LOG_ERR,"Error %m in PHP script %s on line %s\n",__FILE__,__LINE__);
?>
```

NIS (formerly called Yellow Pages)

NIS is a network-based authentication method. It allows one machine to hold all the authentication records for all users in your domain. You must configure PHP with the `--with-yp` setting before compiling to use these functions. More information on using and setting up NIS can be found on Red Hat systems under the `/usr/doc` directory after installing the NIS package, and on the Web at `http://europe.redhat.com/documentation/HOWTO/NIS-HOWTO.php3`.

int yp_get_default_domain(void)

Description: Returns the default domain the computer is in, or `FALSE`.

See Also: `yp_errno`, `yp_err_string`, `yp_master`, `yp_match`, `yp_order`, `yp_first`, `yp_next`

Usage:

```php
<?php
    $NISDomain = yp_get_default_domain();
    if (!$NISDomain)
        {
        echo "Domain request failed! Error number ".yp_errno();
        echo " ".yp_err_string()."<P>";
        }
    else
        echo "NIS Domain is ".$NISDomain."<P>";
?>
```

int yp_order(string Domain, string Map)

Description: Returns the order number for `Domain` in `Map`, or `FALSE`.

See Also: `yp_get_default_domain()`, `yp_errno`, `yp_err_string`, `yp_master`, `yp_match`, `yp_first`

Usage:

```php
<?php
    $order =yp_order($MyDomain, $MyMap) or die(
        "Error number ".yp_errno()." ,".yp_err_string());
    /* $order is availble for use*/
?>
```

string yp_master(string Domain, string Map)

Description: Returns the machine name of the Master NIS server for Map, or FALSE.

See Also: yp_errno, yp_err_string, yp_order, yp_get_default_domain, yp_first, yp_next, yp_match

Usage:

```php
<?php
    $Master = yp_master($MyDomain, $MyMap);
    if (!$Master)
        echo "NIS error number ".yp_errno()." ,".yp_err_string();

?>
```

string yp_match(string Domain, string Map, string Key)

Description: Returns the value for Key in Map in Domain, or FALSE for failure. The Key must be an exact match.

See Also: yp_get_default_domain(), yp_errno, yp_err_string, yp_master

Usage:

```php
<?php
    $NISMatch = yp_match($MyDomain, "password.byname","billsm");
    if (!$NISMatch)
        echo "NIS error number ".yp_errno()." ,".yp_err_string();

?>
```

string[] yp_first(string Domain, string Map)

Description: Returns the first entry in the Map for Domain, or FALSE for failure in a key-value string array.

See Also: yp_get_default_domain(), yp_errno, yp_err_string, yp_master, yp_match, yp_next, yp_order

Usage:

```php
<?php
  $NISEntry = yp_first($MyDomain, $MyMap);
  if (!$NISEntry)
      echo "NIS error number ".yp_errno()." ,".yp_err_string();
```

A

```
    else
        echo "Entry has key ".key($NISEntry)." and value ".value(key($NISEntry));

?>
```

string[] yp_next(string Domain, string Map,string Key)

Description: Returns the next key-value pair in Map in Domain that occurs after Key, or FALSE.

See Also: yp_get_default_domain(), yp_errno, yp_err_string, yp_master, yp_match, yp_order, yp_first

Usage:

```php
<?php
    $NISEntry = yp_first($MyDomain, $MyMap);
    if (!$NISEntry)
        echo "NIS error number ".yp_errno()." ,".yp_err_string();

    else
        {
        echo "Entry has key ".key($NISEntry);
        echo " and value ".value(key($NISEntry));

        $key = key($NISEntry);
        while (1)
            {
            if ( !($NISEntry = yp_next($MyDomain, $MyMap, $key)))
                break; // exit
            $key = key($NISEntry);
            echo "Entry has key ".$key." and value ".value($key);
            }// end of while
        }// end of else
?>
```

int yp_errno(void)

Description: Returns error code for previous NIS operation. The possible error codes are as follows:

- 1—Arguments passed in function are bad
- 2—RPC failure. Domain is unbound
- 3—Can't bind to server on this domain
- 4—No such map in server domain
- 5—No such key in map
- 6—Internal yp_server or client error
- 7—Resource allocation fail
- 8—No more records in map database

- 9—Can't communicate with portmapper
- 10—Can't communicate with yp_bind
- 11—Can't communicate with yp_serv
- 12—Local domain name not set
- 13—yp database is bad
- 14—yp version mismatch
- 15—Access violation
- 16—Database busy

See Also: yp_get_default_domain(), yp_errno, yp_err_string, yp_master, yp_match, yp_order, yp_first, yp_next

Usage:

```php
<?php
    $NISEntry = yp_first($MyDomain, $MyMap);
    if (!$NISEntry)
        echo "NIS error number ".yp_errno()." ,".yp_err_string();

?>
```

string yp_err_string(void)

Description: Returns the error string that describes the last NIS operation error. See the error code list in yp_errno.

See Also: yp_get_default_domain(), yp_errno, yp_master, yp_match, yp_order, yp_first, yp_next

Usage:

```php
<?php
    $NISEntry = yp_first($MyDomain, $MyMap);
    if (!$NISEntry)
        echo "NIS error number ".yp_errno()." ,".yp_err_string();

?>
```

Apache Server-Specific

The functions in this section are specific to the Apache Web server. PHP must be installed as an Apache module for these functions to work.

class apache_lookup_uri(string *FileName*)

Description: Performs a partial request for a URI, and returns the information in a class. The attributes of the class are as follows:

```
class {
    var status;
    var the_request;
    var status_line;
    var method;
    var content_type;
    var handler;
    var uri;
    var filename;
    var path_info;
    var args;
    var boundry;
    var no_cache;
    var no_local_copy;
    var allowed;
    var send_bodyct;
    var bytes_sent;
    var byterange;
    var clength;
    var unparsed_uri;
    var mtime;
    var request_time;
}
```

See Also: apache_note

Usage:

```php
<?php
    $URIInfo = apache_lookup_uri($File);
    echo "Status is ".$URIInfo->status;
?>
```

string apache_note(string NoteName, string [NoteValue])

Description: Gets and sets values in the Apache notes table. If called with a NoteValue, it sets the NoteName in the table to NoteValue. If called without a NoteValue, it retrieves the NoteName from the table.

See Also: apache_lookup_uri, getallheaders

Usage:

```php
<?php
    apache_note("MyNote","This is my note"); // set the note
    echo "My Note is ".apache_note("MyNote");
?>
```

array getallheaders(void)

Description: Returns an associative array of all HTTP headers in the current request.

See Also: apache_note, apache_lookup_uri

Usage:

```php
<?php
$SessionHeaders = getallheaders();
while (list($OneHeader, $HeaderValue) = each($SessionHeaders))
    {
    echo "$OneHeader: $HeaderValue<br>\n";
    }

?>
```

int virtual(string *FileName*)

Description: Includes a filename, identical to the statement `<!--#include virtual ...-->` in Apache. You can use this to include CGI scripts, `.shtml` files, or any other files.

The `virtual()` command will cause the Apache server to perform a sub-request and the resulting *output* of the cgi script, .shtml, .html, .php, or *etc* page will be included in the PHP code.

A `require()` or `include()` command includes the raw file in the PHP code, without processing it first.

This function only works when PHP is installed as a module.

See Also: require, include

Usage:

```php
<?php
    virtual("MyFileName.cgi");
?>
```

Calendar and Date / Time

These functions are available only if you have compiled the calendar extensions in dl/calendar directory under the php main directory, and installed it into your system. For more information, see the `dl()` function in this appendix.

Calendar Conversion

These functions are useful for converting from one calendar system to another. You must first convert your source calendar date to a Julian Day, and then from the Julian Day to your destination calendar date. You are allowed to manipulate days as far back as 4000 BC. A good online reference for calendars is `http://genealogy.org/~scottlee/cal-overview.html`.

string jdtogregorian(int JulianDay)

Description: Converts a Julian Day to a Gregorian calendar day. The result is in the form of mm/dd/yy.

See Also: gregoriantojd, jdtojulian, juliantojd, jdtojewish, jewishtojd, jdtofrench, frenchtojd, jdmonthname, jddayofweek

Usage:

```php
<?php
    $JulianDay = gregoriantojd(2,3,4);
    echo "For JulianDay=$JulianDay, Gregorian is ";
    echo jdtogregorian($JulianDay)."<BR>";
?>
```

int gregoriantojd(int Month, int Day, int Year)

Description: Converts a Month, Day, Year to a JulianDayCount. The year can range from 4714 B.C.–9999 A.D. on the Gregorian Calendar.

See Also: jdtogregorian, jdtojulian, jdtofrench, juliantojd, jdtojewish, jewishtojd, frenchtojd, jdmonthname, jddayofweek

Usage:

```php
<?php
    $JulianDay = gregoriantojd(2,3,4);
    echo "French Republican for ".$JulianDay." is ".jdtofrench($JulianDay);
?>
```

string jdtojulian(int JulianDayCount)

Description: Converts JulianDayCount to the Julian Date.

See Also: jdtogregorian, gregoriantojd, jdtofrench, juliantojd, jdtojewish, jewishtojd, frenchtojd, jdmonthname, jddayofweek

Usage:

```php
<?php
    $JulianDay = gregoriantojd(2,3,4);
    echo "Julian Date for ".$JulianDay." is ".jdtojulian($JulianDay);
?>
```

int juliantojd(int Month, int Day, int Year)

Description: Changes a Julian calendar Month, Day, Year to a JulianDayCount.

See Also: jdtogregorian, gregoriantojd, jdtofrench, jdtojulian, jdtojewish, jewishtojd, frenchtojd, jdmonthname, jddayofweek

Usage:

```php
<?php
 $JulianDay = juliantojd(2,3,1900);
 echo "The Julian Day Count for JulianDate of 2/3/1900 is $JulianDay<br>";

?>
```

string jdtojewish(int JulianDayCount)

Description: Converts a JulianDayCount to a Jewish calendar date.

See Also: jdtogregorian, gregoriantojd, jdtofrench, jdtojulian, juliantodj, jewishtojd, frenchtojd, jdmonthname, jddayofweek

Usage:

```php
<?php
    $JulianDay = gregoriantojd(2,3,4);
    echo "Jewish Date for ".$JulianDay." is ".jdtojewish($JulianDay);
?>
```

int jewishtojd(int Month, int Day, int Year)

Description: Converts a Jewish calendar day to a JulianDayCount.

See Also: jdtogregorian, gregoriantojd, jdtofrench, frenchtojd, jdtojulian, juliantojd, jdtojewish, jdmonthname, jddayofweek

Usage:

```php
<?php
    $JulianDay = jewishtojd(2,3,4);
    echo "Jewish Date for ".$JulianDay." is ".jdtojewish($JulianDay);
?>
```

string jdtofrench(int Month, int Day, int Year)

Description: Converts a French Republican calendar date to a JulianDayCount.

See Also: jdtogregorian, gregoriantojd, jdtojulian, juliantojd, jdtojewish, frenchtojd, jdmonthname, jddayofweek

Usage:

```php
<?php
    $JulianDay = frenchtojd(2,3,4);
    echo "French Date for ".$JulianDay." is ".jdtofrench($JulianDay);
?>
```

int frenchtojd(int Month, int Day, int Year)

Description: Converts a French Republican calendar day to a JulianDayCount.

A

See Also: jdtogregorian, gregoriantojd, jdtojulian, juliantojd, jdtojewish, jdtofrench, jdmonthname, jddayofweek

Usage:

```php
<?php
    $JulianDay = frenchtojd(2,3,4);
    echo "French Date for ".$JulianDay." is ".jdtofrench($JulianDay);
?>
```

string jdmonthname(int JulianDayCount, int Mode)

Description: Takes a JulianDayCount and returns the month it is in. The Mode controls the return format and is one of the following:

- 0—Gregorian, abbreviated
- 1—Gregorian, full
- 2—Julian, abbreviated
- 3—Julian, full
- 4—Jewish
- 5—French Republican

See Also: jdtogregorian, gregoriantojd, jdtojulian, juliantojd, jdtojewish, jdtofrench, frenchtojd, jddayofweek

Usage:

```php
<?php
    $JulianDay = frenchtojd(2,3,4);
    echo "French Month for ".$JulianDay." is ".jdmonthname($JulianDay,5);
?>
```

mixed jddayofweek(int JulianDayCount, int Mode)

Description: Returns the day of the week for JulianDayCount. The return is either a number or a string, depending upon Mode, which is one of the following:

- 0—Return a number from 0–6, with zero being Sunday.
- 1—Return the day of the week as an English name using the Gregorian calendar.
- 2—Return abbreviated English name using the Gregorian calendar.

See Also: jdtogregorian, gregoriantojd, jdtojulian, juliantojd, jdtojewish, jdtofrench, frenchtojd, jdmonthname

Usage:

```php
<?php
    $JulianDay = gregoriantojd(2,3,4);
    echo "Day of week for ".$JulianDay." is ".jddayofweek($JulianDay,1);
?>
```

int easter_date(int year)

Description: Returns the Unix timestamp for midnight on Easter for a given year. The year must be from 1970–2037. See easter_days for years outside this range.

See Also: easter_days

Usage:

```php
<?php
    echo "Easter is on ". date(easter_date(2000));
?>
```

int easter_days(int [year])

Description: Returns the number of days after March 21 that Easter falls on for that year. Use the current year if no year is given.

See Also: easter_date

Usage:

```php
<?php
    echo "Easter is ".easter_days(2000)." days after March 14 for year 2000";
?>
```

Date And Time

int checkdate(int Month, int Day, int Year)

Description: Returns TRUE if a date is valid, FALSE otherwise. The year must be between 0–32767, the month must be between 1–12, and the day must be within the correct number of days for the month. Leap years are understood correctly.

See Also: strftime, date, getdate, gmdate, mktime, gmmktime, time, microtime

Usage:

```php
<?php
    if (checkdate(1,50,32))
        echo "this date is valid";
    else
        echo "this date is invalid";
?>
```

A

`string date(string Format, int [TimeStamp])`

Description: Returns a string controlled by `Format` for the date in `TimeStamp`, or the current system date if `TimeStamp` not given. The `Format` consists of characters, and can be one or more of the following:

- a—am or pm (lowercase)
- A—AM or PM (uppercase)
- d—Day of month with leading zeros
- D—Day of week using three-letter abbreviations: Mon, Tue, Wed, Thu, Fri, Sat, Sun
- F—Name of the month
- h—Hour from 01–12, with leading zeros
- H—Hour from 00–23, with leading zeros
- g—Hour from 1–12, without leading zeros
- G—Hour from 0–23, without leading zeros
- I—Minutes from 00–59, with leading zeros
- j—Day of month from 1–31 without leading zeros
- l—(lowercase L) English text day of week, Monday through Friday
- L—Boolean leap year indicator. 0 is not a leap year, 1 is a leap year.
- m—Month from 01–12, with leading zeros
- n—Month from 1–12, without leading zeros
- M—Month, English text three letter abbreviation, Jan through Dec.
- s—Seconds 00–59
- S—English text suffix, two letters, such as th and nd. The number 2 would print 2nd.
- t—Number of days in the given month.
- U—Seconds since the epoch, which is January 1, 1970 for Unix systems.
- w—Day of week, from 0 (Sunday) to 6 (Saturday)
- Y—The 4 digit year, for example, 1999.
- y—The 2 digit year, for example, 99.
- z—Day of the year, from 0–365
- Z—Time zone offset in seconds. If used with `gmdate()`, will always return 0.

Any characters in the format string that are not recognized are printed as is. You can use `mktime()` to provide the `TimeStamp` argument and deal with dates in the past or future.

See Also: `gmdate`, `checkdate`, `mktime`

Usage:

```php
<?php
    /* print something like
        It is now Monday, Jan 5th, 3:45pm
    */
    echo "It is now".date("D, M jS, g:ia")."<P>";
?>
```

string strftime(string Format,int [TimeStamp])

Description: Returns a string formatted by the Format argument for the time given in TimeStamp. If TimeStamp is not given, use the current local time. Locale-specific words for month, day, and other items follow the settings done using setlocale().

The format string consists of one or more of the following:

- %a—Abbreviated weekday name per current locale
- %A—Full weekday name per current locale
- %b—Abbreviated month name per current locale
- %B—Full month name per current locale
- %c—Preferred date and time per current locale
- %d—Day of month from 01–31
- %H—Hour from 00–23
- %I—Hour from 1–12
- %j—Day of year from 001–366
- %m—Month from 1–12
- %M—Minutes as a decimal number
- %p—am/pm indicator per current locale
- %S—Seconds from 00–59
- %U—Week number in current year, starting with the first Sunday in the year as day 1, week 1.
- %W—Week number in current year, starting with the first Monday in the year as day 1, week 1.
- %w—Day of the week, from 0 (Sunday) to 6 (Saturday).
- %x—Locale-specified date without time
- %X—Locale-specified time without date
- %y—The 2 digit year, 00–99
- %Y—The 4 digit year, that is, 2000–2099
- %Z—Time zone name or abbreviations
- %%—The % character

A

See Also: `setlocale, date`

Usage:

```php
<?php
    /* print something like
        "It is now Monday, January 1, 2000"
    */
    echo "It is now ".strftime("%A, %B %d, %Y")."<P>";
?>
```

`array getdate(int TimeStamp)`

Description: Returns an associative array with the following elements and values:

Array Index	Value
"seconds"	seconds
"minutes"	minutes
"hours"	hours
"mday"	day of month
"wday"	number of day of week
"mon"	number of month
"year"	number of year
"yday"	numeric day of year
"weekday"	day of week, 'Monday' thru 'Sunday'
"month"	month name, 'January' thru 'December'

See Also: `date, gmdate, strftime`

Usage:

```php
<?php
    $TimeNow = getdate(time());
    echo "The time is now ".$TimeNow["hours"].":".$TimeNow["minutes"]."<P>";
?>
```

`string gmdate(string Format, int TimeStamp)`

Description: Returns the date per the `Format` string, using `TimeStamp` as GMT time. In all other respects, it is identical to the `date()` function, using the same formatting.

See Also: `date`

Usage:

```php
<?php
    /* print something like
        It is now Monday, Jan 5th, 3:45pm, Greenwich Mean Time
    */
```

```php
    echo "It is now".date("D, M jS, g:ia")." Greenwich Mean Time<P>";
?>
```

string gmstrftime(string Format, int timestamp)

Description: A string formatted by the Format argument for the time given in TimeStamp as GMT time. This function behaves exactly like strftime() in all other respects, including the Format string.

See Also: strftime

Usage:

```php
<?php
    /* print something like
        "It is now Monday, January 1, 2000, GMT"
    */
    echo "It is now ".strftime("%A, %B %d, %Y")." , GMT<P>";
?>
```

int mktime(int [hour], int [minute], int [second], int [month], int [day], int [year], int [is_dst])

Description: Returns a Unix time in seconds per the time in the argument list. If any or all of the arguments are left out going from right to left, the current time is used to fill in for each missing argument. The only argument that isn't self explanatory is the is_dst, which is set to 1 for daylight savings time, or 0 otherwise.

See Also: date, time

Usage:

```php
<?php
    // change January 1, 1999, 12:30 pm to seconds and back to a day
    echo "Date is ".date("D, M jS, g:ia",mktime(12,30,0,1,1,1999,0));
?>
```

int gmmktime(int [hour], int [minute], int [second], int [month], int [day], int [year], int [is_dst])

Description: Returns the Unix time in seconds for the GMT date passed. This function operates identical to mktime() in all other respects.

See Also: mktime, date, time

Usage:

```php
<?php
    // change January 1, 1999, 12:30 pm GMT to seconds and back to a day
    echo "Date is ".date("D, M jS, g:ia",gmmktime(12,30,0,1,1,1999,0))." , GMT";
?>
```

A

```
int time(void)
```

Description: Returns the current Unix time in seconds.

See Also: `mktime, date`

Usage:

```php
<?php
    // change current time to seconds and back to a day
    echo "Date is ".date("D, M jS, g:ia",time());
?>
```

```
string microtime(void)
```

Description: Returns a string xxx yyy, where yyy is the Unix time in seconds, and the xxx is the number of microseconds that have passed since the second clicked over.

See Also: `time, date`

Usage:

```php
<?php
    echo "Microseconds, Seconds are ".microtime();
?>
```

Databases

LDAP

LDAP stands for Lightweight Directory Access Protocol. It is a partial implementation of the X.500 standard. LDAP was first described in RFC 1777 and RFC 1778, which can be found at `ftp://ftp.isi.edu/in-notes/rfc1777.txt`, and rfc1778.txt at the same location.

Using LDAP, you can implement a centralized database, which contains contact information, public encryption keys, email addresses, and other information. Public LDAP servers are on the Internet. A URL for a list of these servers is `http://www.dante.net/np/pdi.html`.

A good place to start looking for more information on LDAP is `http://www.umich.edu/~dirsvcs/ldap/index.html`. You must retrieve and compile the University of Michigan LDAP client libraries version 3.3, or use the Netscape Directory SDK before LDAP will work. You must also compile LDAP support into PHP. An open source LDAP is at `http://www.openldap.org`. It may work with PHP.

To enable LDAP extensions, you must use the `configure` option —with-`ldap=DIRNAME` before compiling php. If the `=DIRNAME` is left off, the directory will be `/usr/local/ldap`.

An LDAP database has a tree-like structure similar to the directory structure on your hard drive. The root directory is called the world. The directories in the root are called countries. Inside country directories, you will find directories for companies, organizations, or places. Within those directories you will find people or things.

To get to a piece of information within an LDAP database, you must provide enough details to distinguish the information from other information. This is called the distinguished name, and is abbreviated DN.

Assume George Smith works for manufacturing in a company named Global Star, based in the United States. A DN for George Smith would look something like this:

```
cn=George Smith,ou=Manufacturing,o=Global Star,c=US
```

You would read the DN from right to left. The country is the US. The organization is Global Star. The organizational unit is Manufacturing. The common name is George Smith.

No hard and fast rules exist about organizing information in LDAP servers. If you write code to access LDAP servers, you must understand the structure of the information on those servers. Different servers will have different rules. If you apply the wrong rules to a server, you will not get information back.

Many servers allow anonymous access for read of information. Most servers require a password for any other type of access. Before accessing a server, you need to know the name or IP address of the server. You need to know the base dn of the server information you are after, which is the country and the organization. In our previous example, the base dn would be o=Global Star,c=US.

A

int ldap_add(int LinkIdentifier,string DN,array Entry)

Description: Adds entries in an LDAP directory. Returns TRUE for success, FALSE for failure. The Entry array is indexed by attribute. If an attribute has multiple values, it is indexed starting with zero. For example:

```
Entry["AttributeNumber1"]="Attribute Value";
Entry["AttributeNumber2"][0]="Attribute 2, first value";
Entry["AttributeNumber2"][1]="Attribute 2, second value";
```

See Also: ldap_bind

Usage:

```php
<?php
    $LdapServer = ldap_connect("MyMachine"); // mymachine hosts an LDAP server
    if ($LdapServer)
        {
        // obtain write access
        ldap_bind($LdapServer,"cn=root, o=Current CompanyName, c=US","password");
        // now create the entry array
        $Entry["cn"]="User Name";
        $Entry["sn"]="Name"; // the surname
        $Entry["mail"]="user.name@foo.com";// the email address
        $Entry["objectclass"]="person";
```

```
        // now put the data onto the server
        ldap_add($LdapServer,"cn=root, o=Current CompanyName, c=US",$Entry);
        ldap_close($LdapServer);
    }
    else
    echo "did not connect to LDAP server on MyMachine";
?>
```

int ldap_bind(int LinkIdentifier, string [BindRDN], string [BindPassword])

Description: Binds to the specified BindRDN using BindPassword. Returns TRUE on success, FALSE on failure. If the BindRDN and BindPassword arguments are not used, anonymous access is attempted.

See Also: ldap_connect, ldap_close

Usage:

```
<?php
    $LdapServer = ldap_connect("MyMachine"); // mymachine hosts an LDAP server
    if ($LdapServer)
        {
        // obtain write access
        if (!ldap_bind($LdapServer,"cn=root, o=Current CompanyName,
c=US","password"))
        die ("Write access to LDAP server not obtained!");
        // the connection is now ready for write
    }
?>
```

int ldap_close(int LinkIdentifier)

Description: This function is identical to ldap_unbind. It attempts to close the link specified by LinkIdentifier, and returns TRUE on success, FALSE on failure.

See Also: ldap_unbind, ldap_bind

Usage:

```
<?php
    $LdapServer = ldap_connect("MyMachine"); // mymachine hosts an LDAP server
    // other code here
    ldap_close($LdapServer);
?>
```

int ldap_connect(string [HostName],int [PortNumber])

Description: Attempts to connect to LDAP server on HostName on PortNumber. Returns a positive link number on success, FALSE on failure. If HostName and PortNumber are not specified, the already open link number is returned. PortNumber is optional and defaults to 389 if not specified.

See Also: ldap_add, ldap_close, ldap_bind

Usage:

```php
<?php
    $LdapServer = ldap_connect("MyMachine"); // mymachine hosts an LDAP server
    if ($LdapServer)
        {
        // other work here
        }
?>
```

int ldap_count_entries(int LinkIdentifier,int ResultIdentifier)

Description: Returns the number of entries in the previous search results given by
ResultIdentifier, or FALSE on error.

See Also: ldap_search, ldap_bind

Usage:

```php
<?php
    $LdapServer = ldap_connect("MyMachine"); // mymachine hosts an LDAP server
    if ($LdapServer)
        {
        $dn = " o=Current CompanyName, c=US";
        $partialName = "Pe";
        $LookFor = "|(sn=$partialName*)(givenname=$partialName*))";
        $LookInCategories = array("ou","sn","givenname","mail");
        $SearchResult = ldap_search($LdapServer,$dn,$LookFor,$LookInCategories);
        echo "Search returned ".ldap_count_entries($LdapServer,$SearchResult)."
<P>";
        }
?>
```

int ldap_delete(int LinkIdentifier,string DN)

Description: Deletes an entry from an LDAP directory. Returns TRUE on success,
FALSE on failure.

See Also: ldap_add, ldap_bind

Usage:

```php
<?php
    $LdapServer = ldap_connect("MyMachine"); // mymachine hosts an LDAP server
    if ($LdapServer)
        {
        // obtain write accesss
        if (!ldap_bind($LdapServer,"cn=root, o=Current CompanyName, c=US",
                    "password"))
         die ("Write access to LDAP server not obtained!");
        $dn = "sn=Goodby Goodbar, o=Current CompanyName, c=US";
        if (!ldap_delete($LdapServer,$dn))
         echo "delete failed";
        }
?>
```

A

string ldap_dn2ufn(string DN)

Description: Converts the DN to a user-friendly name format by stripping off the identifier type names.

See Also: ldap_bind

Usage:

```php
<?php
    $dn = "sn=Goodby Goodbar, o=Current CompanyName, c=US";
    echo "User friendly format is ".ldap_dn2ufn($dn);
?>
```

array ldap_explode_dn(string DN,int WithAttributes)

Description: Splits the DN returned by ldap_get_dn() into its component parts. Each component part is called a Relative Distinguished Name, or RDN. If WithAttributes is 0, only the RDN is returned. If it is 1, the RDN's are returned with their values.

See Also: ldap_bind

Usage:

```php
<?php
    $dn = "sn=Goodby Goodbar, o=Current CompanyName, c=US";
    $result = ldap_explode_dn($dn, FALSE);
    for ( $i = 1 ; $i <= $result["count"]; $i++)
        echo "item $i = ".$result[$i]."<P>";

?>
```

string ldap_first_attribute(int LinkIdentifier, int ResultEntryIdentifier, int &BERIdentifier)

Description: Returns the first attribute in ResultEntryIdentifier, or FALSE on error. Use ldap_next_attribute() to continue reading attributes.

See Also: ldap_next_attribute, ldap_bind, ldap_first_entry

Usage:

```php
<?php
    $LdapServer = ldap_connect("MyMachine"); // mymachine hosts an LDAP server
    if ($LdapServer)
        {
        $dn = " o=Current CompanyName, c=US";
        $partialName = "Pe";
        $LookFor = "|(sn=$partialName*)(givenname=$partialName*))";
        $LookInCategories = array("ou","sn","givenname","mail");
        $SearchResult = ldap_search($LdapServer,$dn,$LookFor,$LookInCategories);
        $LDAPEntry = ldap_first_entry($LdapServer, $SearchResult);
        $Attribute =
                ldap_first_attribute($LdapServer,$LDAPEntry,&$BERIDPointer);
```

```php
        echo "Search returned first attribute =$Attribute <P>";
        // consume all of the attributes
        while ($Attribute)
         $Attribute =
                ldap_next_attribute($LdapServer,$LDAPEntry,&$BERIDPointer);
        ldap_free_result($SearchResult); // free memory used.
        }
?>
```

int ldap_first_entry(int LinkIdentifier, int Result)

Description: Returns the result entry identifier for the first entry, or FALSE for failure.

See Also: ldap_first_attribute

Usage:

```php
<?php
    $SearchResult = ldap_search($LdapServer,$dn,$LookFor,$LookInCategories);
    $LDAPEntry = ldap_first_entry($LdapServer, $SearchResult);
?>
```

int ldap_free_result(int ResultID)

Description: Frees memory allocated to store the result of a search. Returns TRUE on success, FALSE on error. This call is not strictly required because all memory will be freed when PHP script exits.

See Also: ldap_first_attribute, ldap_search

Usage:

```php
<?php
    $LookInCategories = array("ou","sn","givenname","mail");
    $SearchResult = ldap_search($LdapServer,$dn,$LookFor,$LookInCategories);
    ldap_free_result($SearchResult); // free memory used.
?>
```

array ldap_get_attributes(int LinkIdentifier, int ResultEntryIdentifier)

Description: Returns all entry information in an array, or FALSE on error. The ["count"] index is the number of attributes for the entry. The ["attributename"]["count"] multi-dimensional index is the number of values for attributename.

See Also: ldap_first_attribute, ldap_search

Usage:

```php
<?php
  $E= ldap_first_entry($LdapServer,$SearchResult);
  $att = ldap_get_attributes($LdapServer, $E);
  for ($index = 0; $index < $att["count"]; $index++)
      {
      echo $att[$index]."<P>";// list the attributes
      for ($i2 = 0 ; $i2 < $att[$att[$index]]["count"]; $i2++)
          echo $att[$att[$index]][$i2]."<P>"; // list the values
```

```
        }
?>
```

string ldap_get_dn(int LinkIdentifier, int ResultEntryIdentifier)

Description: Returns the DN of the result entry obtained from a search, or FALSE on error.

See Also: ldap_first_attribute, ldap_search

Usage:

```php
<?php
    $SearchResult = ldap_search($LdapServer,$dn,$LookFor,$LookInCategories);
    echo "DN is ".ldap_get_dn($LdapServer,$SearchResult);
?>
```

array ldap_get_entries(int LinkIdentifier, int ResultIdentifier)

Description: Returns a multidimensional array of all entries, or FALSE on error. The ["count"] index is the number of entries returned. The index [0]["dn"] is the DN of the first entry of the result. The index [0]["count"] is the number of attributes for the first entry. The index [0][0] is the first attribute for the first entry.

See Also: ldap_first_attribute, ldap_search

Usage:

```php
<?php
    $ent = ldap_get_entries($LdapServer, $SearchResult);
    for ($index = 0; $index < $ent["count"]; $index++)
        {
        echo $ent[$index]["dn"]."<P>";// list the entry
        for ($i2 = 0 ; $i2 < $ent[$index]["count"]; $i2++)
            echo $ent[$index][$i2]."<P>"; // list the values
        }
?>
```

array ldap_get_values(int LinkIdentifier, int ResultEntryIdentifier, string Attribute)

Description: Returns an array of values for the Attribute, or FALSE for failure. The index ["count"] is the number of values returned.

See Also: ldap_first_attribute

Usage:

```php
<?php
    $SearchResult = ldap_search($LdapServer,$dn,$LookFor,$LookInCategories);
    $LDAPEntry = ldap_first_entry($LdapServer, $SearchResult);
    $val = ldap_get_values($LdapServer, $LDAPEntry, "mail");
    for ($index = 0 ; $index < $val["count"]; $index++)
        echo "entry number $index is $val[$index]<P>";
?>
```

int ldap_list(int LinkIdentifier, string BaseDN, string Filter, array [Attributes])

Description: Returns a search result identifier, or FALSE if an error occurs. ldap_list uses Filter to search on the BaseDN directory with the scope set to LDAP_SCOPE_ONELEVEL. This is roughly equivalent to doing an ls command on a directory. If you are looking for specific attributes, the Attributes array must be supplied.

See Also: ldap_first_attribute, ldap_search

Usage:

```php
<?php
    // search for organizations in Russia, using previously opened connection
    $BaseDN = "c=RU";
    $Filter = "o=*";
    $Attributes = array("o");
    $SearchResult = ldap_list($LdapServer,$BaseDN,$Filter, $Attributes);
    $ent = ldap_get_entries($LdapServer, $SearchResult);
    for ($index = 0; $index < $ent["count"]; $index++)
        {
        echo $ent[$index]["dn"]."<P>";// list the entry
        for ($i2 = 0 ; $i2 < $ent[$index]["count"]; $i2++)
            echo $ent[$index][$i2]."<P>"; // list the values
        }
?>
```

int ldap_modify(int LinkIdentifier, string DN, array Entry)

Description: Modifies an entry. Works exactly like ldap_add, except existing entry information is replaced. Returns TRUE for success, FALSE for failure.

See Also: ldap_add

Usage:

```php
<?php
    $LdapServer = ldap_connect("MyMachine"); // mymachine hosts an LDAP server
    if ($LdapServer)
        {
        // obtain write access
        ldap_bind($LdapServer,"cn=root, o=Current CompanyName, c=US",
                "password");
        // now create the entry array
        $Entry["cn"]="User Name";
        $Entry["sn"]="Name"; // the surname
        $Entry["mail"]="user.name@foo.com";// the email address
        $Entry["objectclass"]="person";
        // now put the data onto the server
        ldap_modify($LdapServer,"cn=root, o=Current CompanyName, c=US",$Entry);
        ldap_close($LdapServer);
        }
?>
```

A

```
string ldap_next_attribute(int LinkIdentifier, int ResultEntryIdentifier,
int &BERIdentifier)
```

Description: Returns the next attribute in an entry, or FALSE on error. The ResultEntryIdentifier is obtained from the call to ldap_first_attribute.

See Also: ldap_first_attribute

Usage:

```php
<?php
    $Attribute =
            ldap_first_attribute($LdapServer,$LDAPEntry,&$BERIDPointer);
    echo "Search returned first attribute =$Attribute <P>";
    while ($Attribute)
     $Attribute =
            ldap_next_attribute($LdapServer,$LDAPEntry,&$BERIDPointer);


?>
```

```
int ldap_next_entry(int LinkIdentifier, int ResultEntryIdentifier)
```

Description: Returns the entry identifier for the next entry in the ResultEntryIdentifier, which was returned from the ldap_first_entry call. It returns FALSE at the end of the list.

See Also: ldap_first_entry

Usage:

```php
<?php
    $LDAPEntry = ldap_first_entry($LdapServer, $SearchResult);
    while ($LDAPEntry)
        {
        $LDAPEntry = ldap_next_entry($LdapServer, $LDAPEntry);
        // do work here
        }
?>
```

```
int ldap_read(int LinkIdentifier, string BaseDN, string Filter, array
[Attributes])
```

Description: Returns a search result identifier, or FALSE on error. It works like ldap_search or ldap_list, but only searches in the BaseDN.

See Also: ldap_connect, ldap_first_entry, ldap_search

Usage:

```php
<?php
    $dn = " o=Current CompanyName, c=US";
    $partialName = "Pe";
    $LookFor = "|(sn=$partialName*)(givenname=$partialName*))";
    $LookInCategories = array("ou","sn","givenname","mail");
```

```
        $SearchResult = ldap_read($LdapServer,$dn,$LookFor,$LookInCategories);
?>
```

int ldap_search(int LinkIdentifier, string BaseDN, string Filter, array [Attributes])

Description: Returns a search identifier, or FALSE on error. It works like ldap_search or ldap_list, except it searches from the BaseDN down into every tree below BaseDN.

See Also: ldap_list, ldap_connect, ldap_search, ldap_first_attribute

Usage:

```
<?php
        $dn = " o=Current CompanyName, c=US";
        $partialName = "Pe";
        $LookFor = "|(sn=$partialName*)(givenname=$partialName*))";
        $LookInCategories = array("ou","sn","givenname","mail");
        $SearchResult = ldap_read($LdapServer,$dn,$LookFor,$LookInCategories);
?>
```

int ldap_unbind(integer LinkIdentifier)

Description: Closes the connection to the server opened with ldap_connect. Returns TRUE on success, FALSE on failure.

See Also: ldap_connect

Usage:

```
<?php
    $LdapServer = ldap_connect("MyMachine"); // mymachine hosts an LDAP server
    ldap_unbind($LdapServer);
?>
```

MySQL

To use MySQL with PHP, you must configure PHP with the --with-mysql=DIRNAME option before compiling and installing PHP. You must also have MySQL installed and operational.

You have full control over a MySQL database, depending on the privileges of the username you use to log on to the database with. The password is typically in the clear in the PHP script, so it is best to carefully limit the privileges of the script's username.

The mysql functions will typically print an error message if a problem occurs, unless an '@' is prepended to the function call (for example, @mysql_connect()). This error message is also available in $phperrmsg.

int mysql_affected_rows(int LinkIdentifier)

Description: Returns the number of rows affected by the last INSERT, UPDATE, or DELETE SQL query on the server specified by LinkIdentifier. The one exception is a DELETE without a WHERE clause; in that case the number of rows returned is zero.

See Also: mysql_num_rows

Usage:

```php
<?php
    $MySQLLink = mysql_connect("localhost","username", "password");
    mysql_select_db("imp",$MySQLLink);
    $Query = "DELETE FROM names WHERE firstname like %Joe%";
    $result = mysql_query($Query, $MySQLLink);
    echo "There were ".mysql_affected_rows($MySQLLink)." changed<p>";
?>
```

int mysql_close(int LinkIdentifier)

Description: Closes the link to the MySQL database specified by LinkIdentifier, unless the link is a persistent link opened with mysql_pconnect. Returns TRUE on success, FALSE on failure. This call is not absolutely necessary, as non-persistent links will be closed when the PHP script exits.

See Also: mysql_connect, mysql_pconnect

Usage:

```php
<?php
    $MySQLLink = mysql_connect("localhost","username", "password");
    mysql_close($MySQLLink);
?>
```

int mysql_connect(string [Hostname [:port] [:/pathto/socket]],string [UserName], string [Password])

Description: Establishes a connection to a MySQL server. If there are no arguments, the defaults are 'localhost' for Hostname, username of PHP script process for UserName, and an empty password for Password. Returns TRUE on success, FALSE on failure. The Hostname can also include a port number to connect to (for example, localhost:4192), or a path to a socket (for example, localhost:/localsock/mysql).

If this call is made a second time, the already open link identifier will be returned.

See Also: mysql_close, mysql_pconnect

Usage:

```php
<?php
    $MySQLLink = mysql_connect("localhost","username", "password");
    mysql_close($MySQLLink);
?>
```

int mysql_create_db(string DataBaseName, int LinkIdentifier)

Description: Creates a new database on the MySQL server pointed to by LinkIdentifier. You must have logged in as a user with enough privileges for this to work. Returns TRUE on success, or FALSE on failure. You can also use mysql_createdb() for backward compatibility.

See Also: `mysql_connect, mysql_drop_db`

Usage:

```php
<?php
    $MySQLLink = mysql_connect("localhost","username", "password");
    mysql_create_db("NewDatabase",$MySQLLink);
    mysql_close($MySQLLink);
?>
```

int mysql_data_seek(int ResultIdentifier, int RowNumber)

Description: Moves the internal row pointer that is associated with a `ResultIdentifier` to the specified `RowNumber`. Returns `TRUE` on success, `FALSE` on failure. You would typically use `mysql_fetch_row()` as the next call.

See Also: `mysql_fetch_row()`

Usage:

```php
<?php
    $MySQLLink = mysql_connect("localhost","username", "password");
    mysql_select_db("mydb",$MySQLLink);
    $Query = "SELECT * FROM names";
    $result = mysql_query($Query, $MySQLLink);
    mysql_data_seek($result,2); // seek row number 2
    mysql_close($MySQLLink);
?>
```

int mysql_db_query(string DataBaseName, string QueryString, int [LinkIdentifier])

Description: Selects a database and runs a query on it. Returns a result identifier, or `FALSE` on error. If you don't specify the `LinkIdentifier`, it will try to find a previously opened link to use. If it does not find a previously opened link, it will essentially call `mysql_connect()` with no arguments. For backward compatibility, `mysql()` can be used instead of `mysql_db_query()`.

See Also: `mysql_connect`

Usage:

```php
<?php
    $result = myqsl_db_query("MyDB", "SELECT * from names");
    if (!$result)
        echo ("query failed);
?>
```

int mysql_drop_db(string DatabaseName, int [LinkIdentifier])

Description: CAUTION: This call attempts to remove an entire database from the server! Be sure you want to do this! You must be logged on to the server as a user with enough privileges to use this call. For backward compatibility, `mysql_dropdb` can be used instead of `mysql_drop_db`.

Returns TRUE on success, FALSE on failure.

See Also: mysql_connect, mysql_create_db

Usage:

```php
<?php
    $MySQLLink = mysql_connect("localhost","username", "password");
    mysql_drop_db("MyDB");// no more database!
?>
```

int mysql_errno(int LinkIdentifier)

Description: This function retrieves error numbers from the MySQL database backend.

See Also: mysql_error

Usage:

```php
<?php
    mysql_connect("NoSuchServerName");
    echo "Error ".mysql_errorno()." -- ".mysql_error()."<P>";
?>
```

string mysql_error(int LinkIdentifier)

Description: Returns the error string from the last MySQL call.

See Also: mysql_errorno

Usage:

```php
<?php
    mysql_connect("NoSuchServerName");
    echo "Error ".mysql_errorno()." -- ".mysql_error()."<P>";
?>
```

array mysql_fetch_array(int ResultIdentifier, int [ResultType])

Description: Returns an array of the fetched row, or FALSE if there are no more rows. This function stores data in associative indices using the field names as keys, as well as numeric indices. If two or more columns of the result have the same field name, the last field name will be the one indexed by association. You must use the numeric index of the column to retrieve the other columns.

The ResultType argument is optional, and is one of the following defines: MYSQL_ASSOC, MYSQL_NUM, or MYSQL_BOTH.

See Also: mysql_fetch_row, mysql_connect

Usage:

```php
<?php
    $result = myqsl_db_query("MyDB", "SELECT * from names");
```

```
    $RowArray = mysql_fetch_array($result);
    print ("Name = $RowArray["name"]<P>");
?>
```

object mysql_fetch_field(int ResultIdentifier, int [FieldOffset])

Description: Fetches the field at `FieldOffset`, or the next field available if `FieldOffset` not supplied, and returns it in an object. The object has the following properties:

- `name`—Column name
- `table`—The table the column belongs to
- `max_length`—Column maximum length
- `not_null`—Set to 1 if column cannot be null
- `primary_key`—Set to 1 if column is a primary key
- `unique_key`—Set to 1 if column is a unique key
- `multiple_key`—Set to 1 if column is a non-unique key
- `blob`—Set to 1 if column is a BLOB
- `type`—Type of the column
- `unsigned`—Set to 1 if the column is unsigned
- `zerofill`—Set to 1 if column is zero filled

If the indicator fields (for example, `numeric`) are not set to 1; they are set to 0.

See Also: `mysql_field_seek`, `mysql_fetch_lengths`, `mysql_field_len`, `mysql_field_table`, `mysql_field_name`, `mysql_field_type`, `mysql_field_flags`

Usage:

```
<?php
    // using previously opened and selected database
    $result = mysql_query($query, $MySQLLink);
    if ($FieldObj = mysql_fetch_field($result))
        echo "Field name is ".$FieldObj->name." from table ".$FieldObj->table;
?>
```

array mysql_fetch_lengths(int Result)

Description: Returns an array containing the lengths of each field in the last row fetched by `mysql_fetch_row`, or `FALSE` if error. The first field length is at index [0].

See Also: `mysql_fetch_row`, `mysql_fetch_array`, `mysql_fetch_fields`, `mysql_fetch_object`, `mysql_num_fields`

Usage:

```
<?php
    // using previously opened link
    $result = mysql_query($query,$MySQLLink);
    $NumFields = mysql_num_fields($result);
```

```
    $FieldLengths = mysql_fetch_lengths($result);
    for ($index = 0 ; $index < $NumFields ; $index++)
        echo "Field #$index length = ".$FieldLengths[$index]."<P>";
?>
```

object mysql_fetch_object(int Result, int [ResultType])

Description: Returns an object that has attributes that correspond to the fetched row, or FALSE if no more rows exist. ResultType is optional, and can be one of the following values: MYSQL_ASSOC, MYSQL_NUM, or MYSQL_BOTH. The column names become attribute names.

See Also: mysql_fetch_row, mysql_free_result

Usage:

```
<?php
    // using already open connection
    $result = mysql_query($query,$MySQLLink);
    if ($RowObj = mysql_fetch_object($result))
        echo "The Name column contains ".$RowObj->name." <P>";
?>
```

array mysql_fetch_row(int Result)

Description: Returns an array that contains the fetched row, or FALSE if no more rows exist. The first entry in the array is an index [0].

See Also: mysql_fetch_object, mysql_fetch_array, mysql_data_seek, mysql_fetch_lengths, mysql_free_result

Usage:

```
<?php
    // using previously opened connections
    $result = mysql_query($query,$MySQLLink);
    $RowArray = mysql_fetch_array($result);
    $NumFields = mysql_num_fields($result);
    for ($index = 0 ; $index < $NumFields; $index++)
        echo "Field #$index = ".$RowArray[$index]."<P>";
?>
```

string mysql_field_name(int Result, int FieldIndex)

Description: Returns the name of the field specified by FieldIndex in the Result, starting at index [0]. For backward compatibility, mysql_fieldname can be used instead.

See Also: mysql_fetch_object, mysql_fetch_array, mysql_data_seek, mysql_fetch_lengths, mysql_free_result

Usage:

```
<?php
    // using previously opened connection
```

```
    $result = mysql_query($query,$MySQLLink);
    echo "First field name is ".mysql_field_name($result,0);
?>
```

int mysql_field_seek(mysql_field_seek(int Result, int FieldIndex)

Description: Moves the internal field pointer to FieldIndex in Result set. If mysql_fetch_field is called without a FieldIndex parameter, the field pointed to by this function is returned.

See Also: mysql_fetch_field

Usage:

```
<?php
    // using previously opened connection
    $result = mysql_query($query, $MySQLLink);
    mysql_field_seek($result,3) or die ("could not seek to field 3");
    $FieldObj = mysql_fetch_field($result); // fetches field 3
?>
```

string mysql_field_table(int Result, int FieldIndex)

Description: Returns the name of the table for FieldIndex in Result set. For backward compatibility, mysql_fieldtable can be used.

See Also: mysql_fetch_field

Usage:

```
<?php
    // using previously opened connection
    $result = mysql_query($query,$MySQLLink);
    echo "Table name of first field is ".mysql_field_table($result, 0);
?>
```

string mysql_field_type(int Result,int FieldIndex)

Description: Returns the type of the field specified by FieldIndex in the Result, starting at index [0]. For backward compatibility, mysql_fieldtype can be used instead.

See Also: mysql_field_name

Usage:

```
<?php
    // using previously opened connection
    $result = mysql_query($query,$MySQLLink);
    echo "Type of first field is ".mysql_field_type($result,0);
?>
```

string mysql_field_flags(int Result, int FieldIndex)

Description: Returns the field flags for the FieldIndex in Result set, separated by spaces. The following flag words can be returned: auto_increment, binary, blob, enum, multiple_key, not_null, primary_key, timestamp, unique_key, unsigned, zero-fill. For backward compatibility, mysql_fieldflags can be used instead. The explode() function can be used to break up the long string.

See Also: mysql_field_name, mysql_fetch_object

Usage:

```php
<?php
    // using previously opened connection
    $result = mysql_query($query,$MySQLLink);
    echo "Flags of first field is ".mysql_field_Flags($result,0);
?>
```

int mysql_field_len(int Result, Int FieldIndex)

Description: Returns the length of the field specified by FieldIndex for Result set. For backward compatibility mysql_fieldlen can be used.

See Also: mysql_fetch_field

Usage:

```php
<?php
    // using previously opened connection
    $result = mysql_query($query,$MySQLLink);
    echo "Length of first field is ".mysql_field_len($result,0);
?>
```

int mysql_free_result(int Result)

Description: Frees the memory that was used by Result set. This function only needs to be used if you are using too much memory during the execution of a script. All memory used during execution of a script is freed when the script exits. For backward compatibility mysql_freeresult can be used.

See Also: mysql_fetch_row, mysql_connect, mysql_close

Usage:

```php
<?php
    // using previously opened link
    $result = mysql_query($query,$MySQLLink);
    mysql_free_result($result); // release memory occupied by this call
?>
```

int mysql_insert_id(int [LinkIdentifier])

Description: Returns the ID generated by the last INSERT SQL query for an AUTO_INCREMENT field. The LinkIdentifier is the identifier from the mysql_connect call, and is entirely optional.

See Also: mysql_fetch_field

Usage:

```php
<?php
    // using previously opened link
    $query = "INSERT into demographics (income, age) values (1111.11,22);
    $result = mysql_query($query,$MySQLLink);
    echo "Auto Increment key value is ".mysql_insert_id($MySQLLink)."<P>";
?>
```

int mysql_list_fields(string DatabaseName, string TableName,int [LinkIdentifier])

Description: Returns a result identifier that contains information about the TableName in DatabaseName, or -1 if an error occurs. To retrieve the information you would use the functions mysql_field_flags, mysql_field_len, mysql_field_name, or mysql_field_type. If an error occurs, the error string will be placed in $phperrmsg. For backward compatibility mysql_listfields can be used.

See Also: mysql_field_flags, mysql_field_len, mysql_field_name, mysql_field_type, mysql_connect

Usage:

```php
<?php
    // using previously opened connection
    $result = mysql_list_fields("MyDB", "MyTable",$MySQLLink);
    echo "Flags of first field is ".mysql_field_Flags($result,0);
    echo "Type of first field is ".mysql_field_type($result,0);
?>
```

int mysql_list_dbs(int [LinkIdentifier])

Description: Returns a result identifier containing the databases the MySQL daemon identified by LinkIdentifier is hosting. You will use the mysql_tablename function to retrieve information from the result set. For backward compatibility mysql_listdbs can be used.

See Also: mysql_tablename

Usage:

```php
<?php
    // using previously opened connection
    $result = mysql_list_dbs($MySQLLink);
    echo "First database name is ".mysql_tablename($result,0)." <P>";
?>
```

int mysql_list_tables(string DatabaseName, int [LinkIdentifier])

Description: Returns a result pointer containing the tables in DatabaseName for connection specified by optional LinkIdentifier. You use the mysql_tablename function to get the table names from the result set. For backward compatibility mysql_listtables can be used.

See Also: mysql_tablename, mysql_db_query

Usage:

```php
<?php
    // using previously opened connection
    $result = mysql_list_tables("MyDB",$MySQLLink);
    echo "First table name is ".mysql_tablename($result,0)." <P>";
?>
```

int mysql_num_fields(int Result)

Description: Returns the number of fields in Result set. For backward compatibility mysql_numfields can be used.

See Also: mysql_fetch_row, mysql_db_query

Usage:

```php
<?php
    // using previously opened connection
    $result = mysql_query($query,$MySQLLink);
    $NumFields = mysql_num_fields($result);
    echo "There are $NumFields number of fields<P>";
?>
```

int mysql_num_rows(int Result)

Description: Returns the number of rows in Result set. For backward compatibility mysql_numrows can be used.

See Also: mysql_db_query, mysql_query, mysql_fetch_row, mysql_connect

Usage:

```php
<?php
    // using a previously opened link
    $result = mysql_query($query,$MySQLLink);
    echo "The number of rows returned is ".mysql_num_rows($result)."<P>";
?>
```

int mysql_pconnect(string [Hostname [:port] [:/path/tosocket]], string UserName, string Password)

Description: This function works exactly like mysql_connect, except the persistent link identifier returned will not be closed when the PHP script exits. This provides quicker startup if the link was previously opened by the same or different script. The hostname, username, and password must all match; otherwise a new connection is attempted.

See Also: mysql_connect, mysql_pclose

Usage:

```php
<?php
    $PersistentLink = mysql_pconnect("Hostname", "username", "password");
?>
```

int mysql_query(string QueryString, int [LinkIdentifier])

Description: Sends the QueryString to the database specified by the optional LinkIdentifier and returns the result set. If LinkIdentifier is missing, the last opened link is used. If no link exists, a link is attempted using mysql_connect with no arguments. The return is FALSE if an error occurred.

See Also: mysql_connect, mysql_db_query

Usage:
```php
<?php
    $MySQLLink = mysql_connect("localhost","username", "password");
    $result = mysql_query("select * from MyTable",$MySQLLink);
?>
```

mixed mysql_result(int Result, int Row, mixed [Field])

Description: Returns one cell from a Result set. 'Field' can be the field index (as an integer), the field name (as a string), or the field table dot name (for example, "TableName.FieldName"). If the column name is aliased, use the alias to retrieve the field. For example if you used "SELECT * from names as FirstName," then you would use "FirstName" for the Field argument.

This function should not be used because it is such a slow way to retrieve data. Also, you should not use this function with other functions that fetch fields from the Result set. It is better to use the functions mysql_fetch_row, mysql_fetch_array, or mysql_fetch_object.

See Also: mysql_fetch_row, mysql_fetch_array, mysql_fetch_object

Usage:
```php
<?php
    // using previously opened link
    $result = mysql_query($query,$MySQLLink);
    echo "first field in first row is ".mysql_result($result,0,0);
?>
```

int mysql_select_db(string DatabaseName, int [LinkIdentifier])

Description: Selects the current active database on server specified by optional LinkIdentifier. Each mysql_query call after this uses the currently active database. If LinkIdentifier is not provided, the last opened link is used. If no link exists, a connection is attempted using mysql_connect called with no arguments. The function returns TRUE on success, or FALSE on failure. For backward compatibility mysql_selectdb can be used.

See Also: mysql_connect, mysql_pconnect, mysql_query

A

Usage:

```php
<?php
    $MySQLLink = mysql_connect("localhost","username", "password");
    mysql_select_db("mydb",$MySQLLink);
    $Query = "SELECT * FROM names";
    $result = mysql_query($Query, $MySQLLink);// query is made on "mydb"
?>
```

string mysql_tablename(int Result, int ItemIndex)

Description: Returns the name of a table from the last `Result` set when used with `mysql_list_tables`. The function `mysql_num_rows` can be used to determine the number of tables returned in `Result`.

See Also: `mysql_list_tables`, `mysql_list_dbs`

Usage:

```php
<?php
    // using previously opened connection
    $result = mysql_list_tables("MyDB",$MySQLLink);
    echo "First table name is ".mysql_tablename($result,0)." <P>";
?>
```

SNMP

To use SNMP on Red Hat, you must install the SNMP package. SNMP server functionality is available on Windows NT, but not Windows 95/98. You will find more about SNMP at the commercial site, `http://www.snmp.com`.

The snmp package provided with the PHP download is in the dl/snmp directory. You must get the ucd-3.2 snmp library and compile and install it. Take the header files `asn1.h`, `snmp_api.h`, `snmp_client.h`, `snmp_impl.h`, `snmp.h`, `parse.h` from the snmp library and copy them to /usr/local/include. Change into the dl/snmp library in the PHP distribution and build the library. See the `README` file in the dl/snmp directory for more information.

To use SNMP, use the `dl` command, `dl("/path/to/snmp.so")` in your script. Alternatively, you can specify the snmp library in the `PHP3.ini` file.

string snmpget(string HostName, string Community, string ObjectID, int [Timeout], int [Retries])

Description: Returns the SNMP object value or `FALSE` on error. The object is specified by `ObjectID`. The SNMP agent is specified by `HostName`. The SNMP read community is specified by `Community`. The optional `Timeout` specifies how long to wait for an answer. The optional `Retries` specifies how many times to try before giving up.

See Also: `snmp_walk`

Usage:

```php
<?php
    $SystemContact=snmpget("HostName.com","public","system.SysContact.0");
?>
```

int snmpset(string HostName, string Community, string ObjectID, string Type, mixed Value, int [Timeout], int [Retries])

Description: Sets the SNMP object named `ObjectID` of `Type` to `Value` on `HostName` in `Community`. The optional `Timeout` specifies how long to wait for an answer. The optional `Retries` specifies how many times to try before giving up. Returns `TRUE` for success or `FALSE` for failure.

See Also: snmpget

Usage:

```php
<?php
    $result = snmpset("HostName.com","private","system.SystContact.0",
              "OID","Bill Smith");
?>
```

array snmpwalk(string HostName, string Community, string ObjectID, int [Timeout], int [Retries])

Description: Returns an array of SNMP values starting from `ObjectID` on `HostName` in `Community`, or `FALSE` if an error occurs. The optional `Timeout` specifies how long to wait for an answer. The optional `Retries` specifies how many times to try before giving up.

If `Community` is null, the SNMP values start from the root of the SNMP tree, and the entire tree is returned.

See Also: snmpget

Usage:

```php
<?php
    $ResultArray = snmpwalk("Hostname.com","public",""); // get entire tree
    for ($index = 0 ; $index < count(ResultArray); $index++)
        echo "Item number $index = ".$REsultArray[$index]."<P>";
?>
```

array snmpwalkoid(string HostName, string Community, string ObjectID, int [Timeout], int [Retries])

Description: Returns an associative array with object IDs and values starting from `ObjectID` on `HostName` for `Community`, or `FALSE` if an error occurs. The optional `Timeout` specifies how long to wait for an answer. The optional `Retries` specifies how many times to try before giving up.

If `Community` is null, the SNMP values start from the root of the SNMP tree, and the entire tree is returned.

A

See Also: snmpget, snmpwalk

Usage:

```php
<?php
    $ResultArray = snmpwalkoid("hostname.com","public","");
    // look at each part of the array and print its name and value
    for (reset($ResultArray);
        $Identifier = key($ResultArray);
        next($ResultArray))
            echo "For $Identifier, value is = $ResultArray[$Identifier]<P>";
?>
```

boolean snmp_get_quick_print(void)

Description: If you are using the UCD Library, this returns the current quick_print value. The value of quick_print is 0 by default (off).

See Also: snmpget

Usage:

```php
<?php
    $QPValue = snmp_get_quick_print();
?>
```

void snmp_set_quick_print(boolean QuickPrintValue)

Description: Sets the value of quick_print in the UCD library to QuickPrintValue. If it is a 1, the library will return "quick printed" values. In other words, only the value will be printed. If the value is 0, which is the default, all the information about the object will be printed, including the type. Also, when the value is 0, additional hex values are printed for all strings less than four characters in length.

See Also: snmpget

Usage:

```php
<?php
    snmp_set_quick_print(0);
    echo snmpget("hostname.com","public","system.SysContact.0")."<P>";
?>
```

Data Manipulation

PHP allows you to create constants to be used in your code. Constants cannot be changed once created. A set of pre-defined constants is also available to the user.

Defined("CONSTANT_NAME", "Constant Value")

Description: Associate CONSTANT_NAME with 'Constant Value'. PHP will replace every occurrence of CONSTANT_NAME with 'Constant Value' before parsing the script. C-like macro definitions are not currently supported.

See Also: `defined constants`

Usage:

```php
<?php
    define("MY_SCRIPT_NAME", "PHP define test script");
    define("NUMBER_OF_ITEMS", 3);
    echo MY_SCRIPT_NAME." has ".NUMBER_OF_ITEMS." in it<P>";
?>
```

Defined Constants

Description: The following constants are defined whenever a PHP script starts executing:

- `E_ERROR`—An error other than parsing, from which recovery is not possible. Used with the `error_reporting()` function.
- `E_WARNING`—An error which PHP recognizes. PHP will continue executing. Used with the `error_reporting()` function.
- `E_PARSE`—An error where PHP can't parse the script because of a syntax error. Recovery is not possible. Used with the `error_reporting()` function.
- `E_NOTICE`—Something happened. It might not be an error. PHP continues executing. Used with the `error_reporting()` function.
- `FALSE`—A false value. Can be used in any PHP statement. Always a 0 under PHP.
- `__FILE__`—The PHP file currently being parsed. If the constant is in an included file, it is the name of the `include` file.
- `__LINE__`—The number of the current line being parsed.
- `PHP_VERSION`—The version of PHP currently being used.
- `PHP_OS`—The name of the operating system PHP is running under.
- `TRUE`—A true value. Can be used in any PHP statement. Always a 1 under PHP.

See Also: `define`

Usage:

```php
<?php
    if ($MyErrorIndicater == TRUE)
        echo "Detected an error at "._LINE_." in "._FILE_."<P>";
?>
```

Imaging

You can get the size of images in PHP without the GD library installed. For all of the other functionality, the GD library is required. The latest GD library is available at `http://www.boutell.com/gd/`. This library is included with the standard Red Hat distribution and is usually installed by default.

array getimagesize(string *FileName*, array [&ImageInformation])

Description: Returns the size of a GIF, JPG, or PNG image file, the dimensions of the image, the file type, and a height or width text string that can be used within an HTML IMG tag.

The array returned contains the following indexed elements:

- Index 0—Width of the image in pixels
- Index 1—Height of image in pixels
- Index 2—The image type. 1 = GIF, 2 = JPG, 3 = PNG
- Index 3—Text string containing the height and width parameters: "height=xxx width=xxx". This string can be used directly in an IMG tag.

The ImageInformation is optional, and allows you to obtain extended information from the file. It currently gives you the JPG APP markers in an associative array. You can recover IPTC information that has been embedded in the APP13 marker. See http://www.xe.net/ipc/. You can use the iptcparse function to read the binary APP13 marker information.

The GD library is not required to use this function.

Usage: iptcparse

```php
<?php
    $ImgSize = getimagesize("file.jpg",&InfoArray);
    // if the image contains an APP13 marker, display it
    if (isset($InfoArray["APP13"]))
        {
        $iptc = ipctparse($InfoArray["APP13"]);
        var_dump($iptc);
        }
?>
```

int imagearc(int Image, int CoordX, int CoordY, int Width, int Height, int StartDegrees, int EndDegrees, int Color)

Description: Draws a partial ellipse of Color centered at CoordX, CoordY, with the top left being (0,0) in the image specified by Image. The ellipses width and height are specified by Width and Height. The start and end points are specified in degrees by StartDegrees and EndDegrees.

The Color argument must be created by ImageColorAllocate.

See Also: imagecreate, imagecolorallocate

Usage:

```php
<?php
    $Image = imagecreate(100,200); // create a 100 by 200 pixel imageCharUp
    $black = imagecolorallocate($Image,0,0,0);
```

```
    $white = imagecolorallocate($image,255,255,255);
    imagearc($Image,50,100, 25, 50, 270, 30, $white);
?>
```

int imagechar(int Image, int Font, int X, int Y, string Char, int Color)

Description: Horizontally draws the first character of Char in the Image with upper-left corner at X,Y with Color. If the font number is 1, 2, 3, 4, or 5, a built-in font is used. If higher numbers are used, the fonts are larger.

See Also: imageloadfont, imagecreate

Usage:

```
<?php
    $Image = imagecreate(100,200); // create a 100 by 200 pixel imageCharUp
    $black = imagecolorallocate($Image,0,0,0);
    $white = imagecolorallocate($image,255,255,255);
    imagechar($Image,1,20, 20, "H", $white);
?>
```

int imagecharup(int Image, int Font, int X, int Y, string Char, int Color)

Description: Vertically draws the first character of Char in the Image with upper-left corner at X,Y with Color. If the font number is 1, 2, 3, 4, or 5, a built-in font is used. If higher numbers are used, the fonts are larger.

See Also: imagecreate, imagechar, imageloadfont

Usage:

```
<?php
    $Image = imagecreate(100,200); // create a 100 by 200 pixel imageCharUp
    $black = imagecolorallocate($Image,0,0,0);
    $white = imagecolorallocate($image,255,255,255);
    imagecharup($Image,1,40, 40, "H", $white);
?>
```

int imagecolorallocate(int Image, int Red, int Green, int Blue)

Description: Returns a color identifier for the color composed of the Red, Green, and Blue components. Image is the return from imagecreate. You must call this function for each color that is to be used in the image.

See Also: imagecreate, imagechar, imageloadfont

Usage:

```
<?php
    $Image = imagecreate(100,200); // create a 100 by 200 pixel imageCharUp
    $black = imagecolorallocate($Image,0,0,0);
    $white = imagecolorallocate($image,255,255,255);
```

```php
    $red = imagecolorallocate($image,255,0,0);
    $green = imagecolorallocate($image,0,255,0);
    $blue = imagecolorallocate($image,0,0,255);
?>
```

int imagecolortransparent(int Image, int [Color])

Description: Sets the transparent color in `Image` to `Color`. If `Color` is not specified, the current transparent color is returned.

See Also: creatimage, imagecolorallocate

Usage:

```php
<?php
    $Image = imagecreate(100,200); // create a 100 by 200 pixel imageCharUp
    $black = imagecolorallocate($Image,0,0,0);
    $white = imagecolorallocate($image,255,255,255);
    $red = imagecolorallocate($image,255,0,0);
    $green = imagecolorallocate($image,0,255,0);
    $blue = imagecolorallocate($image,0,0,255);
    imagecolortransparent($Image,$green); // green is now transparent
?>
```

int imagecopyresized(int DestinationImg, int SourceImg, int DestX, int DestY, int SourceX, int SourceY, int DestWidth, int DestHeight, int SourceWidth, int SourceHeight)

Description: Copies a rectangular portion of `SourceImg` to `DestImg`. If `SourceX`, `SourceY` are different from `DestX`, `DestY`, the image is stretched or shrunk to fit. The coordinates refer to the upper-left corner of the images. You can copy within an image by using the same parameter for `SourceImg` and `DestImg`. If the copied regions overlap, the results cannot be predictable.

See Also: imagecreate, imagecolorallocate

Usage:

```php
<?php
    $Image = imagecreate(100,200); // create a 100 by 200 pixel imageCharUp
    $Image2 = imagecreate(200,400); // create a 200 by 400 pixel imageCharUp
    $black = imagecolorallocate($Image,0,0,0);
    $white = imagecolorallocate($image,255,255,255);
    $red = imagecolorallocate($image,255,0,0);
    $green = imagecolorallocate($image,0,255,0);
    $blue = imagecolorallocate($image,0,0,255);

    $black = imagecolorallocate($Image2,0,0,0);
    $white = imagecolorallocate($image2,255,255,255);
    $red = imagecolorallocate($image2,255,0,0);
    $green = imagecolorallocate($image2,0,255,0);
    $blue = imagecolorallocate($image2,0,0,255);
    imagecharup($Image2,1,40, 40, "H", $white);
    imagecopyresized($Image,$Image2,0,0,0,0,100,200,200,400);
?>
```

int ImageCreate(int Width, int Height)

Description: Returns an image identifier representing a blank image `Width` pixels by `Height` pixels. The `Width` is also referred to as `X`, the `Height` is also referred to as `Y`. The concepts for drawing images are borrowed from Euclidean geometry.

See Also: imagecolorallocate, imagedestroy

Usage:

```
<?php
    $Image = imagecreate(100,200); // create a 100 by 200 pixel imageCharUp
    $Image2 = imagecreate(200,400); // create a 200 by 400 pixel imageCharUp
?>
```

int imagecreatefromgif(string *FileName*)

Description: This function is removed starting with version 1.6 of the GD library because of patent restrictions. The patent holder for compressed GIF technology is charging fees for the use of compressed GIF technology on Web sites. Before you use compressed GIFS on your Web site, you must obtain an agreement that can involve payment of fees. For this reason, most free Web sites are moving to the PNG format.

int imagedashedline(int Image, int X1, int Y1, int X2, int Y2, int Color)

Description: Draws a dashed line of `Color` in `Image` starting at coordinates X1,Y1 to coordinates X2,Y2

See Also: imagecreate, imageline

Usage:

```
<?php
    $Image = imagecreate(100,200); // create a 100 by 200 pixel imageCharUp
    $black = imagecolorallocate($Image,0,0,0);
    $white = imagecolorallocate($image,255,255,255);
    imagedashedline($Image,1,1,30,40,$white);
?>
```

int imagedestroy(int Image)

Description: Frees the memory associated with `Image`. `Image` is the image identifier returned from imagecreate.

See Also: imagecreate

Usage:

```
<?php
    $Image = imagecreate(100,200); // create a 100 by 200 pixel imageCharUp
    imagedestroy($Image);
?>
```

int imagefill(int Image, int X, int Y, int Color)

Description: Floods an `Image` with `Color` starting at coordinates X,Y.

See Also: `imagecreate`

Usage:

```php
<?php
    $Image = imagecreate(100,200); // create a 100 by 200 pixel imageCharUp
    $black = imagecolorallocate($Image,0,0,0);
    $white = imagecolorallocate($image,255,255,255);
    imageflood($Image,$white);
?>
```

int imagefilledpolygon(int Image, array Points, int NumberOfVertices, int Color)

Description: Creates a polygon filled by `Color` at the array specified by `Points` for the `NumberOfVertices` in `Image`. The `Points` array is in pairs. Points[0]=X1, Points[1]=Y1, Points[2]=X2, Points[3]=Y2, and so forth.

See Also: `imagecreate, imagecolorallocate`

Usage:

```php
<?php
    $Image = imagecreate(100,200); // create a 100 by 200 pixel imageCharUp
    $black = imagecolorallocate($Image,0,0,0);
    $white = imagecolorallocate($image,255,255,255);
    $Points = array(10,10,20,20,10,20);
    imagefilledpolygon($Image,Points,3,$white);
?>
```

int imagefilledrectangle(int Image, int X1, int Y1, int X2, int Y2, int Color)

Description: Creates a rectangle filled with `Color` in `Image` starting at upper-left corner Y1,Y1 to lower-right corner X2,Y2. The upper-left corner of the image is 0,0.

See Also: `imagecreate, imagecolorallocate`

Usage:

```php
<?php
    $Image = imagecreate(100,200); // create a 100 by 200 pixel imageCharUp
    $black = imagecolorallocate($Image,0,0,0);
    $white = imagecolorallocate($image,255,255,255);
    imagefilledrectangle($image,5,5,50,50,$white);
?>
```

int imagefilltoborder(int Image, int X, int Y, int Border, int Color)

Description: Floods `Image` with `Color` using a border color of `Border`, starting at upper-left corner X,Y.

See Also: imagecreate

Usage:

```php
<?php
    $Image = imagecreate(100,200); // create a 100 by 200 pixel imageCharUp
    $black = imagecolorallocate($Image,0,0,0);
    $white = imagecolorallocate($image,255,255,255);
    imagefloodfill($Image,5,5,$white,$black);
?>
```

int imagefontheight(int Font)

Description: Returns the height in pixels of the specified font.

See Also: imagecreate, imageloadfont, imagefontwidth, imagechar, imagecharup

Usage:

```php
<?php
    $Height = imagefontheight(1);// get height of built in font
    $FontNumber = imageloadfont("MyFont.file");
    $Height2 = imagefontheight($FontNumber); // get height of loaded font
?>
```

int imagefontwidth(int Font)

Description: Returns the width in pixels of a character in Font.

See Also: imagefontheight, imageloadfont, imagecreate

Usage:

```php
<?php
    $Width = imagefontwidth(1);// get height of built in font
    $FontNumber = imageloadfont("MyFont.file");
    $Width2 = imagefontwidth($FontNumber); // get height of loaded font
?>
```

int imagegif(int Image, string *FileName*)

Description: This function was removed from the GD library starting with version 1.6 because of patent restrictions. See the note on imagecreatefromgif.

int imageinterlace(int Image, int [Interlace])

Description: Sets interlace for Image to Interlace value. If Interlace is 1, the Image will be interlaced. If Interlace is 0, the Image will not be interlaced. If the optional Interlace parameter is not provided, the current Interlace setting is returned.

Usage:

```php
<?php
    $CurrentInterlace = imageinterlace($Image);
    imageinterlace($Image,1);// set interlace
?>
```

int imageline(int Image, int X1, int Y1, int X2, int Y2, int Color)

Description: Draws a line using `Color` from X1,Y1 to X2,Y2 in Image. The coordinate 0,0 is the top left corner of the images.

See Also: imagecreate, imagecolorallocate, imagedashedline

Usage:

```php
<?php
    $Image = imagecreate(100,200); // create a 100 by 200 pixel imageCharUp
    $black = imagecolorallocate($Image,0,0,0);
    $white = imagecolorallocate($image,255,255,255);
    imageline($Image,0,0, 25,25,$white);
?>
```

int imageloadfont(string *FileName*)

Description: Loads a user-defined bitmap font and returns a font identifier number for it. This number is always greater than 5. Built-in fonts have numbers from 1–5.

Bitmapped fonts are architecture dependent, and do not scale well. You must generate the font file on the same type of machine you will be running PHP on. For example, a bitmap font file created on an Alpha CPU might not work on a X86 (Intel) CPU.

See Also: imagefontheight, imagefontwidth, imagecreate

Usage:

```php
<?php
    $FontNumber = imageloadfont("MyFont.file");
    $Width2 = imagefontwidth($FontNumber); // get height of loaded font
?>
```

int imagepolygon(int Image, array Points, int NumberOfVertices, int Color)

Description: Creates a polygon using `Color` at the array specified by `Points` for the `NumberOfVertices` in Image. The `Points` array is in pairs. Points[0]=X1, Points[1]=Y1, Points[2]=X2, Points[3]=Y2, and so forth.

See Also: imagecreate, imagefilledpolygon

Usage:

```php
<?php
    $Image = imagecreate(100,200); // create a 100 by 200 pixel imageCharUp
    $black = imagecolorallocate($Image,0,0,0);
    $white = imagecolorallocate($image,255,255,255);
    $Points = array(10,10,20,20,10,20);
    imagepolygon($Image,Points,3,$white);
?>
```

int ImageRectangle(int Image, int X1, int Y1, int X2, int Y2, int Color)

Description: Creates a rectangle using Color in Image starting at upper-left corner Y1,Y1 to lower-right corner X2,Y2. The upper-left corner of the image is 0,0.

See Also: imagecreate

Usage:

```php
<?php
    $image = imagecreate(100,200); // create a 100 by 200 pixel imageCharUp
    $black = imagecolorallocate($Image,0,0,0);
    $white = imagecolorallocate($image,255,255,255);
    imagerectangle($image,5,5,50,50,$white);
?>
```

int ImageSetPixel(int Image, int X, int Y, int Color)

Description: Draws a pixel in Image at X,Y using Color. The top left of the image is 0,0.

See Also: imagecreate, imagecolorallocate

Usage:

```php
<?php
    $image = imagecreate(100,200); // create a 100 by 200 pixel imageCharUp
    $black = imagecolorallocate($Image,0,0,0);
    $white = imagecolorallocate($image,255,255,255);
    imagesetpixel($image,5,5,$white);
?>
```

int ImageString(int Image, int Font, int X, int Y, string String, int Color)

Description: Draws the String in Image using Color at coordinates X,Y. The top left of the image is 0,0. Fonts 1–5 specify a built-in font.

See Also: imagecreate, imageloadfont

Usage:

```php
<?php
    $Image = imagecreate(100,200); // create a 100 by 200 pixel imageCharUp
    $black = imagecolorallocate($Image,0,0,0);
    $white = imagecolorallocate($image,255,255,255);
    imagestring($Image,50,50,"Hi",$white);
?>
```

ImageStringUp

Description: Draws the String vertically in Image using Color at coordinates X,Y. The top left of the image is 0,0. Fonts 1–5 specify a built-in font.

See Also: imagestring, imagecreate, imageloadfont

Usage:

```php
<?php
    $Image = imagecreate(100,200); // create a 100 by 200 pixel imageCharUp
    $black = imagecolorallocate($Image,0,0,0);
    $white = imagecolorallocate($image,255,255,255);
    imagestringup($Image,100,50,"Hi",$white);
?>
```

int imagesx(int Image)

Description: Returns the width of the image specified by Image.

See Also: imagecreate

Usage:

```php
<?php
    $Image = imagecreate(100,200); // create a 100 by 200 pixel imageCharUp
    echo "image is ".imagesx($Image)." pixels wide";
?>
```

int imagesy(int Image)

Description: Returns the height of the image specified by Image.

See Also: imagecreate

Usage:

```php
<?php
    $Image = imagecreate(100,200); // create a 100 by 200 pixel imageCharUp
    echo "image is ".imagesy($Image)." pixels tall";
?>
```

array imagettfbbox(int Size, int Angle, string Font*FileName*, string Text)

Description: Calculates and returns in an array the box that bounds a TrueType Font in Font*FileName* using font Size along the Angle. The Font*FileName* can also be a URL.

The array contains the X,Y coordinates of the lower-left corner in indexes 0,1, X,Y coordinates of the lower-right corner in 2,3, X,Y coordinates of upper-right corner in 4,5, and the X,Y coordinates of upper-left corner in 6,7.

You must have the GD library and the Freetype library installed.

See Also: imagettftext

Usage:

```php
<?php
    $BR = imagettfbbox(10,0,"TimesRoman","Test!");
    echo "Upper left corner is at X= $BR[0], Y=$BR[1]";
?>
```

array imagettftext(int Image, int Size, int Angle, int X, int Y, int Color, String "Font*FileName*", string Text)

Description: Draws the string Text in Image starting a coordinate X,Y on Angle in Color using TrueType font in Font*FileName*. The X,Y coordinates are more or less the lower-left of the first character, also known as the base point. The image string function's X,Y coordinates specify the upper-right corner of the first character.

The Angle is in degrees. Zero (0) degrees is left to right, horizontally printed text. The degrees increment counter-clockwise, with 90 degrees being straight up, bottom to top.

The Text string can also contain UTF-8 character sequences, similar to &#354, to allow you to print more than 255 individual characters.

The array contains the X,Y coordinates of the upper-left corner in indexes 0,1, X,Y coordinates of the upper-right corner in 2,3, X,Y coordinates of lower-right corner in 4,5, X,Y coordinates of lower-left corner in 6,7.

See Also: imagettfbbox

Usage:

```php
<?php
    $Image - imagecreate(400,400);
    $white = imagecolorallocate($Image,255,255,255);
    imagettftext($image,10,0,20,10,$white,"TimesRoman.TTF","Test!");
?>
```

int ImageColorAt(int Image, int X, int Y)

Description: Returns the index of the color of the pixel at X,Y in Image.

See Also: imagecolorallocate, imagecolorset, imagecolorsforindex

Usage:

```php
<?php
    $Image - imagecreate(400,400);
    $white = imagecolorallocate($Image,255,255,255);
    $ColorIndex = imagecolorat($Image, 10,10);
?>
```

int ImageColorClosest(int Image, int Red, int Green, int Blue)

Description: Returns the index of the color specified by Red, Green, Blue that is in Image. The closest color to the requested RGB value is returned.

See Also: imagecolorallocate, imagecolorset, imagecolorsexact

Usage:

```php
<?php
    $Image - imagecreate(400,400);
    $white = imagecolorallocate($Image,255,255,255);
    $red = imagecolorallocate($Image,255,0,0);
```

```
    $ColorIndex = imagecolorclosest($image,255,0,0); //returns the index of red
?>
```

int ImageColorExact(int Image, int Red, int Red, int Blue)

Description: Returns the index of the color specified by Red, Green, Blue in the palette of Image. If the color does not exists, a -1 is returned.

See Also: imagecolorclosest

Usage:

```
<?php
    $Image - imagecreate(400,400);
    $white = imagecolorallocate($Image,255,255,255);
    $ColorIndex = imageColorExact($Image, 255,255,255); //return white's index
?>
```

int ImageColorResolve(int Image, int Red, int Green, int Blue)

Description: Returns a color index for the color specified by Red, Green, Blue. The closest color index will be returned.

See Also: imagecreate, imagecolorset

Usage:

```
<?php
    $Image - imagecreate(400,400);
    $white = imagecolorallocate($Image,255,255,255);
    $ColorIndex = imagecolorresolve($Image, 255,255,255);
                            // returns index for white
?>
```

array ImageColorsForIndex(int Image, int ColorIndex)

Description: Returns an associative array containing red, green, and blue keys containing the values for the ColorIndex in Image.

See Also: imagecreate, imagecolorset

Usage:

```
<?php
    $Image - imagecreate(400,400);
    $white = imagecolorallocate($Image,255,255,255);
    $ColorIndex = imagecolorresolve($Image, 255,255,255);
        // return index for white
    $RGBArray = imagecolorsforindex($Image,$ColorIndex);
        // return RGB for white
    echo "Red value for white is ".$RGBArray["red"];
?>
```

int ImageColorsTotal(int Image)

Description: Returns the total number of colors in Image's palette.

See Also: `imagecolorat, imagecolorsforindex, imagecreate`

Usage:

```php
<?php
    $Image - imagecreate(400,400);
    $white = imagecolorallocate($Image,255,255,255);
    $red = imagecolorallocate($Image,255,0,0);
    $black = imagecolorallocate($Image,0,0,0);
    $blue = imagecolorallocate($Image,0,0,255);
    $NumOfColors = imagecolorstotal($Image);
?>
```

boolean ImageColorSet(int Image, int Index, int Red, int Green, int Blue)

Description: Sets the specified index in `Image` to specified color. You can use this to change the background color instantly, creating a flood fill effect.

See Also: `imagecolorat, imagecolorsforindex, imagecreate`

Usage:

```php
<?php
    $Image = imagecreate(400,400);
    $black = imagecolorallocate($Image,0,0,0);
    imagecolorset($Image,$black,255,0,0); // change black to red
?>
```

array imagepsbbox(string Text, int Font, int Size, int [Space], int [Tightness], float [Angle])

Description: Returns the bounding box for the string `Text` using `Font` index (from `imagepsloadfont`), at an `Angle` in degrees, and returns the bounding box in an array.

The `Size` argument is in pixels. The optional `Space` and `Tightness` arguments are expressed in units, which are fractions of em-square units. A value of 1 is 1/1000th of an em-square.

The `Space` parameter is signed, and added to the default value of a space in the font. The `Tightness` parameter is also signed, and is added to the amount of whitespace between characters.

The returned array contains the X,Y coordinates of the lower-left corner in indexes 0,1, and the X,Y coordinates of the upper-right corner in index 2,3. You need to add 1 pixel to each direction in the returned box if the `Angle` parameter is zero degrees.

See Also: `imagecreate, imagepsfreefont, imagepsloadfont`

Usage:

```php
<?php
    $FontIndex = imagepsloadfont("MyPSType1Font");
    $Image = imagecreate(400,400);
```

```
    imagepsbbox("Display This!", $FontIndex, 10, 3, 2, 0);
?>
```

void imagepsencodefont(string FontEncoding*FileName*)

Description: Changes the fonts encoding vector to the character encoding vector found in FontEncoding*FileName*. This is most typically used to allow support for languages other than English. The exact format of the encoding format is fount in T1libs documentation. The ps.default_encoding configuration entry also controls this behavior.

See Also: imagecreate, imagepsloadfont

Usage:

```
<?php
    imagepsencodefont("MyPS1EncodeFile");// modify PS1 encoding
?>
```

void imagepsfreefont(int FontIndex)

Description: Frees the memory allocated by imagepsloadfont.

See Also: imagecreate, imagepsloadfont

Usage:

```
<?php
    $FontIndex = imagepsloadfont("MyPSType1Font");
    imagepsfreefont($FontIndex);// free the font
?>
```

int imagepsloadfont(string Font*FileName*)

Description: Returns a font index for the PostScript Type 1 font loaded, or FALSE upon error. An error message is printed describing the error.

See Also: imagecreate, imagepsfreefont

Usage:

```
<?php
    $FontIndex = imagepsloadfont("MyPSType1Font");
?>
```

array imagepstext(int Image, string Text, int Font, int Size, int Foreground, int Background, int X, int Y, int [Space], int [Tightness], float [Angle], int [AntiAliasSteps])

Description: Draws the string Text on top of Image using Font index (from imagepsloadfont), using Foreground and Background colors at an Angle in degrees, and returns the bounding box in an array.

The Size argument is in pixels. The optional Space and Tightness arguments are expressed in units, which are fractions of em-square units. A value of 1 is 1/1000th of an em-square.

The text will try to fade into the Background color using AntiAliasingSteps, although no pixels with the Background color are actually painted. The allowed values are between 4–16. You should use higher values for fonts smaller than 20 points. For larger fonts, use the value of 4. The larger the value of AntiAliasingSteps, the more computation time is required.

The X, Y arguments are roughly the lower-left corner of the first character. The Space parameter is signed, and added to the default value of a space in the font. The Tightness parameter is also signed, and is added to the amount of whitespace between characters.

The array contains the X,Y coordinates of the lower-left corner in indexes 0,1, and the X,Y coordinates of the upper-right corner in index 2,3.

See Also: imagecreate, imagepsfreefont, imagepsloadfont

Usage:

```php
<?php
    $FontIndex = imagepsloadfont("MyPSType1Font");
    $Image = imagecreate(400,400);
    $white = imagecolorallocate($Image,255,255,255);
    $red = imagecolorallocate($Image,255,0,0);
    $black = imagecolorallocate($Image,0,0,0);
    $blue = imagecolorallocate($Image,0,0,255);
    imagepstext($Image,"Display This!", $FontIndex, 10, $white,
        $black, 200, 10, 3, 2, 0, 12);
?>
```

New Image Functions in PHP 4

The Image functions ImageColorClosestHWB(), ImageCopyMerge(), ImagePaletteCopy() and ImageCreateFromWBMP() were recently added to PHP 4.0.1, so are now in the current version. Because they are so new, they have not been documented. A basic synopsis of the functions is included in this section.

int imagecolorclosesthwb(int image, int red, int green, int blue)

Description: Gets the index of the color, which has the hue, white, and blackness nearest to the given color.

See Also: ImageColorClosest

int imagecopymerge(int sourceImage, int destinationImage, int destinationX, int destinationY, int sourceX, int sourceY, int sourceWidth, int sourceHeight, int percentage)

Description: Merges one part of an image with another. Also based on the percentage indicated. If set to 100, it will function identically to imagecopy. If 0, it will take no action.

See Also: ImageCopy

int imagepalettecopy(int destination, int source)

Description: Copies a palette from one image to another, attempting to match the colors in the target image to the colors in the source palette.

int imagecreatefromwbmp(string *filename*)

Description: Creates a new image from a WBMP file or URL.

See Also: ImageCreateFromGIF, ImageCreateFromJPEG, ImageCreateFromPNG

IMAP

IMAP functionality requires PHP configuration and ancillary package installment. All of the necessary functions required to enable PHP to use IMAP are covered in the PHP installation chapter in this book.

IMAP stands for *Internet Message Access Protocol*. The IMAP implemented by PHP is IMAP 4. You can get more information at http://www.imap.org.

int imap_alerts(void)

Description: Returns an array containing the IMAP alert messages generated by this script, or since the last imap_alerts call. The errors are cleared by this call.

See Also: imap_errors, imap_last_error

Usage:

```
<?php
    $MyBox = imap_open("{MyMail.server.com}INBOX",$MyUserName,$Password);
    imap_delete($MyBox1,1);// mark message 1 for deletion
    imap_close($MyBox1,CL_EXPUNGE);// remove deleted messages
    $IA = imap_alerts();
    echo "first imap alert is $IA[0]";
?>
```

int imap_append(int ImapStream, string MailBox, string Message, string [Flags])

Description: Appends the string Message to MailBox along with the optional string Flags. The end of line terminator in a string is "\n", except for the Cyrus IMAP server, which requires "\r\n". ImapStream is the value returned from imap_open.

See Also: imap_open

Usage:

```
<?php
    $MyBox = imap_open("{MyMail.server.com}INBOX",$MyUserName,$Password);
    imap_append($MyBox,"INBOX","A Brand New Message in in your mbox!");
    imap_close($MyBox);
?>
```

string imap_base64(string Text)

Description: Decode a BASE-64 encoded text and return the message as a string.

See Also: base64_decode

Usage:

```php
<?php
    $ClearTextString = imap_base64($Base64EncodedString");
?>
```

string imap_body(int ImapStream, int MessageNumber, int [Flags])

Description: Returns the body of the message with number MessageNumber in the current open mailbox specified by ImapStream. The optional Flags argument is a bitmask with one or more of the following values OR'd together:

- FT_UID—The MessageNumber is a User ID.
- FT_PEEK—Do not change the state of the Seen flag. This allows you to "peek" at a message.
- FT_INTERNAL—The return string is in internal format. Do not change ending to CRLF.

See Also: imap_open

A

Usage:

```php
<?php
    $MyBox = imap_open("{MyMail.server.com}INBOX",$MyUserName,$Password);
    $BodyText = imap_body($MyBox,1); // read the first message
    imap_close($MyBox);
?>
```

object imap_check(int ImapStream)

Description: Returns information about the current mailbox in an array, or FALSE on failure. The object returned has the following properties:

```
object {
    var $Date;
    var $Driver;
    var $Mailbox;
    var $Nmsgs;
    var $Recent;
    };
```

See Also: imap_open

Usage:

```php
<?php
    $MyBox = imap_open("{MyMail.server.com}INBOX",$MyUserName,$Password);
    $MyMail = imap_check($MyBox);
```

```
    echo "My box contains ".$MyMail->Nmsgs." messages<P>";
    imap_close($MyBox);
?>
```

int imap_close(int ImapStream, int [Flag])

Description: Closes the mailbox specified by ImapStream. If the optional contains CL_EXPUNGE, the mailbox will be silently cleared of deleted messages before closing.

See Also: imap_open

Usage:

```
<?php
    $MyBox = imap_open("{MyMail.server.com}INBOX",$MyUserName,$Password);
    $MyMail = imap_check($MyBox);
    echo "My box contains ".$MyMail->Nmsgs." messages<P>";
    imap_close($MyBox,CL_EXPUNGE);
?>
```

int imap_createmailbox(int ImapStream, string MboxName)

Description: Creates a new mailbox specified by MboxName on the IMAP server specified by ImapStream. A mailbox can be thought of as a folder to store a message in. Returns TRUE on success, FALSE on failure.

See Also: imap_open

Usage:

```
<?php
    $MyBox = imap_open("{MyMail.server.com}INBOX",$MyUserName,$Password);
    if (!imap_createmailbox($MyBox,"Personal"))//create mailbox named personal
        echo "Mailbox create failed!<P>";
    imap_close($MyBox,CL_EXPUNGE);
?>
```

int imap_delete(int ImapStream, int MessageNumber)

Description: Marks MessageNumber for deletion from IMAP account specified by ImapStream. Returns TRUE.

See Also: imap_expunge, imap_close, imap_open

Usage:

```
<?php
    $MyBox = imap_open("{MyMail.server.com}INBOX",$MyUserName,$Password);
    imap_delete($MyBox,1);// mark message 1 for deletion
    imap_close($MyBox,CL_EXPUNGE);// remove deleted messages
?>
```

int imap_deletemailbox(int ImapStream, string MailBoxName)

Description: Deletes the mailbox MailBoxName in IMAP account specified by ImapStream. Returns TRUE on success, FALSE on failure.

See Also: imap_open

Usage:

```php
<?php
    $MyBox = imap_open("{MyMail.server.com}INBOX",$MyUserName,$Password);
    if (!imap_deletemailbox($MyBox,"Personal"))// delete mailbox 'Personal'
        echo "could not delete mailbox!<P>";
    imap_close($MyBox,CL_EXPUNGE);
?>
```

array imap_errors(void)

Description: Returns an array of all the IMAP error messages generated since the beginning of the session, or since the last call to imap_errors. When imap_errors is called, the errors are cleared.

See Also: imap_last_error, imap_open

Usage:

```php
<?php
    $MyBox = imap_open("{MyMail.server.com}INBOX",$MyUserName,$Password);
    imap_delete($MyBox1,1);// mark message 1 for deletion
    imap_close($MyBox1,CL_EXPUNGE);// remove deleted message
    $IMAPErrors = imap_errors();
    echo "the first error is $IMAPErrors[0]";
?>
```

int imap_expunge(int ImapStream)

Description: Remove all mail previously marked for deletion from IMAP account specified by ImapStream. Returns TRUE.

See Also: imap_open, imap_delete, imap_close

Usage:

```php
<?php
    $MyBox = imap_open("{MyMail.server.com}INBOX",$MyUserName,$Password);
    imap_delete($MyBox,1);// mark message 1 for deletion
    imap_expunge($MyBox);// remove the message
    imap_close($MyBox);
?>
```

array imap_getmailboxes(int ImapStream, string Reference, string Pattern)

Description: Returns an array of objects containing mailbox information. The objects have the following attributes:

```
object {
    var $name; // name of the mailbox
    var $delimiter; // hiearchy delimiter for this mailbox
    var $attributes;
    }
```

The name is the name of the mailbox. The delimiter is the hierarchy delimiter for the hierarchy the mailbox is in. The attribute is a bitmask consisting of one or more of the following:

- `LATT_NOINFERIORS`—This mailbox has no mailboxes below it.
- `LATT_NOSELECT`—This is a container, not a mailbox. It cannot be opened.
- `LATT_MARKED`—This mailbox is marked by UW-IMAPD.
- `LATT_UNMARKED`—This mailbox was unmarked by UW-IMAPD.

Reference is the IMAP server using the format `"{ImapServer:ImapPort}"`. The `Pattern` argument specifies where to start searching, with an empty string or the `*` character specifying all mailboxes. If you pass the `%` character in `Pattern`, you are specifying only mailboxes in the current level, and none of the mailboxes below that level. A pattern argument of `"~/mail/%"` will return all the mailboxes in the ~mail directory.

Usage:

```php
<?php
    $MyBox = imap_open("{MyMail.server.com}INBOX",$MyUserName,$Password);
    $Mailbox = imap_getmailboxes($MyBox,"{MyMail.server.com:143}","*");
    echo "First Mailbox is ".$Mailbox[0]->name."<P>";
    imap_close($MyBox);
?>
```

array imap_getsubscribed(int ImapStream, string Reference, string Pattern)

Description: This function works identically to `imap_getmailboxes`, except that it returns just the mailboxes the user is subscribed to.

See Also: `imap_getmailboxes`, `imap_open`

Usage:

```php
<?php
    $MyBox = imap_open("{MyMail.server.com}INBOX",$MyUserName,$Password);
    $Mailbox = imap_getsubscribed($MyBox,"{MyMail.server.com:143}","*");
    echo "First Subscribed Mailbox is ".$Mailbox[0]->name."<P>";
    imap_close($MyBox);
?>
```

string imap_fetchbody(int ImapStream, int MessageNumber, string PartNumber,int [Flags])

Description: Fetches a particular section of the body of the message specified by `MessageNumber` in account specified by `ImapStream`, and returns the section as a string. The `PartNumber` is a string of integers delimited by a period. These integers index into the body part list per the IMAP4 specification. The body parts are not decoded by this function. The `Flags` are a bit mask with one or more of the following `OR`'d together:

- `FT_UID`—The `MessageNumber` is a UserID.

- FT_PEEK—Do not change the state of the Seen flag. This allows you to "peek" at a message.

- FT_UID—The returned string is in internal format, without the ending changed to CRLF.

See Also: imap_open, imap_body, imap_close

Usage:

```php
<?php
    $MyBox = imap_open("{MyMail.server.com}INBOX",$MyUserName,$Password);
    $PartOfMessage = imap_fetchbody($MyBox,1,1);
    imap_close($MyBox);
?>
```

object imap_fetchstructure(int ImapStream, int MessageNumber)

Description: Return all of the structured information for Message number in account specified by ImapStream in an object. The object has the following attributes:

```
object    {
    var $type; // integer
    var $encoding; // integer
    var $ifsubtype; // boolean
    var $subtype;     //string subtype
    var $ifdescription; // boolean
    var $description; // string
    var $ifid; // integer
    var $id; // String
    var $lines; // Integer
    var $bytes;// Integer
    var $ifparameters; // boolean
    var $parameters; // array of objects
    var $parts; // array of objects
    }
```

If the message is a multipart message, an array of objects of all the properties is returned in the attribute parts[]. The array of objects called parameters[] consists of objects having the following attributes:

```
object {
    var $attribute; // attribute of the parameter
    var $value;     // value of the parameter
    }
```

See Also: imap_open, imap_body, imap_close

Usage:

```php
<?php
    $MyBox = imap_open("{MyMail.server.com}INBOX",$MyUserName,$Password);
    $MsgStructure = imap_fetchstructure($MyBox,1);
    echo "Message type is ".$MsgStructure->type."<P>";
    imap_close($MyBox);
?>
```

A

object imap_header(int ImapStream, int MessageNumber, int [FromLength], int [SubjectLength], string [DefaultHost])

Description: Returns an object containing header elements from MesssageNumber in account specified by ImapStream. The optional FromLength and SubjectLength are used to limit the number of characters read from each of these attributes. Some of the header elements returned are

- remail
- date
- Date
- subject
- Subject
- in_reply_to
- message_id
- newsgroups
- followup_to
- references
- message flags
- toaddress
- to[]—An array of objects from the To line containing personal, adl (address list), mailbox, and host.
- fromaddress
- from[]—An array of objects on the From line containing personal, adl (address list), mailbox, and host.
- ccaddress—Up to 1024 characters
- cc[]—An array of objects on the Cc line, containing personal, adl (address list), mailbox, and host.
- bccaddress—Up to 1024 characters
- bcc[]—An array of objects on the Bcc line, containing personal, adl (address list), mailbox, and host.
- reply_toaddress—Up to 1024 characters
- reply_tp[]—An array of objects on the Reply_to_line, containing personal, adl (address list), mailbox, and host.
- senderaddress—Up to 1024 characters
- sender[]—An array of objects on the sender line, containing personal, adl (address list), mailbox, and host.
- return_path—Up to 1024 characters

- return_path[]—An array of objects on the return_path line, containing personal, adl (address list), mailbox, and host.
- udate—Unix time format mail message date
- fetchfrom—From line of maximum fromlength characters.
- fetchsubject—From line of maximum subjectlength characters.

The message flags attribute previously listed is an object containing the following attributes:

- Recent— R —Recent message, has been seen; N —Recent message, has not been seen, ' '—Message is not recent.
- Unseen— U —Unseen message that is also not recent; —Message is recent.
- Answered—A —Message has been answered; ' '—Message has not been answered.
- Deleted— D —Deleted; ' '—not deleted.
- Draft— X —Message is a draft; ' '—Message is not a draft.
- Flagged— F —Message is flagged; ' '—Message is not flagged.

The Recent and Unseen flags have interesting combinations. To know that a message is Unseen, you use this combinational test: Unseen == 'U' || Recent == 'N'.

See Also: imap_open

Usage:

```php
<?php
    $MyBox = imap_open("{MyMail.server.com}INBOX",$MyUserName,$Password);
    $MsgHeader = imap_header($MyBox,1);
    echo "Message To Address is ".$MsgHeader->toaddress."<P>";
    imap_close($MyBox);
?>
```

array imap_headers(int ImapStream)

Description: Returns an array of strings containing header information, with one array element per mail message.

See Also: imap_open

Usage:

```php
<?php
    $MyBox = imap_open("{MyMail.server.com}INBOX",$MyUserName,$Password);
    $Msgs = imap_headers($MyBox);
    echo "Message header info for first msg is ".$Msgs[0]."<P>";
    imap_close($MyBox);
?>
```

string imap_last_error(void)

Description: Returns the text of the last IMAP error that occurred in the current script page. The error information is not reset; repeated calls return the same information unless new errors occur.

See Also: imap_open, imap_errors

Usage:

```php
<?php
    $MyBox = imap_open("{MyMail.server.com}INBOX",$MyUserName,$Password);
    $Msgs = imap_headers($MyBox1);
    echo "Last error Message ".imap_last_error()."<P>";
    imap_close($MyBox);
?>
```

array imap_listmailbox(int ImapStream, string Reference, string Pattern)

Description: Returns an array containing mailbox names. The Reference and Pattern have the same format as described in imap_getmailboxes.

See Also: imap_open, imap_getmailboxes

Usage:

```php
<?php
    $MyBox = imap_open("{MyMail.server.com}INBOX",$MyUserName,$Password);
    $Mbox = imap_listmailbox($MyBox,"{MyMail.server.com:143}","*");
    echo "The first mailbox is ".$Mbox[0]."<P>";
    imap_close($MyBox);
?>
```

array imap_listsubscribed(int ImapStream, string Reference, string Pattern)

Description: Returns an array of all of the mailboxes that you have subscribed. The Reference and Pattern have the same format as described in imap_getmailboxes.

Usage: imap_open, imap_getmailboxes

```php
<?php
    $MyBox = imap_open("{MyMail.server.com}INBOX",$MyUserName,$Password);
    $Mbox = imap_listsubscribed($MyBox,"{MyMail.server.com:143}","*");
    echo "The first mailbox is ".$Mbox[0]."<P>";
    imap_close($MyBox);
?>
```

int imap_mail_copy(int ImapStream, string MsgList, string Mailbox, int Flags)

Description: Copies messages specified by the list or range specified by MsgList to Mailbox for server specified by ImapStream. Returns TRUE on success, FALSE on error. The Flags parameter is a bitmask containing one or more of the following:

- `CP_UID`—The sequence numbers are UIDS (User ID's).
- `CP_MOVE`—Delete the messages from the current mailbox after copying.

Usage:

```php
<?php
    $MyBox = imap_open("{MyMail.server.com}INBOX",$MyUserName,$Password);
    $Mbox = imap_mail_copy($MyBox,"2","SAVED",CP_MOVE);
                                        // move to the saved mailbox
    imap_close($MyBox);
?>
```

int imap_mail_move(int ImapStream, string MsgList, string Mailbox)

Description: Copies messages specified by the list or range specified by `MsgList` to `Mailbox` for server specified by `ImapStream`. Returns `TRUE` on success, `FALSE` on error.

Usage:

```php
<?php
    $MyBox = imap_open("{MyMail.server.com}INBOX",$MyUserName,$Password);
    $Mbox = imap_mail_move($MyBox,"2","SAVED");// move to the saved mailbox
    imap_close($MyBox);
?>
```

int imap_num_msg(int ImapStream)

Description: Returns the number of messages in the current mailbox.

See Also: `imap_open`, `imap_num_recent`

Usage:

```php
<?php
    $MyBox = imap_open("{MyMail.server.com}INBOX",$MyUserName,$Password);
    $Mbox = imap_num_msg($MyBox);
    echo "Number of messages in mailbox is $Mbox<P>";
    imap_close($MyBox);
?>
```

int imap_num_recent(int ImapStream)

Description: Returns the number of recent messages in the current mailbox.

See Also: `imap_open`, `imap_num_msg`

Usage:

```php
<?php
    $MyBox = imap_open("{MyMail.server.com}INBOX",$MyUserName,$Password);
    $Mbox = imap_num_recent($MyBox);
    echo "Number of recent messages in mailbox is $Mbox<P>";
    imap_close($MyBox);
?>
```

int imap_open(string MailBox, string UserName, string Password, int [Flags])

Description: Returns an IMAP stream on success or FALSE on error. You can also open a connection to a POP3 or an NNTP server. The Mailbox is in the form of "{server.domain.com:143}INBOX", where 143 is the port for the IMAP server, and INBOX is the mailbox name. The UserName is the login name for the user, and Password is the password on the account.

To use this function to log on to a POP3 server on the local machine, you would use "{localhost/pop3:110}INBOX" for the MailBox parameter. To log into an NNTP server on the local machine, you would use "{localhost/nntp:119}newsgroup.name" for the MailBox parameter. The 'localhost' string can be replaced with a name or IP address to connect to other machines.

The optional Flags parameter is a bitmask with one or more of the following OR'd together:

- OP_READONLY—Open mailbox for reading only.
- OP_ANONYMOUS—Don't use the .newsrc file, and don't update it, when reading news.
- OP_HALFOPEN—Used with IMAP and NNTP: Open the connection, but don't open a mailbox.
- CL_EXPUNGE—Expunge deleted messages automatically when the mailbox is closed.

See Also: imap_close

Usage:

```php
<?php
    $MyBox = imap_open("{MyMail.server.com}INBOX",
                        $MyUserName,$Password,CL_EXPUNGE);
    imap_close($MyBox);
?>
```

int imap_ping(int ImapStream)

Description: Returns TRUE if the stream is still valid. This can be used as a keep alive for servers which have an automatic timeout because of inactivity. It can cause the server to notify you of new mail.

See Also: imap_open, imap_close

Usage:

```php
<?php
    $MyBox = imap_open("{MyMail.server.com}INBOX",$MyUserName,$Password);
    $Mbox = imap_ping($MyBox);
    if ($Mbox)
        echo "mailbox connection is still active<P>";
```

```
    else
        echo "mailbox connection is NOT active<P>";
    imap_close($MyBox);
?>
```

int imap_renamemailbox(int ImapStream, string OldMailboxName, string NewMailboxName)

Description: Renames OldMailboxName to NewMailboxName on server specified by ImapStream. Returns TRUE on success and FALSE on error.

See Also: imap_open

Usage:

```
<?php
    $MyBox = imap_open("{MyMail.server.com}INBOX",$MyUserName,$Password);
    $Mbox = imap_renamemailbox($MyBox,"PERSONAL", "OLDPERSONAL");
    imap_close($MyBox);
?>
```

int imap_reopen(string ImapStream, string Mailbox, string [Flags])

Description: Reopens the specified stream to the new mailbox. Returns TRUE on success, or FALSE on failure.

The optional Flags parameter are a bitmask with one or more of the following OR'd together:

- OP_READONLY—Open mailbox as read only.
- OP_ANONYMOUS—Don't use the .newsrc file, and don't update it, when reading news.
- OP_HALFOPEN—Used with IMAP and NNTP: Open the connection, but don't open a mailbox.
- CL_EXPUNGE—Expunge deleted messages automatically when the mailbox is closed.

See Also: imap_open

Usage:

```
<?php
    $MyBox = imap_open("{MyMail.server.com}INBOX",$MyUserName,$Password);
    $Mbox = imap_reopen($MyBox,"{MyMail.server.com}INBOX");
    imap_close($MyBox);
?>
```

int imap_subscribe(int ImapStream, string Mailbox)

Description: Subscribes you to a new Mailbox on server specified by ImapStream. Returns TRUE on success and FALSE on error.

See Also: imap_open

Usage:

```php
<?php
    $MyBox = imap_open("{MyMail.server.com}INBOX",$MyUserName,$Password);
    $Mbox = imap_subscribe($MyBox,"PERSONAL");
    imap_close($MyBox);
?>
```

int imap_undelete(int ImapStream, int MsgNumber)

Description: Removes the deletion flag for the message specified by MsgNumber on server specified by ImapStream. Returns TRUE on success, or FALSE on error.

See Also: imap_delete, imap_open

Usage:

```php
<?php
    $MyBox = imap_open("{MyMail.server.com}INBOX",$MyUserName,$Password);
    $Mbox = imap_undelete($MyBox,1);
    imap_close($MyBox);
?>
```

int imap_unsubscribe(int ImapStream, string Mailbox)

Description: Unsubscribes you from the Mailbox on the server specified by ImapStream.

See Also: imap_delete, imap_open

Usage:

```php
<?php
    $MyBox = imap_open("{MyMail.server.com}INBOX",$MyUserName,$Password);
    $Mbox = imap_unsubscribe($MyBox,"PERSONAL");
    imap_close($MyBox);
?>
```

string imap_qprint(string StringToConvert)

Description: Converts a quoted-printable string to an 8 bit (binary). Returns the string.

Usage:

```php
<?php
    $ConvertedString = imap_qprint($QuotedPrintableString);
?>
```

string imap_8bit(string StringEightBit)

Description: Converts an 8 bit string to a quoted printable string. Returns the quoted-printable string.

See Also: imap_open

Usage:

```php
<?php
    $QuotedPrintableString = imap_8bit($EightBitBinaryString);
?>
```

string imap_binary(string EightBitBinaryString)

Description: Converts an 8-bit binary string to a Base64 string. Returns the Base64 string.

See Also: imap_8bit, imap_open

Usage:

```php
<?php
    $Base64String = imap_binary($EightBitBinaryString);
?>
```

array imap_scanmailbox(int ImapStream, string SearchString)

Description: Returns an array containing the names of mailboxes that have SearchString in the text of the mailbox.

Usage:

```php
<?php
    $MyBox = imap_open("{MyMail.server.com}INBOX",$MyUserName,$Password);
    $Mbox = imap_scanmailbox($MyBox,"in");???
    imap_close($MyBox);
?>
```

array imap_mailboxmsginfo(int ImapStream)

Description: Returns information about the mailbox specified by ImapStream in an array of objects, or FALSE on failure. The object contains the following attributes:

```
object {
    var $Date; // date of the message
    var $Driver; // driver
    var $Mailbox; // name of the mailbox
    var $Nmsgs; // number of messages
    var $Recent; // number of recent messages
    var $Unread; // number of unread messages
    var $Size; // mailbox size
    }
```

See Also: imap_open

Usage:

```php
<?php
    $MyBox = imap_open("{MyMail.server.com}INBOX",$MyUserName,$Password);
    $MboxInfo = imap_mailboxmsginfo($MyBox);
    echo "Date of first message is ".$MboxInfo[0]->Date;
    imap_close($MyBox);
?>
```

int imap_msgno(int ImapStream, int UID)

Description: Returns the message number for the given UID. It is the complement of imap_uid.

See Also: imap_open, imap_uid

Usage:

```php
<?php
    $MyBox = imap_open("{MyMail.server.com}INBOX",$MyUserName,$Password);
    $MboxUID = imap_uid($MyBox,1);
    $MboxNumber = imag_msgno($MyBox,$MboxUID);
    echo "Msg Number of UID $MboxUID is $MboxNumber<P>";
    imap_close($MyBox);
?>
```

string imap_rfc822_write_address(string Mailbox, string HostName, string PersonalInfo)

Description: Returns an email address given the Mailbox, HostName, and PersonalInfo. The Mailbox parameter is the account name which is the login ID under Linux. The HostName parameter is the machine and domain name, the PersonalInfo is the user's real name.

See Also: imap_open, imap_rfc822_parse_adrlist

Usage:

```php
<?php
    $Address =
        imap_rfc822_write_address("jsmith","host.domain.com","John Smith");
?>
```

array imap_rfc822_parse_adrlist(string Address, string DefaultHost)

Description: Parses the addresses that are in the AddressString, and returns an array of objects containing the addresses. The attributes of each of the objects are as follows:

```
object {
    var $mailbox;// username
    var $host; // host name
    var $personal; // person's name
    var $adl; // domain source route
    }
```

See Also: imap_open, imap_rfc822_write_address

Usage:

```php
<?php
    $AdrInfo = imap_rfc822_parse_adrlist($AddressList, "mydomain.com")
    echo "First mailbox is ".$AdrInfo[0]->mailbox;
?>
```

string imap_setflag_full(int ImapStream, string Sequence, string Flag, int Options)

Description: Adds the Flag parameter to the messages specified by Sequence for mailbox specified by ImapStream. The Options parameter can be set to ST_UID to indicate the Sequence parameter contains user ID's (UID's) as opposed to sequence numbers.

See Also: imap_open

Usage:

```php
<?php
    $MyBox = imap_open("{MyMail.server.com}INBOX",$MyUserName,$Password);
    $MboxInfo = imap_setflag_full($MyBox,"1","R");
    imap_close($MyBox);
?>
```

string imap_clearflag_full(int ImapStream, int Sequence, string Flag, int Options)

Description: Deletes the Flag parameter from the messages specified by Sequence for mailbox specified by ImapStream. The Options parameter can be set to ST_UID to indicate the Sequence parameter contains user IDs (UIDs) as opposed to sequence numbers.

See Also: imap_setflag_full

Usage:

```php
<?php
    $MyBox = imap_open("{MyMail.server.com}INBOX",$MyUserName,$Password);
    $MboxInfo = imap_setflag_full($MyBox,"1","R");
    imap_close($MyBox);
?>
```

string imap_sort(int ImapStream, int Criteria, int Reverse, int Options)

Description: Returns an array of message numbers sorted by Reverse and Criteria. If Reverse is 1, the sorting is in reverse. If Reverse is 0, sorting is normal. The Criteria parameter can be only one of the following:

- SORTDATE—Message date
- SORTARRIVAL—Arrival date
- SORTFROM—Sort using first FROM address in messages
- SORTSUBJECT—Sort by message subject
- SORTTO—Sort by first TO address in messages
- SORTCC—Sort by first CC address in messages
- SORTSIZE—Sort by size of messages in octets

The Options parameter is one or more of the following OR'd together:

- SE_UID—Return UID's (user ID's) instead of sequence numbers
- SE_NOPREFETCH—Don't pre-fetch searched messages

Usage:

```php
<?php
    $MyBox = imap_open("{MyMail.server.com}INBOX",$MyUserName,$Password);
    $MboxInfo = imap_sort($MyBox, SORTFROM, 0, SE_NOPREFETCH);
    echo "First message sorted by From address is message number $MboxInfo<P>";
    imap_close($MyBox);
?>
```

string imap_fetchheader(int ImapStream, int MessageNumber, int Flags)

Description: Returns the unfiltered RFC822 format header of the specified `MessageNumber` as a text string. The `Flags` parameter can be one of the following:

- `FT_UID`—The `MessageNumber` is a UID.

- `FT_INTERNAL`—The string returned is in internal format.

- `FT_PREFETCH`—The RFC822 text should be pre-fetched at the same time the header is returned. This can save some time when reading all of a message.

See Also: imap_open

Usage:

```php
<?php
    $MyBox = imap_open("{MyMail.server.com}INBOX",$MyUserName,$Password);
    $MboxInfo = imap_fetchheader($MyBox, 1,FT_INTERNAL);
    echo "Message number 1 header is $MboxInfo<P>";
    imap_close($MyBox);
?>
```

array imap_search(int ImapStream, string Criteria, int Flags)

Description: Searches the mailbox specified by `ImapStream` using `Criteria`, returning an array of message numbers. `Criteria` is a string containing keywords separated by spaces. A multiword argument contained in the string must be quoted (for example, "Chery Marie"). The keywords are one or more of the following:

- `ALL`—Return all messages matching rest of the criteria list.

- `ANSWERED`—Match messages with the `\\ANSWERED` flag set.

- `BCC "search string"`—Match messages with "search string" in the Bcc: field.

- `BEFORE "date"`—Match messages with Date: before "date."

- `BODY "search string"`—Match messages with "search string" in the message body.

- `CC "search string"`—Match messages with "search string" in the Cc: field.

- `DELETED`—Match messages that are deleted.

- FLAGGED—Match messages with the \\FLAGGED flag set. This is also known as the "Important" or "Urgent" flag.

- FROM "search string"—Match messages with the "search string" in the From: field.

- KEYWORD "search string"—Match messages with "search string" as a keyword.

- NEW—Match messages that are new.

- OLD—Match messages that are old.

- ON "date"—Match messages with Date: field matching "date."

- RECENT—Match messages with the \\RECENT flag set.

- SEEN—Match messages that have been seen (the \\SEEN flag is set).

- SINCE "date"—Match messages with Date: field later than "date."

- SUBJECT "search string"—Match messages with search string in the Subject: field.

- TEXT "search string"—Match messages with "search string" in the text.

- TO "search string"—Match messages with "search string" in the To: field.

- UNANSWERED—Match messages that have not been answered.

- UNDELETED—Match messages that are not deleted.

- UNFLAGGED—Match messages that are not flagged.

- UNKEYWORD "keyword"—Match messages that do not have the keyword "keyword."

- UNSEEN—Match messages not yet seen.

According to the online documentation, this list was derived from reading the UW c-client code, and may contain errors. The search strings are case sensitive: "Sue" and "sue" are two different names.

The Flags argument can be the value SE_UID, which forces the returned array to contain user ID's (UID's) rather than message sequence numbers.

See Also: imap_open

Usage:

```php
<?php
    $MyBox = imap_open("{MyMail.server.com}INBOX",$MyUserName,$Password);
    $Mbox = imap_search($MyBox,"UNSEEN FROM joe",0);
    echo "First unread message from joe is message number $Mbox<P>";
    imap_close($MyBox);
?>
```

object imap_status(int ImapStream, string MailBox, int FLAGS)

Description: Returns information on an arbitrary mailbox specified by MailBox. The object has the following attributes:

```
object {
    var $messages;// number of messages
    var $recent;// number of recent messages
    var $unseen;// new messages
    var uidnext;// next uid
    var uidvalidity;// changes when uid not valid
    var $flags;// which of the attributes are valid
    }
```

The `flags` argument controls the information returned in the object, and can be one or more of the following OR'd together:

- `SA_MESSAGES`—Return the number of messages in the mailbox in the attribute `messages`.

- `SA_RECENT`—Return the number of recent messages in the mailbox in the attribute `recent`.

- `SA_UNSEEN`—Return the number of unseen messages in the mailbox in the attribute `unseen`.

- `SA_UIDNEXT`—Return the next uid to be used in the mailbox in the attribute `uidnext`.

- `SA_UIDVALIDITY`—Set the attribute `uidnext` to a constant that changes when UIDs for the mailbox may no longer be valid.

- `SA_ALL`—Set all of the above flags.

The `flags` attribute contains the previous flags. You can test using the above bitmasks to determine which attributes have been filled in.

See Also: `imap_open`

Usage:

```php
<?php
    $MyBox = imap_open("{MyMail.server.com}INBOX",$MyUserName,$Password);
    $Status = imap_status($MyBox,"PERSONAL",SA_UNSEEN);
    echo "You have ".$Status->unseen." unseen messages in mailbox PERSONAL<P>";
    imap_close($MyBox,CL_EXPUNGE);// remove deleted messages
?>
```

int imap_uid(int ImapStream, Int MsgNumber)

Description: Returns the UID (user ID) for the given `MessageNumber`. This function is the complement to `imap_msgno`.

See Also: `imap_msgno`, `imap_open`

Usage:

```php
<?php
    $MyBox = imap_open("{MyMail.server.com}INBOX",$MyUserName,$Password);
    $MboxUID = imap_uid($MyBox,"1");
```

```
        echo "User ID of message number 1 is $MboxUID<P>";
        imap_close($MyBox);
?>
```

Math

mixed abs(mixed Number)

Description: Returns the absolute value of Number. The return type is float if the Number argument is float; otherwise the return type is int.

See Also: min, max

Usage:

```php
<?php
    $A = -32;
    echo "absolute value of $A is ".abs($A)."<P>";
?>
```

float acos(float Number)

Description: Returns the arc cosine of Number in radians.

See Also: asin, atan, tan, sin, cos

Usage:

```php
<?php
    $a = 30.0;
    echo "Arc Cosing of $a is ".acos($a)."<P>";
?>
```

float asin(float Number)

Description: Returns the arc sine of Number in radians.

Usage: acos, atan, sin, cos

```php
<?php
    $a = 30.0;
    echo "Arc sine of $a is ".asin($a)."<P>";
?>
```

float atan(float Number)

Description: Returns the arc tangent of Number in radians.

See Also: acos, asin, tan

Usage:

```php
<?php
    $a = 30.0;
    echo "Arc tangent of $a is ".atan($a)."<P>";
?>
```

float atan2(float X, float Y)

Description: Returns the arc tangent in radians of coordinates X and Y. This is similar to calculating arc tangent of X,Y, except the signs of X and Y are used to determine the quadrant of the answer.

See Also: atan, tan

Usage:

```php
<?php
    $At2 = atan2(3.0,4.0);
?>
```

string base_convert(string Number, int FromBase, int ToBase)

Description: Returns a string containing Number changed to base specified by ToBase. The parameters FromBase and ToBase must be numbers from 2–36. Bases higher than base 10 will have numbers represented by letters a–z, with 10 being the letter a, 11 b, 12 c, and so forth.

See Also: bindec

Usage:

```php
<?php
    $dec = base_convert("FF",16,10); // convert from base 16 to base 10
?>
```

int bindec(string BinaryString)

Description: Returns the binary number in BinaryString converted to decimal. The largest binary number that can be converted is 31 1's in a row.

See Also: octdec, base_convert

Usage:

```php
<?php
    $decimal = bindec("1111");// $decimal is now 15
?>
```

int ceil(float Number)

Description: Returns the next highest integer value from floating point Number.

See Also: floor, round

Usage:

```php
<?php
    $Num = ceil(3.2); // $Num is now 4
?>
```

float cos(float Number)

Description: Returns the cosine of `Number` in radians.

See Also: `sin, tan, atan, acos, asin`

Usage:

```php
<?php
    $Cosine = cos(1.0);
?>
```

string decbin(int Number)

Description: Returns a string which is decimal `Number` converted to binary. The largest number that can be converted is 2147483647.

See Also: `bindec, octdec, base_convert`

Usage:

```php
<?php
    $Binary = decbin(15); // $Binary is now "1111"
?>
```

string dechex(int Number)

Description: Returns `Number` converted to hexadecimal in a string. The largest number that can be converted to hexadecimal is 2147483647.

See Also: `base_convert, hexdec, decbin, bindec`

Usage:

```php
<?php
    $Hex = dechex(16); // $Hex is now "10"
?>
```

string decoct(int Number)

Description: Returns `Number` converted to octal in a string. The largest number that can be converted to octal is 2147483647.

See Also: `base_convert, octdec`

Usage:

```php
<?php
    $Octal = decoct(8); // $Octal is now "10"
?>
```

float exp(float Number)

Description: Returns e raised to the power of `Number`.

See Also: `pow`

A

Usage:

```php
<?php
    $Esquared = exp(2);
?>
```

int floor(float Number)

Description: Returns the next lowest integer value from floating point Number.

See Also: ceil, round

Usage:

```php
<?php
    $FloorInt = floor(3.4); // $FloorInt is now 3
?>
```

int getrandmax(void)

Description: Returns the largest value that can be returned by a call to rand().

See Also: rand

Usage:

```php
<?php
    $MaxRand = getrandmax();
?>
```

int hexdec(string HexadecimalNumber)

Description: Returns HexadecimalNumber converted to decimal from base 16. The largest number that can be converted is 2147483647.

Usage: base_convert, dechex

```php
<?php
    $DecimalNumber = hexdec("FF"); // $DecimalNumber is now 255
?>
```

float log(float Number)

Description: Returns the log to the base e of Number.

See Also: log10, exp, pow

Usage:

```php
<?php
    $LogBaseE = log(2);
?>
```

float log10(float Number)

Description: Returns the log base 10 of Number.

See Also: log10, log, pow, exp

Usage:

```php
<?php
    $LogBase10 = log10(20);
?>
```

mixed max(mixed Number1, mixed [Number2], mixed [Number3], ...)

Description: Returns the highest value from the arguments. If Number1 is an array, the highest value in the array is returned. You must have Number2 if Number1 is a string, integer, or float. You can have as many arguments as you want.

See Also: min

Usage:

```php
<?php
    $MaxValue = max(1,2,3,12);// $MaxValue is 12
?>
```

mixed min(mixed Number1, Mixed [Number2], mixed [Number3],...)

Description: Returns the lowest value from the argument list. If the first argument is an array, the lowest value from the array is returned. If Number1 is a string, integer, or float, Number2 must be provided. You can have an unlimited number of arguments.

See Also: max

Usage:

```php
<?php
    $MinNumber = min ( 4, 3, 7, 22, 1);
?>
```

int mt_rand(int [Minimum], int [Maximum])

Description: Returns a random number using a Mersenne Twister random generator. This should be suitable for cryptographic purposes, and is faster than the default libc random number generator. If this function is called without Minimum and Maximum parameters, the number returned will be between 0–RAND_MAX. You need to seed the random number generator with mt_srand().

See Also: mt_srand

Usage:

```php
<?php
    mt_srand((double)microtime()*1000000); // seed a pseudo random value
    $Random = mt_rand();
?>
```

void mt_srand(int SeedValue)

Description: Seed the mt random number generator with a starting value.

See Also: mt_rand

Usage:

```php
<?php
    mt_srand((double)microtime()*1000000); // seed a pseudo random value
?>
```

int mt_getrandmax(void)

Description: Returns the maximum value that a call to mt_rand() will produce.

See Also: mt_rand, mt_srand

Usage:

```php
<?php
    $MaxValue = mt_getrandmax();
?>
```

string number_format(float Number, int [Decimals], string [DecimalPoint], string [ThousandsSeparator])

Description: Returns Number formatted per the arguments. You can have 1, 2, or 4 arguments to this function. With one argument supplied, Number will be formatted without a decimal point, but with a comma between each group of thousands. If two arguments are supplied, Number will be formatted with Decimals number of decimals, with a period (".") in front and a comma (",")between every group of thousands. If all arguments are supplied, Number will be formated with Decimals number of decimals, the DecimalPoint string will be used instead of a period ("."), and the ThousandsSeparator string will be used instead of a comma between groups of thousands.

See Also: max

Usage:

```php
<?php
    $Num = number_format(10000); // $Num is now "10,000"
?>
```

int octdec(string OctalString)

Description: Returns the decimal number represented by OctalString. The largest number that can be converted is 017777777777 octal, or 2147483647 decimal.

See Also: decoct, base_convert

Usage:

```php
<?php
    $Dec = octdec("1773");
?>
```

double pi(void)

Description: Returns an approximation of `pi`, which is an irrational number that starts 3.14159265358979323846….

See Also: sin, cos, tan

Usage:
```php
<?php
    echo "pi is approximately ".pi()."<P>";
?>
```

float pow(float Base, float Exponent)

Description: Returns the result of raising `Base` to the power of `Exponent`.

Usage:
```php
<?php
    $Answer = pow(2,3);//$Answer is 8
?>
```

int rand(int [Minimum],int [Maximum])

Description: Returns a pseudo random number between 0–RAND_MAX when no parameters are provided. When `Minimum` and `Maximum` are provided, the random number is a value from `Minimum` to `Maximum`.

See Also: srand, mt_rand

Usage:
```php
<?php
    srand(microtime()*1000);
    $Random = rand();
?>
```

float round(float Number)

Description: Returns the rounded value of `Number`.

See Also: ceil, floor

Usage:
```php
<?php
    $Answer = round(2.3); // $Answer is 2
    $Answer = round(2.5); // $Answer is 3
?>
```

float sin(float Number)

Description: Returns the sine of `Number` in radians.

See Also: cos, tan

Usage:

```php
<?php
    $Answer = sin(1);
?>
```

float sqrt(float Number)

Description: Returns the square root of `Number`.

See Also: pow

Usage:

```php
<?php
    $Answer = sqrt(4); // returns 2
?>
```

void srand(int RandomSeedValue)

Description: Seeds the random number generator with `RandomSeedValue`.

See Also: rand

Usage:

```php
<?php
    srand(time());
?>
```

float tan(float Angle)

Description: Returns the tangent of `Angle` in radians.

See Also: sin, cos

Usage:

```php
<?php
    $Answer = tan(1);
?>
```

Miscellaneous

void eval(string CodeString)

Description: Executes the PHP code in `CodeString`. One possible use for this function is to store code in files or databases for later execution.

The statements within the string must end with a semicolon. You might also have to escape characters in the string (such as the $ character) to avoid substituting a string value for a string name. To include quotes in a string you might have to escape the "" character with a backslash. Any variable created or assigned a value in a `CodeString` retains its value throughout the rest of the script.

See Also: include, require

Usage:

```php
<?php
    $CodeString = "echo 'this is a test<P>';";
    eval(CodeString); // will echo "this is a test<P>"
?>
```

mixed func_get_arg(int ArgumentNumber)

Description: Returns the argument specified by ArgumentNumber. The number 0 is the first argument. When used with func_num_args, you can create variable length user defined functions.

See Also: func_num_args

Usage:

```php
<?php
function foo(){
    $NumberOfArguments = func_num_args();
    echo "Argument number 1 passed to foo() is ".func_get_arg(0)."<P>";
}
 foo(10, 11, 12, 13); // prints Argument number 1 passed to foo is 10
?>
```

array func_get_args(void)

Description: Returns an array containing each of the arguments passed to the current user-defined function.

See Also: func_num_args

Usage:

```php
<?php
function foo(){
    $NumberOfArguments = func_num_args();
    $ArgArray = function_get_args();
    echo "Argument number 1 passed to foo() is ".$ArgArray[0]."<P>";
}
 foo(10, 11, 12, 13); // prints Argument number 1 passed to foo is 10
?>
```

int func_num_args(void)

Description: Returns the number of arguments passed to the current user-defined function.

See Also: func_get_arg

Usage:

```php
<?php
function foo(){
    $NumberOfArguments = func_num_args();
    echo "Number of arguments passed to foo() is $NumberOfArguments<P>";
```

```
}
 foo(10, 11, 12, 13); // prints Number of arguments passed to foo() is 4
?>
```

int function_exists(string FunctionName)

Description: Returns TRUE if the function has been defined, FALSE otherwise.

See Also: function_num_args

Usage:

```
<?php
function foo() {
    $a = 3;
}
  if (function_exists("foo"))
    echo "foo() does exist<P>";

  if (!function_exists("foo2"))
    echo "foo2() does not exist<P>";
?>
```

void leak(int NumberOfBytes)

Description: Wastes the specified NumberOfBytes in an unrecoverable fashion while the current script is running. This memory will only be recovered when the script ends. It is useful for testing your PHP application under adverse conditions.

See Also: free

Usage:

```
<?php
    echo "leaking a lot of memory !<P>";
    leak(10000000);
?>
```

int mail(string ToAddress, string SubjectLine, string MessageBody, string [AdditionalHeaders])

Description: Sends email addressed ToAddress with the subject SubjectLine containing the MessageBody, along with the optional AdditionalHeaders. The ToAddress can be a list of addresses separated by commas. If you include ExtraHeaders, the headers should be separated by the newline character. Returns TRUE on success, FALSE on failure.

See Also:

Usage:

```
<?php
    $Result = mail("bill.smith@company.com","This is a test message",
                    "Hello there!");
    if (!$Result)
        echo "Message was not sent<P>";
?>
```

string pack(string Format, mixed [Argument1],mixed [ArgumentN])

Description: Returns a binary string containing Argument1...N packed into it per the Format string. This function is similar to the Perl pack function, and the formatting codes work the same. The format code is a character that defines what you are formatting, followed by an optional number that specifies how many characters are in the Argument. For example, a format code of a10 specifies a NUL (ASCII 0) padded string of 10 characters in length. The format codes are as follows:

- '@'—Fill the packed string with NUL bytes to the position specified by the repeat count.
- 'a'—NUL padded string—The repeat count following the 'a' is the number of characters in the string. If fewer than repeat count number of characters, the string is filled out with NULs.
- 'A'—Space-padded string—The repeat count following the 'a' is the number of characters in the string. If fewer than repeat count number of characters, the string is filled out with spaces (ASCII ' ').
- 'c'—Signed character—Convert the number argument to a signed character.
- 'C'—Unsigned character—Convert the number argument to an unsigned character.
- 'd'—Double (float)—The number argument will be stored as a double width floating point number.
- 'f'—Float—The number argument will be stored as a floating pointer number.
- 'h'—Hexadecimal string conversion—The number argument will be stored as a hex string, low nibble first.
- 'H'—Hexadecimal string conversion—The number argument will be stored as a hex string, high nibble first.
- 'i'—Signed integer—The number argument will be stored as a signed integer (native byte order).
- 'I'—Unsigned integer—The number argument will be stored as an unsigned integer (native byte order).
- 'l'—Signed long—The number argument will be stored as a signed long (32 bits, native byte order).
- 'L'—Unsigned long—The number argument will be stored as an unsigned long (32 bits, native byte order).
- 'n'—Unsigned short—The number argument will be stored as an unsigned short (16 bits, big endian byte order).
- 'N'—Unsigned long—The number is saved as an unsigned long (32 bits, big endian byte order).

A

- 's'—Signed short—The number is saved as a signed short (16 bits, native byte order).

- 'S'—Unsigned short—The number is saved as an unsigned short (16 bits, native byte order).

- 'v'—Unsigned short—The number is saved as an unsigned short (16 bits, little endian byte order).

- 'V'—Unsigned long—The number is saved as an unsigned long (32 bits, little endian byte order).

- 'x'—NUL byte (ASCII 0)—Store an ASCII 0.

- 'X'—Back up the packed string storage pointer 1 byte. The next directive will overwrite the previous directive.

See Also: unpack

Usage:

```
<?php
    $Binary = pack("a5a5","hello","this I");// $Binary has "hello this "
?>
```

Program Execution

The following functions aid in the execution of external programs. You must be careful when executing external commands due to the inherent security risks involved. In the past, programs have inadvertantly allowed a cracker to copy system files from arbitrary locations.

`string escapeshellcmd(string Command)`

Description: Returns a string containing backslashes in front of any characters in the Command string that can cause problems when executed by a shell program.

See Also: quotemeta, pack

Usage:

```
<?php
    $Command = "wrong; format; for ; command";
    $BetterCommand = escapeshellcmd($Command);
    echo "The command '$Command' was changed to '$BetterCommand'<P>";
?>
```

`string exec(string Command, string [ResultArray], int [ReturnVariable])`

Description: Executes the command and returns the last line from the resulting output of the command. If the optional ResultArray argument is supplied, all of the resulting output lines from the command will be stored in it, one element per line, starting at the end of the array. To clear the array, use unset on it first. If the optional ReturnVariable argument is supplied, the return value of the command will be stored in it.

See Also: `passthru, unset`

Usage:

```php
<?php
    $Command = "ls";
    exec ($Command, $ReturnArray, $ReturnValue);
    echo "The first line of return is $ReturnArray[0]<P>";
?>
```

`string system(string Command, int [ReturnValue])`

Description: Returns the result of executing `Command`, exactly like the C version of the function. If the optional `ReturnValue` argument is supplied, the return value of the executed command is stored there.

See Also: `passthru, exec`

Usage:

```php
<?php
    system("ls",$ReturnValue); // run the ls command
?>
```

`string passthru(string Command, int [ReturnValue])`

Description: Executes `Command` and returns the result to the browser without filtering. This is useful for calling programs that generate images. For example, you could set the content-type to "image/gif" and call a program that generates a gif image stream. This would put the image directly to the browser.

See Also: `exec, fpassthru`

Usage:

```php
<?php
    passthru("ls",$ReturnValue); // run the ls command and display
?>
```

A

`int register_shutdown_function(string FunctionName)`

Description: Registers the function specified by `FunctionName` to be executed when the PHP script processing is complete. No output to the browser can be done by this function. This function will be called when the user presses STOP on the browser, or when the script terminates for any reason.

See Also: `exec`

Usage:

```php
<?php
    function MyShutdownFunction() {
        $Exit = TRUE;
        // do other work here
    }
```

```
        register_shutdown_function("MyShutdownFunction");
                                    // to be called when quitting
?>
```

string serialize(mixed SomeValue)

Description: Returns a string containing a byte-stream representation of `SomeValue` that can be stored on any storage device. You use this function to store PHP data without losing type, structure, or value information. To recover the `SomeValue`, use the `unserialize()` function.

You can serialize integers, floats, strings, arrays, and objects. Object attributes are saved, but object methods are lost.

See Also: `unserialize`

Usage:

```
<?php
    $MyData = "This is a test";
    $SaveData = serialize($MyData);
    // The $SaveData string may be written to a file or database here
?>
```

Semaphore and Shared Memory

Semaphores are used by tasks to communicate with each other. You can think of them in the same term as Railway Flags, being set or reset. Shared memory is a memory region that several programs can read and write simultaneously. Sharing information using shared memory is very fast.

If you are executing a daemon on the same system the Web server is running on, the daemon can communicate with a PHP script using semaphores and shared memory, greatly expanding what the PHP script can do. Alternatively, PHP can execute a program and communicate with that program using semaphores and shared memory.

As always, you must look at such activities with the security risks in mind.

int sem_get(int Key, int [MaximumAcquire], int [PermissionBits])

Description: Returns a semaphore ID that is used to access a System V semaphore with the given key. If the semaphore exists, it is created with the permissions specified by `PermissionBits`. If no `PermissionBits` argument exists, the permissions are set to 0666. The number of processes that can acquire this semaphore simultaneously is set by the `MaximimumAcquire` argument. If the argument does not exist, the default is set to 1 if the process finds it is the only process attached to the semaphore.

If you call `sem_get()` a second time using the same key, a new sempahore identifier will be returned. The same semaphore will be accessed.

See Also: `sem_acquire, sem_release`

Usage:

```php
<?php
    $Key = microtime()*100000;
    $Semaphore = sem_get($Key,2,0666);
?>
```

int sem_acquire(int SemaphoreIdentifier)

Description: Acquires a semaphore, and returns TRUE on success, or FALSE on failure. This function will hang the PHP script until the semaphore can be acquired. If the PHP script attempts to acquire an already acquired, it can hang forever, if the MaxAcquire value provided in sem_get is exceeded. If you do not explicitly release the semaphore before exiting the PHP script, it will be automatically released, and a warning message will be generated.

To use a semaphore in conjunction with another application, get the semaphore, then acquire it. Do some work while it is acquired, and place the result of the work in shared memory or in a file on the disk. Then release the semaphore. When the semaphore is released, the other application can acquire it and then pick up the information you have placed in shared memory or on disk.

See Also: sem_get, sem_release

Usage:

```php
<?php
    $Key = microtime()*100000;// random key
    $Semaphore = sem_get($Key,2,0666);
    if (sem_acquire($Semaphore))
        echo "semaphore acquired<P>";
    else
        echo "semaphore not acquired<P>";
?>
```

int sem_release(int SemaphoreIdentifier)

Description: Release a semaphore previously acquired, and return TRUE on success or FALSE on failure. If the semaphore was not previously acquired, a warning message will be generated.

See Also: sem_acquire, sem_get

Usage:

```php
<?php
    $Key = microtime()*100000;// random key
    $Semaphore = sem_get($Key,2,0666);
    if (sem_acquire($Semaphore))
        echo "semaphore acquired<P>";
    else
        echo "semaphore not acquired<P>";
    // do some work here
```

A

```
    sem_release($Semaphore);
?>
```

int shm_attach(int Key, int [MemorySize], int [Permissions])

Description: Returns an ID that can be used to access System V shared memory using the given Key. The first call will create the memory of size `MemorySize` with optional permission bits specified by `Permissions`. If `Permissions` is not specified, the default permissions are `0666`.

A second call to `shm_attach` using the same Key will return a different ID, but will refer to the same memory. In this case, the `MemorySize` and `Permissions` arguments will be ignored.

See Also: shm_detach

Usage:

```
<?php
    $Key = 91055;
    $MemoryID =shm_attach($Key, 1000, 0666); // get 1000 bytes of memory
    if (!$MemoryID)
        echo "could not get shared memory!<P>";
?>
```

int shm_detach(int SharedMemoryID)

Description: Detach from the shared memory as specified by the `SharedMemoryID` obtained from `shm_attach`. This does not delete the shared memory.

See Also: shm_attach, shm_remove

Usage:

```
<?php
    $Key = 91055;
    $MemoryID =shm_attach($Key, 1000, 0666); // get 1000 bytes of memory
    if (!$MemoryID)
        {
        echo "could not get shared memory!<P>";
        exit;
        |
    shm_detach($MemoryID); // remove self from memory
?>
```

int shm_remove(int SharedMemoryID)

Description: Removes shared memory from the Unix system. All data in the memory is deleted.

See Also: shm_attach, shm_detach

Usage:

```php
<?php
    $Key = 91055;
    $MemoryID =shm_attach($Key, 1000, 0666); // get 1000 bytes of memory
    if (!$MemoryID)
        {
        echo "could not get shared memory!<P>";
        exit;
        }
    shm_detach($MemoryID); // detach self from memory
    shm_remove($MemoryID); // delete the memory
?>
```

int shm_put_var(int SharedMemoryID, int VariableKey, mixed Variable)

Description: Inserts or changes Variable in shared memory using VariableKey. All variable types are supported.

See Also: shm_get, shm_acquire

Usage:

```php
<?php
    $Key = 91055;
    $MemoryID =shm_attach($Key, 1000, 0666); // get 1000 bytes of memory
    if (!$MemoryID)
        {
        echo "could not get shared memory!<P>";
        exit;
        }
    $VariableKey = 121212;
    $MyData = "This is a test";
    shm_put_var($MemoryID, $VariableKey, $MyData);
?>
```

mixed shm_get_var(int SharedMemoryID, int VariableKey)

Description: Returns the variable from shared memory specified by SharedMemoryID using VariableKey. This does not delete the variable from memory.

See Also: shm_get, shm_acquire, shm_remove_var

Usage:

```php
<?php
    $Key = 91055;
    $MemoryID =shm_attach($Key, 1000, 0666); // get 1000 bytes of memory
    if (!$MemoryID)
        {
        echo "could not get shared memory!<P>";
        exit;
        }
    $VariableKey = 121212;
    $MyData = shm_get_var($MemoryID, $VariableKey); // see shm_put_var
?>
```

A

```
int shm_remove_var(int SharedMemoryID, int VariableKey)
```

Description: Removes the variable from shared memory. The space occupied by the variable is available for reuse.

See Also: shm_get, shm_acquire, shm_get_var

Usage:

```php
<?php
    $Key = 91055;
    $MemoryID =shm_attach($Key, 1000, 0666); // get 1000 bytes of memory
    if (!$MemoryID)
        {
        echo "could not get shared memory!<P>";
        exit;
        }
    $VariableKey = 121212;
    $MyData = shm_remove_var($MemoryID, $VariableKey); // see shm_put_var
?>
```

void sleep(int Seconds)

Description: This function delays program execution for the number of seconds specified by Seconds.

See Also: usleep

Usage:

```php
<?php
    sleep(10); // wait 10 seconds
?>
```

int uniqid(string Prefix)

Description: Returns a unique identifier with Prefix string on front, based on the current time in microseconds. The prefix string is limited to 114 characters.

See Also: rand

Usage:

```php
<?php
    $UniqueKey = uniqid("Me");
    $UniqueKey2 = uniqid(mt_rand());
?>
```

array unpack(string FormatString, string BinaryDataString)

Description: Unpacks data from BinaryDataString as specified by FormatString and returns the result in an array.

See Also: pack

Usage:

```php
<?php
    $BinaryDataString = pack("c1",10);
    $ResultArray = unpack("c1", $BinaryDataString);
    echo "ResultArray[0]= ".$ResultArray[0]."<P>";
?>
```

mixed unserialize(string String)

Description: Changes a serialized variable and changes it back into a PHP variable. The variable type is the same as when it was serialized. If an object is serialized, its methods are not saved in the serial string.

See Also: serialize

Usage:

```php
<?php
    $MyData = 12;
    $Serial = serialize($MyData);
    $MyRecoveredData = unserialize($Serial);
    // $MyRecoveredData == $MyData
?>
```

void usleep(int Microseconds)

Description: This function halts program execution for the given number of microseconds. The results of this call are unpredictable, as it can take hundreds of micro-seconds to call the underlying code and return from it. Also, operating system scheduling activities can cause you to sleep much longer. The sleep function tends to be much more accurate.

See Also: sleep

Usage:

```php
<?php
    usleep(1000); // sleep 1000 microseconds
?>
```

PHP Information and Options

The following functions allow you to set runtime parameters that affect how PHP processes scripts and get runtime parameter information from your system. These functions are useful for debugging or for tuning system performance.

int error_log(string Message, int MessageType, string [Destination], string [ExtraHeaders])

Description: Sends the error message specified by Message to the location specified by MessageType and Destination. The ExtraHeaders parameter specifies extra information to send with the error message when the error message is being sent by email.

The Destination parameter specifies where the message should go as follows:

- 0—Sends Message to the PHP system logger or a file, depending on the error_log configuration directive in the php3.ini file.
- 1—Sends the message by email to the address specified by Destination, using ExtraHeaders information. It uses the same internal functions as the mail() function does.
- 2—Sends the message though the PHP debugging connection to the address:port specified by Destination, if remote debugging has been enabled.
- 3—Appends the message to the end of the file specified by Destination.

See Also: debugger_on

Usage:

```php
<?php
    error_log("My very own Error Message",0); // log an error to the system
logger
?>
```

int error_reporting(int [Level])

Description: Returns the current error reporting level, and sets PHP's error reporting level to the Level argument, if given. The error reporting level is a bit-mask of the following values OR'd together:

- 1—E_ERROR
- 2—E_WARNING
- 4—E_PARSE
- 8—E_NOTICE
- 16—E_CORE_ERROR
- 32—E_CORE_WARNING

The warning level can also be set in the PHP3.ini file.

See Also: error_log

Usage:

```php
<?php
    error_reporting(E_ERROR | E_WARNING);
?>
```

string getenv(string VariableName)

Description: Returns the value of an environment variable specified by VariableName, or FALSE on failure.

See Also: phpinfo

Usage:

```php
<?php
    $Path = getenv("PATH"); // returns the current path
?>
```

string get_cfg_var(string VariableName)

Description: Returns the value of the configuration variable specified by VariableName, or FALSE on failure, as set in the configuration file specified by cfg_file_path configuration variable.

See Also: phpinfo

Usage:

```php
<?php
    $ConfigFile = get_cfg_var("cfg_file_path"); // if set, configuration file is
used
?>
```

string get_current_user(void)

Description: Returns the name of the owner running the current PHP script.

See Also: getmyuid, getmypid, getmyinode, getlastmod

Usage:

```php
<?php
    $UserName = get_current_user();
?>
```

int getlastmod(void)

Description: Returns a Unix timestamp which is the time of the last modification of the current page the PHP script is running on, or FALSE on error.

See Also: date

Usage:

```php
<?php
    $LastMod = getlastmod();
    echo "This page modified on ".date("F d Y",$LastMod)."<P>";
?>
```

array getrusage(int [Who])

Description: Calls the system function getrusage, and returns an associative array containing the data returned from that function. A value of 1 for the optional Who argument will call getrusage with RUSAGE_CHILDREN. See the man pages for getrusage for the field name definitions, which are the associative array indexes.

See Also: getmyuid

Usage:

```php
<?php
    $RUsage = getrusage();// call for me
    echo "Current time used is ".$RUsave["ru_utime.tv_sec"]." seconds<P>";
?>
```

long get_magic_quotes_gpc(void)

Description: Returns the current active configuration setting for magic_quotes_gpc. The function returns a 1 if quotes are on, 0 if off.

See Also: get_magic_quotes_runtime, set_magic_quotes_runtime

Usage:

```php
<?php
    $MagicSetting = get_magic_quotes_gpc();
?>
```

long get_magic_quotes_runtime(void)

Description: Returns the current active magig_quotes_runtime setting. The function returns a 1 if quotes are on, 0 if off.

See Also: get_magic_quotes_gpc, set_magic_quotes_runtime

Usage:

```php
<?php
    $MagicRuntime = get_magic_quotes_runtime();
?>
```

long set_magic_quotes_runtime(int NewSetting)

Description: Sets the current active magig_quotes_runtime setting to NewSetting. The NewSetting should be a 1 if quotes are to be on, 0 if off.

See Also: get_magic_quotes_gpc, get_magic_quotes_runtime

Usage:

```php
<?php
    set_magic_quotes_runtime(1);// turn quotes on
?>
```

int getmyinode(void)

Description: Returns the inode of the current page the PHP script is running on, or FALSE on error. This value can be used as a unique but determinable key for feeding to shm_get.

See Also: getmypid, getlastmod, getmyuid, get_current_user

Usage:

```php
<?php
```

```
        $MyInode = getmyinode();
?>
```

int getmypid(void)

Description: Returns the process ID of the current PHP script, or FALSE on error. If PHP is running as a server module, it is not guaranteed that separate invocations of the script will have different process IDs.

See Also: getmyinode, getlastmod, getmyuid, get_current_user

Usage:

```
<?php
?>
```

int getmyuid(void)

Description: Returns the user ID of the PHP script, or FALSE on error. Under Apache on Red Hat systems, this is usually the user nobody.

See Also: getmypid, getlastmod, getmyinode, get_current_user

Usage:

```
<?php
        $MyUID = getmyuid();
?>
```

int phpinfo(void)

Description: This function sends almost all information about the current state of PHP to a Web browser. It is useful for determining whether you have certain features enabled. It also gives you OS information, server information, environment information, and master and local configuration information.

See Also: phpversion

Usage:

```
<?php
        phpinfo();
?>
```

string phpversion(void)

Description: Returns a string containing the currently running PHP's version.

See Also: phpinfo

Usage:

```
<?php
        $Ver = phpversion();
        echo "Current PHP version is ".$Ver."<P>";
?>
```

int extension_loaded(string ExtensionName)

Description: Returns TRUE if the extension specified by ExtensionName is loaded, FALSE otherwise.

See Also: phpinfo

Usage:

```php
<?php
    $ImapIn = extension_loaded("imap");
    if ($ImapIn)
        echo "Imap extension is loaded<P>";
    else
        echo "Imap extension is not loaded<P>";
?>
```

void putenv(string EnvironmentSetting)

Description: Adds the EnvironmentSetting string to the environment.

See Also: getenv

Usage:

```php
<?php
    $MyID = getmyuid();
    putenv("MYID=$MyID");
?>
```

void set_time_limit(int Seconds)

Description: Sets the number of seconds a script is allowed to run before being terminated with a fatal error. A value of 0 disables the time limit. The default is 30 seconds, or the value defined in the configuration file setting for max_execution_time.

When this function is called, it resets the timeout counter to zero. If you were to continuously call this function, the script would never time out.

See Also: phpinfo

Usage:

```php
<?php
    set_time_limit(15); // the script will now timeout in 15 seconds
    set_time_limit(0);// the script will never timeout now
?>
```

String Functions

string AddSlashes(string String)

Description: Returns a string with backslashes in front of characters that need to be quoted for database queries or exec calls. The characters escaped are backslash (\), single quote ('), double quote ("), and NUL (ASCII 0).

See Also: `stripslashes, htmlspecialchars, quotemeta`

Usage:

```php
<?php
    $MyString = " This \ string 'requires' backslashes";
    $MyNewString = addslashes($MyString);
?>
```

string bin2hex(string StringToBeConverted)

Description: Returns an ASCII string containing the bytewise, high nibble first hexadecimal representation of the binary string specified by `StringToBeConverted`.

See Also: `octdec, decoct`

Usage:

```php
<?php
    $MyKey = mhash(MHASH_SHA1,"This is a test");
    echo "The hash value is ".bin2hex($MyKey)."<P>\n";
?>
```

string chop(string StringToBeTrimmed)

Description: Returns the `StringToBeTrimmed` without any trailing whitespace.

See Also: `trim`

Usage:

```php
<?php
    $TrimedString = chop("This is a test                    ");
?>
```

string chr(int ASCIICharacter)

Description: Returns a one-character string containing the character specified by `ASCIICharacter`.

See Also: `ord, sprintf`

Usage:

```php
<?php
    $MyChar = chr(0x41); // the letter A is in $MyChar
?>
```

string chunk_split(string String, int [ChunkLength], string [EndOfLineString])

Description: Splits the `String` argument into smaller chunks, inserting every optional `ChunkLength` characters, which defaults to 76, the optional `EndOfLineString`, which defaults to `"\r\n"`. The `String` argument is untouched.

See Also: `ereg_replace`

Usage:

```php
<?php
    $ConvertedString = chunk_split(base64_encode($MyData));
?>
```

string convert_cyr_string(string String, string FromCharSet, string ToCharSet)

Description: Converts the `String` argument from one Cyrillic character set specified by `FromCharSet` to the set specfied by `ToCharSet`. The allowable values for the from and to set are as follows:

- k—koi8-r
- w—windows \1251
- I—iso8859-5
- a—x-cp866
- d—x-cp866
- m—x-mac-cyrillic

Usage:

```php
<?php
    $NewString = convert_cyr_string($OldCyrillicString,"k","a");
?>
```

string crypt(string String, string [Salt])

Description: Encrypts a string using standard Unix DES encryption. The optional `Salt` string is a two-character string that will be randomly generated by PHP if you do not provide it. If your system supports multiple encryption types, the following constants will be set. If they are set to 0, the type is not supported. If they are set to 1, the type is supported.

- CRYPT_STD_DES—Standard DES encryption with a 2 character SALT
- CRYPT_EXT_DES—Standard DES encryption with a 9 character SALT
- CRYPT_MD5—MD5 encryption with a 12 character SALT starting with 1
- CRYPT_BLOWFISH—Extended DES encryption with a 16 character SALT starting with 2

There is no decryption function, because `crypt` uses a one-way algorithm. If you feed it the same data with the same SALT, you will get the same encryption out. The encryption values can then be compared for a match.

See Also: mt_srand

Usage:

```php
<?php
```

```
    $EncryptedString = crypt("This is a test");
    echo "The encrypted string for 'This is a test' is $EncryptedString<P>";
?>
```

echo(string Argument1, string [Argument2], ...)

Description: Echoes all arguments to the browser. You do not have to use parentheses with echo because echo is not really a function.

See Also: print, printf, flush

Usage:

```
<?php
    echo "This is a test", " of the echo "," command <P>";
?>
```

int ereg(string Pattern, string String, array [Regs])

Description: This function does a case-sensitive search of String for matches to the regular expression in Pattern and returns TRUE if a match for Pattern was found, or FALSE if no matches were found or an error occurred. If the optional array argument Regs is given, the substring matches will be stored in it. $Regs[0] will contain a copy of String. $Regs[1] will contain the first substring match, and so on.

See Also: eregi, ereg_replace, eregi_replace

Usage:

```
<?php
    // locate the year from the date function
    $d = date("M, Y");
    ereg("([0-9]{4})",$d,$Regs);
    echo "Year is $Regs[1]<P>";
?>
```

string ereg_replace(string Pattern, string Replacement, string String)

Description: Scans String for matches to Pattern, then replaces the matches with Replacement, and returns the modified string. If no matches are found, String is returned unchanged.

If Pattern contains substrings in parentheses, then Replacement can contain references that govern replacement. The references are of the form \\number, where number is 0–9. A \\0 will be replaced by the entire contents of String. A \\1 will be replaced by the text matching the first parenthesized substring. A \\2 will be replaced by the text matching the second parenthesized substring, and so on.

See Also: ereg, eregi, eregi_replace

Usage

```
<?php
```

```
    // print The brown dog is not pink
    $String = "The red dog is not pink";
    echo ereg_replace(" red", " brown", $String);
    // print The red dog is not blue
    echo ereg_replace("( )pink", "\\1blue",$String);
    // print The brown dog is not pink
    echo ereg_replace("(( )red)", "\\2brown",$String);
?>
```

int eregi(string Pattern , string String, array [Regs])

Description: This function works identically to ereg, except that it is not case sensitive.

See Also: ereg

Usage:

```
<?php
    // find BlUe
    $String = "I feel BlUe";
    if (eregi("blue",$String))
        echo "Found blue!<P>";
?>
```

string eregi_replace(string Pattern, string Replacement, string String)

Description: This function works the same as ereg_replace, except that it is not case sensitive.

See Also: ereg_replace

Usage:

```
<?php
    // print The brown dog is not pink
    $String = "The RED dog is not pink";
    echo eregi_replace(" red", " brown", $String);
?>
```

array explode(string Separator, string String)

Description: Returns an array of strings created by splitting String apart at the Separator characters.

See Also: split, implode

Usage:

```
<?php
    $String = "item1,item2,item3";
    $Items = explode(",",$String);
    echo "Items[0]=".$Items[0]."<P>";
?>
```

void flush(void)

Description: Flushes the output buffers, causing all text held by PHP or anything behind PHP (such as a CGI script, Web server, and so forth) to be pushed to the user's browser. Using this function ensures the user sees all generated output to date.

See Also: printf, print, echo

Usage:

```php
<?php
    echo "this is a test";
    flush();
?>
```

array get_meta_tags(string *FileName*, int [UseInclude*Path*])

Description: Opens FileName and parses it line by line for meta tags of the form `<meta name="myname" content="Bill Smith">` and returns an array. The value of the `'name='` property becomes the key in the array. The value of the `'content='` property becomes the value in the array. Special characters are changed to '_', and all characters are converted to lowercase. If the optional UseIncludePath is set to 1, PHP will try to open the file using the standard include path.

See Also: include, replace

Usage:

```php
<?php
    $MetaArray = get_meta_tags("MyFileName",1);
        echo "my name is ".$MetaArray["myname"]."<P>";
?>
```

string htmlspecialchars(string String)

Description: Returns a string that converts certain characters to HTML entities. You can use this function to avoid a user hijacking of your Web site by preventing user-supplied text from containing HTML markup commands. The following characters are translated:

- '&' becomes '&'
- '"' becomes '"'
- '<' becomes '<'
- '>' becomes '>'

See Also: htmlentities

Usage:

```php
<?php
    $String = "<HREF http://www.somewhere.com>";
    $NewString =  htmlspecialchars($String);
```

```
    echo $String." becomes ".$NewString."<P>";
?>
```

string htmlentities(string String)

Description: This function works the same as htmlspecialchars, except that all characters are replaced by entities which have HTML entity equivalents using the ISO-8559-1 characters, if the replacements exists.

See Also: htmlspecialchars, nl2br

Usage:

```php
<?php
    $String = "<HREF http://www.somewhere.com>";
    $NewString = htmlentities($String);
    echo $String." becomes ".$NewString."<P>";
?>
```

string implode(string ConcatString, array StringFragments)

Description: Returns a string containing StringFragments joined together with ConcatString between each fragment.

See Also: explode, split, join

Usage:

```php
<?php
    $List[0]="ball";
    $List[1]="doll";
    $NewString = implode(", ",$List);
    echo $NewString."<P>";// echo "ball, doll"
?>
```

string join(string ConcatString, array StringFragments)

Description: join is identical to implode in every respect

See Also: implode

Usage:

```php
<?php
    $List[0]="ball";
    $List[1]="doll";
    $NewString = join(", ",$List);
    echo $NewString."<P>";// echo "ball, doll"
?>
```

string ltrim(string String)

Description: Trims spaces from the start of a string and returns the string.

See Also: chop, trim

Usage:

```php
<?php
    $Str = "  this is a test  ";
    echo ltrim($Str)."<P>";// prints "this is a test"
?>
```

string md5(string String)

Description: Calculates the MD5 hash of String.

See Also: crypt

Usage:

```php
<?php
    $Hash = md5("This is a test");
?>
```

string nl2br(string String)

Description: Converts newline characters to the HTML <BR> line break, and returns a string with the HTML break before all newline characters.

See Also: htmlspecialchars

Usage:

```php
<?php
    $Str = "This is\na test \n of this\n";
    echo nl2br($Str);
?>
```

int Ord(string Character)

Description: Returns the ASCII value of the first character in Character string. This is the complement to chr.

See Also: chr

Usage:

```php
<?php
    $Str = "0";
    if (ord($Str) == 0x30)
        echo "The first character is 0!";
?>
```

void parse_str(string String)

Description: Parses String and sets variables as if the string were a URL being passed to a PHP page starting up.

See Also: getenv

Usage:

```php
<?php
    $String = "Page=1&Word[]=the&Word[]=best&line=the+best";
    parse_str($String);
    echo "Page = $Page<P>";
    echo $Word[0]; // echos the
    echo $Word[1]; // echos best
    echo $line; // echos "the best"
?>
```

Perl-Compatible Regular Expression

PHP implements a set of regular expression parser functions that are compatible with how Perl operates. An entire book could be written on Perl regular expressions. I will cover enough information to get you started. For help, http://engpub1.bu.edu/bioinfo/BE561/PERL5.html is a good beginning resource. Another good thing to do is visit your favorite search site (www.mamma.com, www.yahoo.com, www.google.com, www.excite.com, www.dogpile.com) and look for "Perl regular expression."

You must enclose the expression in delimiters. A forward slash (/) is a good delimiter, and is commonly used in Perl. You cannot use an alphabetic character or a backslash (\) as a delimiter, but all other characters are fair game. If you use a delimiter within an expression, you must escape it with a backslash. You can follow the end delimiter with pattern modifiers that affect how the regular expression is processed.

Within the delimiters, the following character sequences affect the pattern match. This is not an exhaustive list, but will suffice for most uses:

- \A—Matches only at the beginning of the string.
- \b—Matches a word boundary, unless looking for a character. If looking for a character, \b represents a backspace.
- \B—Matches a non-word boundary.
- \d—Matches a numeric character.
- \D—Matches a non-numeric character.
- \w—Matches any alphanumeric character, including an underline (_).
- \W—Matches any non-alphanumeric character.
- \s—Matches a whitespace.
- \S—Matches a non-white space.
- \Z—Matches only at the end of a string.
- \n, \r, \f, \t, \NNN—Matches newline, return, form feed, tab, arbitrary number (as you would expect).
- \<n'th>—Within a pattern, matches the n'th occurrence of substring. Use $<n'th> outside of a pattern.

- $+—Returns whatever the last bracket match matched.
- $&—Returns the entire matched string.
- $`—Returns everything before the matched string.
- $'—Returns everything after the matched string.
- ^—Matches the beginning of the string.
- $—Matches the end of the string.
- .*—Matches everything following.
- .—Matches any character except newline.
- |—The "OR" function, separating alternatives in the pattern match.
- ()—Groups items together.
- []—Looks for characters (character-class matching).
- *—A quantifier that matches 0 or more times, equivalent to writing {0,}.
- +—A quantifier that matches 1 or more times, equivalent to writing {1,}.
- ?—A quantifier that matches 0 or 1 times, equivalent to writing {0,1}. It is also a modifier that forces the minimum number of matches possible. You follow the quantifier with the ? (for example, *?).
- {n}—A quantifier that matches exactly n times. Limited to 65536.
- {n,}—A quantifier that matches at least n times. Limited to 65536.
- {n,m}—A quantifier that matches at least n but not more than m times. Limited to 65536 for both n and m.
- I—Pattern modifier—Ignores case.
- g—Pattern modifier—Replaces all possible matches rather than the first match.
- U—Pattern modifier—Has the same effect as following quantifiers by a ?, but operates on the entire pattern.
- x—Pattern modifier—Ignores whitespaces except when escaped or inside a character class.

A

int preg_match(string Pattern, string SearchedString, array [MatchesFound]

Description: Searches SearchedString for regular expression in Pattern, and places the information in optional MatchesFound array. $MatchesFound[0] will contain the text that matched the full Pattern. Index [1] will contain the text that matches the first parenthetical subpattern. Index [2] will contain the next parenthetical subpattern, and so on. Returns TRUE if a match was found, FALSE otherwise.

See Also: preg_match_all, preg_replace, preg_split

Usage:

```php
<?php
    $Found = preg_match("/page\s+#(\d+)/i","found on page #12.",$text);
```

```
    if ($Found)
        echo "Item is found on page ".$text[1]."<P>";
?>
```

int preg_match_all(string Pattern, string SearchedString, array MatchesFound, int [Order])

Description: Searches `SearchedString` for matches to `Pattern` and puts the result in `MatchesFound` in the order specified by optional `Order`. Returns the number of full pattern matches found, or `FALSE` otherwise. Order can be one of the following:

- `PREG_PATTERN_ORDER`—In this order, `$MatchesFound[0]` is an array of full-pattern matches, `$MatchesFound[1]` is an array of strings matched by the first parenthetical subpattern. Index `[2]` is an array of strings matched by the second parenthetical subpattern, and so on. This is the default.

- `PREG_SET_ORDER`—In this order, `$MatchesFound[0]` is an array of the first set of matches. Index `[1]` is an array of the second set of matches, and so on.

See Also: preg_match, preg_replace, preg_split

Usage:

```php
<?php
    preg_match_all("/<[^>]+>(.*)<\/[^>]+>/U","<b>Name: </b>",
                                    $text, PREG_SET_ORDER);
    echo $text[0][1]."<P>\n"; // will echo "name:"
?>
```

mixed preg_replace(mixed Pattern, mixed Replacement, mixed Searched)

Description: Searches `Searched` for matches to `Pattern` and replaces the matches with `Replacement`. Every argument can be an array, or all can be strings.

If `Pattern` contains substrings in parentheses, then `Replacement` can contain references that govern replacement. The references are of the form \\number, where number is 0–99. A \\0 will be replaced by the entire contents of matched pattern. A \\1 will be replaced by the text matching the first parenthesized substring. A \\2 will be replaced by the text matching the second parenthesized substring, and so on.

If no matches are found in `Searched`, the function returns it unchanged. If `Pattern` and `Replacement` are arrays, then a value is sequentially taken from each array and used to do search and replace on `Searched`. If `Replacement` has fewer values than `Pattern`, then an empty string is used for the missing entries. If `Pattern` is an array and `Replacement` is a string, `Replacement` is used for every value of `Pattern`.

See Also: preg_match_all

Usage:

```php
<?php
    $Pattern =
```

```
        array("/(19|20\d{2})\/(\d{1,2})\/(\d{1,2})/", "/^\s*{(\w+)}\s*=/");
    $Replacement = array("\\3/\\4/\\1", "\\1 =");
    $S =print preg_replace($Pattern, $Replacement, "{Date} = 2000/6/19");
    echo $S."<P>\n";// echos Date = 6/19/2000
?>
```

array preg_split(string Pattern, string SearchedString, int [Limit]

Description: Returns an array of substrings of SearchedString split around Pattern matches. If optional Limit is given, then only a maximum Limit substrings are returned.

See Also: explode, split, preg_match, preg_replace

Usage:

```
<?php
    $S = "this is a test";
    $Words = preg_split("/[\s]+/",$S);
?>
```

string preg_quote(string String)

Description: preg_quote puts a backslash in front of every character that is part of a regular expression syntax in String. This allows you to search a regular expression string for a match. The regular expression characters escaped are '. \\ + * ? [^] $ ( ) { } = ! < > | :'

See Also: AddSlashes

Usage:

```
<?php
    $S = "/<[\s,]+>";
    $S2 = preg_quote($S);
?>
```

array preg_grep(string Pattern, array SearchedArray)

Description: Returns an array consisting of the elements in SearchedArray that match the Pattern. This function only exists in PHP 4.0 or above.

See Also: preg_match_all

Usage:

```
<?php
    $SearchedArray = array(1.0,2,3.0);
    $Pattern = "|^(\d+)?\.\d+$|";
    $SA=print preg_replace($Pattern, $SearchedArray);
    // $SA contains all floating point numbers in $SearchedArray
?>
```

string quoted_printable_decode(strng String)

Description: Returns an 8-bit binary string that is the result of decoding the quoted printable string. This function is similar to imap_qprint.

See Also: `imap_qprint`

Usage:

```php
<?php
    $DecodedString = quoted_printable_decode($EncodedString);
?>
```

string quotemeta(string String)

Description: Returns a string with a backslash character in front of every one of the following characters: . \ + * ? [^] ($)

See Also: `addslashes, htmlspecialchars, nl2br, stripslashes`

Usage:

```php
<?php
    $Str = "Hello, Are you jim?";
    $QMString = quotemeta($Str);// put a \ before ?
?>
```

string rawurldecode(string String)

Description: Returns a string with URL percent (%) sequences decoded into characters. The string `"hello%20mr%20Bill"` is decoded into `"hello mr Bill"`.

See Also: `htmlspecialchars, rawurlencode`

Usage:

```php
<?php
    $DecodedString = rawurldecode($EncodedString);
?>
```

string rawurlencode(string String)

Description: Returns `String` modified according to RFC1738, where most non-alphanumeric characters are replaced by percent (%) escape sequences. This prevents characters from being interpreted as special URL delimiters, or being mangled by email systems.

See Also: `rawurldecode`

Usage:

```php
<?php
    $EncodedString = rawurlencode("This is a test (</ &) today");
?>
```

string setlocale(string Category, string Locale)

Description: Sets the local as specified by `Locale`, with the categories specified by `Category`, and returns the current locale or `FALSE` if locale functionality is not implemented. An invalid category name will return `FALSE` and generate a warning message.

The Category argument must be one of the following:

- "LC_COLLATE"—String comparison (not yet implemented in PHP)
- "LC_CTYPE"—Character classification and conversion in functions like strtoupper()
- "LC_MONETARY"—Not yet implemented in PHP, for the function localconv()
- "LC_NUMERIC"—For decimal separator
- "LC_TIME"—For date and time formatting with strftime()
- "LC_ALL"—For all of the previous combined

If Locale is an empty string, the locale names will be set from the environment variables of the same name, or from 'LANG'. If Locale is "0", the locale setting is not changed, but the current setting is returned.

See Also: strtolower, strtoupper, ucfirst, strftime, gmstrftime,

Usage:

```php
<?php
    setlocale("LC_TIME","de_DE");
    echo "Time in German is ".strftime("%A."))."<P>";
?>
```

int similar_text(string First, string Second, double [Percent])

Description: Calculates the similarity between the string argument First and the string argument Second and returns the similarity in percent in the Percent argument. The function returns the number of matching characters in both strings.

See Also: soundex

Usage:

```php
<?php
    $NumChars = similar_text("red","read",$P);
    echo "the similarity in percent between red and read is $P<P>";
?>
```

string soundex(string String)

Description: Returns the four-character soundex key of String. Words that are pronounced similarly produce the same soundex key.

See Also: similar_text

Usage:

```php
<?php
    $S1 = soundex("Knuth");
    $S2 = soundex("Kant");
    echo "Knuth soundex = $S1, Kant soundex = $S2<P>";
?>
```

A new function added in PHP 4.0.1 is similar to similar_text, but much more powerful. It is called levenshtein and calculates the levenshtein distance between two strings. Such applications include fuzzy searches, spell checking, and recommending different search words.

int levenshtein (string str1, string str2)

Description: This function returns the Levenshtein-Distance between the two argument strings or -1 if one of the argument strings is longer than the limit of 255 characters.

The Levenshtein distance is defined as the minimal number of characters you have to replace, insert, or delete to transform *str1* into *str2*. The complexity of the algorithm is O(m*n), where n and m are the length of *str1* and *str2* (rather good when compared to `similar_text()`, which is O(max(n,m)**3), but still expensive).

See Also: `soundex()`, `similar_text()` and `metaphone()`.

Usage:

```php
<?php
    $Distance = levenshtein("red","read");
    echo "The levenshtein distance is $Distance";
?>
```

array split(string Pattern, string String, int [Limit])

Description: Returns an array of maximum size `Limit` of strings split apart at `Pattern`, or `FALSE` on failure.

See Also: `explode, implode`

Usage:

```php
<?php
    $Str= "create an array of first 5 words";
    $MyArray = split(" ",$Str,5);
?>
```

string sprintf(string FormatString, mixed [Argument1], mixed [Argument2],...)

Description: Returns a string formatted by the rules in `FormatString`. This function works exactly like `printf()` in all respects (except `printf` outputs to a browser, and `sprintf` puts the result in a string). See `printf()` for the formatting rules.

See Also: `printf`

Usage:

```php
<?php
    $TryNumber = 1;
    $Str = sprintf("This is try number %d<P>\n",$TryNumber);
    echo $Str;
?>
```

string sql_regcase(string String)

Description: Returns a regular expression which will match the argument String, regardless of case.

See Also: ereg

Usage:

```php
<?php
    echo sql_regcase("This ");
?>
```

string strchr(string SearchedString, string SearchFor)

Description: This function is an alias for strstr and works identically.

See Also: strstr

Usage:

```php
<?php
    $Found = strchr("Look for one in this", "one");
?>
```

int strcmp(string String1, string String2)

Description: Returns a negative number if String1 is less than String2, a positive number if String1 is greater than String2, and 0 if they are equal. This function does a case-sensitive comparison.

See Also: ereg, substr, strstr

Usage:

```php
<?php
    if (strcmp("abb","abc")<0)
        echo "String 1 comes before String 2 in the alphabet.";
?>
```

int strcspn(string String1, string String2)

Description: counts the number of characters that occur before String2 is found in String1.

See Also: strspn

Usage:

```php
<?php
    $Num = strcspn("abcdef","def");
    echo "There were $Num characters in string 1 before 'def'<P>";
?>
```

string strip_tags(string String)

Description: Strips all HTML and PHP tags from the given string, using the same functionality as is found in `fgetss`. This function can be used to prevent user hijacking of a Web page that provides bulletin board or message board functionality.

See Also: `fgetss`

Usage:

```php
<?php
    $MyStr = '<?php kill("/etc/passwd")?>';
    $MyNewStr = strip_tags($MyStr);
    echo "The clean string is $MyNewStr";
?>
```

string StripSlashes(string String)

Description: Returns a string with backslashes removed. For example, \" becomes ", and \\ becomes \.

See Also: `addslashes`

Usage:

```php
<?php
    $S = "\'This is a test\'";
    $S1 = stripslashes($S);
    echo $S1;
?>
```

int strlen(string String)

Description: Returns the length of argument `String`.

See Also: `substr`

Usage:

```php
<?php
    $Len = strlen("This is a test");
?>
```

int strrpos(string SearchedString, mixed SearchChar)

Description: Returns the last occurrence of `SearchChar` in `SearchedString`, or `FALSE`. If `SearchChar` is a string of more than one character, only the first character is used. If `SearchChar` is an integer, it is taken as an ordinal and the character it represents is searched for.

See Also: `strpos`, `strrchr`, `substr`, `strstr`

Usage:

```php
<?php
    $S ="This is a string";
```

```php
    $Pos = strrpos($S,"s");
    echo "The last s in $S is at position $Pos<P>";
?>
```

int strpos(string SearchedString, string SearchFor, int [Offset])

Description: Returns the position of SearchFor in SearchedString, or FALSE if not found. All of SearchFor is used in the check, unlike strrpos. If SearchChar is an integer, it is taken as an ordinal and the character it represents is searched for. The optional Offset argument specifies the character position in the string to start searching.

See Also: strrpos, strrchr, substr, strstr

Usage:

```php
<?php
    $S ="This is a string";
    $Pos = strpos($S,"s a");
    echo "'s a' is found at position $Pos<P>";
?>
```

string strrchr(string SearchedString, mixed SearchFor)

Description: Returns the rest of SearchedString starting at the last occurrence of SearchFor, or FALSE if not found. If SearchFor is a string of more than one character, only the first character is used. If SearchChar is an integer, it is taken as an ordinal and the character it represents is searched for.

See Also: substr, strstr, strpos

Usage:

```php
<?php
    $S ="This is a string";
    $Pos = strrchr($S,"s");
    echo "$Pos<P>";// echos "string"
?>
```

string strrev(string String)

Description: Returns a reversed String.

See Also: strrpos, substr

Usage:

```php
<?php
    $Rev = "madam im adam";
    echo "Palindrome of $Rev is ".strrev($Rev)."<P>";
?>
```

int strspn(string String1, string String2)

Description: Returns the length of the first part of String1 that consists entirely of characters in String2.

See Also: strcspn

Usage:

```php
<?php
    $S ="This is a string";
    $Pos = strspn($S,"s a");
    echo "length is $Pos<P>";
?>
```

string strstr(string SearchedString, mixed SearchFor)

Description: Returns the rest of SearchedString from the first occurrence of SearchFor, or FALSE if no match found. If SearchFor is an integer, it is converted as an ordinal and that character is searched for.

See Also: strrchr, substr, ereg

Usage:

```php
<?php
    $Found = strchr("Look for one in this", "one");
?>
```

string strtok(string [String], string TokenDelimiters)

Description: Returns the next token from String split apart at any one of the delimiters in TokenDelimiters. The first call to strtok requires the String to break apart. The subsequent calls only require the TokenDelimiter. The functions split and explode can also be used, except strtok allows multiple delimiters.

See Also: split, explode

Usage:

```php
<?php
    $S = "This string containg 5 tokens";
    $Token = strtok($S," "); // grab tokens at the space
    $c=0;
    while ($Token)
    {
    $c++;
    echo "Token number $c is $Token<P>";
    $Token=strtok(" ");
    }
?>
```

string strtolower(string String)

Description: Returns the argument String converted to lowercase. Only alphabetic characters as defined by the current locale are converted.

See Also: ucfirst, strtoupper

Usage:

```php
<?php
    $S = "ThIS IS a TesT";
    $lc = strtolower($S);
    echo "'$S' in lower case is '$lc'<P>";
?>
```

string strtoupper(string String)

Description: Returns argument String converted to uppercase. Only alphabetic characters as defined by the current locale are converted.

See Also: strtolower, ucfirst

Usage:

```php
<?php
    $S = "This is a TesT";
    $lc = strtoupper($S);
    echo "'$S' in uppet case is '$lc'<P>";
?>
```

string str_replace(string SearchFor, string ReplaceWithString, string SearchedString)

Description: This function replaces all occurrences of SearchFor string with the ReplaceWithString in the SearchedString. This function is much faster than ereg_replace, and can be used on binary strings.

See Also: ereg_replace

Usage:

```php
<?php
    $S = "The brown dog is not blue";
    $S2 = str_replace("brown", "red", $S);
    echo $S2;
?>
```

string strtr(string SearchedString, string From, string To)

Description: This function translates all occurrences of the From string into the To string in the SearchedString argument. It is similar to str_replace, except that if From and To are of different lengths, the longer string is truncated to the same length as the shorter before the translation.

See Also: str_replace, ereg_replace

Usage:

```php
<?php
    $S = "The brown dog is not blue";
    $S2 = strtr($S,"bro","red");
    echo $S2;// you get "The redwn ddg is ndt rlud"
?>
```

string substr(string SearchedString, int StartOffset, int [Length])

Description: Returns the part of SearchedString specified by StartOffset for the optional Length. If Length is not given, the rest of the string after counting StartOffset characters into the string is returned.

If StartOffset is negative, the starting point is the end of the string counting backwards. For example, a -1 specifies the last character in the string. A -2 specifies the second character from the end of the string, and so on. If StartOffset is incorrect for the size of the string, one character will be returned.

If Length is negative, the returned string will end Length characters from the end of the string. If Length, being too large of a negative value, would cause a negative length string to be returned, one character at StartOffset will be returned.

See Also: strstr

Usage:

```php
<?php
    $RS = substr("123456", -1); // $RS= "6"
    $RS = substr("123456", -2); // $RS= "56"
    $RS = substr("123456", -1); // $RS= "6"
    $RS = substr("123456",-4, 1); // $RS= "3"
    $RS = substr("123456", 2); // $RS= "3456"
    $RS = substr("123456", 2,2); // $RS= "34"
?>
```

string trim(string String)

Description: This function returns String with spaces removed from the beginning and end of a string.

See Also: chop, ltrim

Usage:

```php
<?php
    $S = "   this is a test    ";
    $S1 = trim($S);//$S1 == "this is a test"
?>
```

string ucfirst(string String)

Description: This function capitalizes the first letter of String, if that letter is alphabetic per the current locale setting.

See Also: strtoupper, strtolower, ucword

Usage:

```php
<?php
    $S = "this is a test.";
```

```
    $S2 = ucfirst($S); // $S2=="This is a test."
?>
```

string ucwords(string String)

Description: This function capitalizes the first letter of each word in String, if that letter is alphabetic per the current locale setting.

See Also: strtoupper, strtolower, ucfirst

Usage:

```
<?php
    $S = "this is a test.";
    $S2 = ucfirst($S); // $S2=="This Is A Test."
?>
```

URL Functions

array parse_url(string URLString)

Description: Returns an associative array containing the various parts of URLString. The components returned are "scheme," "host," "port," "user," "pass," "path," "query," and "fragment."

See Also: urldecode

Usage:

```
<?php
    $U = "http://www.mydomain.com:80/start/index.html";

    $UArray = parse_url($U);
    echo "Host is ".$Uarray["host"];
?>
```

string urldecode(string URLString)

Description: Decodes the %xx encoding in a string (where xx is a number), and returns the decoded string.

See Also: urlencode

Usage:

```
<?php
    $U = "%32";
    echo "The value of encoded string '%U' is ";
    echo htmlspecialchars(urldecode($U))."<P>";
?>
```

string urlencode(string String)

Description: Returns String modified mostly according to RFC1738, where most non-alphanumeric characters are replaced by percent (%) escape sequences. The difference in the encoding is that spaces are encoded as a plus sign (+). This prevents characters from being interpreted as special URL delimiters, or being mangled by email systems. This function can be used to encode a URL string query to pass variables to another Web page.

See Also: `rawurlencode`, `urldecode`

Usage:

```php
<?php
    // encode a url, allowing the user to click on it
    echo '<A HREF=webpageurl?Var1=',urlencode($SomeData),'>';
?>
```

string base64_encode(string DataString)

Description: Encodes binary string `DataString` using base64 encoding. Base64 encoding allows binary data to be transported through email systems that strip the most significant bits from characters.

See Also: `base64_decode`, `chunk_split`

Usage:

```php
<?php
    $EncodedString = base64_encode($BinaryString);
?>
```

string base64_decode(string EncodedDataString)

Description: Decodes `EncodedDataString` and returns a binary data string.

See Also: `base64_encode`

Usage:

```php
<?php
    $DecodedDataString = base64_decode($EncodedString);
?>
```

Variable Functions

The following functions operate on variables. You can query or change the type of a variable. You can also test for the existence of variables, or destroy them so they don't exist within PHP.

string gettype(mixed Variable)

Description: Returns the PHP variable type for `Variable`. The possible returns are as follows:

- `integer`
- `double`
- `string`

- array
- object
- unknown type

See Also: setttype

Usage:

```php
<?php
    $V = 32;
    $T = gettype($V); // $T == "integer"
?>
```

double doubleval(mixed Variable)

Description: Returns the floating point value of Variable. Variable can be any scalar type, and cannot be an array or an object.

See Also: intval, strval, settype, getttype

Usage:

```php
<?php
    $V = 31;
    $DV = doubleval($V); // $DV == 31.00
?>
```

int intval(mixed Variable, int [Base])

Description: Returns the integer value of Variable using the optional Base as the numeric base for the conversion. If Base is not provide, base 10 is assumed. Variable can be any scalar type, and cannot be an array or an object.

See Also: doubleval, strval, settype, gettype

Usage:

```php
<?php
    $V = 32.34;
    $IV = intval($V,10); // $IV == 32
?>
```

int empty(mixed Variable)

Description: Returns FALSE if Variable is set, and is not empty and non-zero value, TRUE otherwise.

See Also: isset, unset

Usage:

```php
<?php
    $S = empty($T); // if $T is not set or is zero, it is empty
    if ($S)
        echo "\$T is empty";
?>
```

int is_array(mixed Variable)

Description: Returns TRUE if Variable is an array, FALSE otherwise.

See Also: is_double, is_float, is_int, is_integer, is_real, is_string, is_long, is_object

Usage:

```php
<?php
    if (is_array($ArrayVariable))
        echo "\$ArrayVariable is an array<P>";
?>
```

int is_double(mixed Variable)

Description: Returns TRUE if Variable is a double, FALSE otherwise. is_float and is_real are aliases for this function.

See Also: is_array, is_float, is_int, is_integer, is_real, is_string, is_long, is_object

Usage:

```php
<?php
    $ID = is_double($DoubleVar);
    if ($ID)
        echo "\$DoubleVar is a double";
?>
```

int is_float(mixed Variable)

Description: This function is an alias for is_double. It works exactly the same.

See Also: is_double, is_real, is_int, is_integer, is_string, is_object, is_array, is_long

Usage:

```php
<?php
    $ID = is_float($DoubleVar);
    if ($ID)
        echo "\$DoubleVar is a float";
?>
```

int is_int(mixed Variable)

Description: This function is an alias for is_long. It works exactly the same as is_long.

See Also: is_double, is_real, is_int, is_integer, is_string, is_object, is_array, is_long

Usage:

```php
<?php
    $I = is_int($LongVar);
    if ($I)
        echo "\$LongVar is an int";
?>
```

int is_integer(mixed Variable)

Description: This function is an alias for is_long. It works exactly the same as is_long.

See Also: is_double, is_real, is_int, is_integer, is_string, is_object, is_array, is_long

Usage:

```php
<?php
    $I = is_integer($LongVar);
    if ($I)
        echo "\$LongVar is an integer";
?>
```

int is_long(mixed Variable)

Description: Returns TRUE if Variable is a long integer, FALSE otherwise. is_int and is_integer are aliases for is_long and can be used in its place.

See Also: is_double, is_float, is_string, is_array, is_object

Usage:

```php
<?php
    if (is_long($LongVar))
        echo "\$LongVar is a Long integer";
?>
```

int is_object(mixed Variable)

Description: Returns TRUE if Variable is an object, FALSE otherwise.

See Also: is_double, is_float, is_string, is_array, is_long

Usage:

```php
<?php
    if (is_long($ObjVar))
        echo "\$ObjVar is an object";
?>
```

int is_real(mixed Variable)

Description: Returns TRUE if Variable is a float, FALSE otherwise. This function is an alias for is_double.

See Also: is_double, is_float, is_string, is_array, is_long, is_object

Usage:

```php
<?php
    $ID = is_real($DoubleVar);
    if ($ID)
        echo "\$DoubleVar is a real number (float)";
?>
```

int is_string(mixed Variable)

Description: Returns TRUE if Variable is a string, FALSE otherwise.

See Also: is_double, is_float, is_array, is_long, is_object

Usage:

```php
<?php
    if (is_string($StringVar))
        echo "\$StringVar is a string";
?>
```

int isset(mixed Variable)

Description: Returns TRUE if Variable exists, FALSE otherwise. Variables don't exist until they have been assigned a value or had a value put into them by a function. If a variable has been unset(), then isset() will return FALSE.

See Also: empty, unset

Usage:

```php
<?php
    $a = 1;
    if (isset($a))
        echo "\$a exists";
    unset($a);
    if (!isset($a))
        echo "\$a does not exist now";
    if (!isset($b))
        echo "\$b does not exist";
?>
```

int settype(mixed Variable, string Type)

Description: Sets Variable to Type. Returns TRUE if successful, FALSE if failure. The Type string can be one of the following:

- array
- double
- integer
- object
- string

See Also: gettype

Usage:

```php
<?php
    $a = 3;
    settype($a,"string");
    echo "$a is now a string";
?>
```

string strval(mixed Variable)

Description: Returns the string value of Variable, which can be any scalar type. Variable cannot be an array or an object.

See Also: doubleval, intval, setttype

Usage:

```php
<?php
    $a = 33;
    $S = strval($a);
    echo "\$a is now $S<P>";
?>
```

int unset(mixed Variable)

Description: Removes Variable from PHP and returns TRUE. The variable no longer exists.

See Also: settype, isset

Usage:

```php
<?php
    $a = 3;
    unset($a); // a no longer exists
?>
```

void var_dump(mixed expression)

Description: This function returns structured information about an expression that includes its type and value. Arrays are explored recursively with values indented to show structure.

See Also: print_r()

Usage:

```php
<pre>
<?php
    $a = array (1, 2, array ("a", "b", "c"));
    var_dump ($a);
?>
</pre>
```

SWF Functions

Using the SWF module from http://reality.sgi.com/grafica/flash/, PHP has extensive Shockwave Flash Support. Upon compiling PHP (after libswf has been installed), all you need to do is configure --with-swf[=DIR], where DIR is a location containing the directories include and lib. The include directory **must** contain the swf.h and libswf.a files.

Many functions are available through PHP to the libswf module. Documenting them all would probably be pointless. Here is a quick listing of the important functions:

- swf_openfile—Opens a new Shockwave Flash file.
- swf_closefile—Closes the current Shockwave Flash file.
- swf_labelframe—Labels the current frame.
- swf_showframe—Displays the current frame.
- swf_setframe—Switches to a specified frame.
- swf_getframe—Gets the frame number of the current frame.
- swf_addcolor—Sets the global add color to the rgba value specified.
- swf_placeobject—Place an object onto the screen.
- swf_modifyobject—Modify an object.
- swf_removeobject—Remove an object.
- swf_nextid—Return the next free object ID.
- swf_defineline—Defines a line.
- swf_definerect—Defines a rectangle.
- swf_definepoly—Defines a polygon.
- swf_startshape—Starts a complex shape.
- swf_shapefillsolid—Sets the current fill style to the specified color.
- swf_shapemoveto—Moves the current position.
- swf_shapelineto—Draws a line.
- swf_shapecurveto—Draws a quadratic Bèzier curve between two points.
- swf_shapecurveto3—Draws a cubic Bèzier curve.
- swf_shapearc—Draws a circular arc.
- swf_endshape—Completes the definition of the current shape.
- swf_definefont—Defines a font.
- swf_setfont—Change the current font.
- swf_fontsize—Changes the font size.
- swf_definetext—Defines a text string.
- swf_textwidth—Gets the width of a string.

- `swf_pushmatrix`—Pushes the current transformation matrix back onto the stack.
- `swf_popmatrix`—Restores a previous transformation matrix.
- `swf_scale`—Scale the current transformation.
- `swf_translate`—Translates the current transformations.
- `swf_rotate`—Rotates the current transformation.

A

Index

Other Related Titles

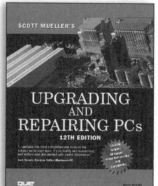

JESSE LIBERTY'S

from scratch

PROGRAMMING SERIES

Best selling C++ author, Jesse Liberty and accompanying authors teach novice programmers how to program in today's hottest languages in the context of building a complete application. Learn how to architect efficient and scalable projects before you start coding and then see when and how to apply critical programming concepts and techniques to bring your application to life.

OTHER UPCOMING *FROM SCRATCH* TITLES INCLUDE:

C++ from scratch: is designed to walk novice programmers through the analysis, design and implementation of a functioning object-oriented application using C++. You will learn all the critical programming concepts and techniques associated with the language in the context of creating a functioning application.

C++ FROM SCRATCH
JESSE LIBERTY
ISBN: 0-7897-2079-5
$29.99 USA/$44.95 CAN

X Window Programming from scratch shows how to create a graphical user interface and accomplish graphic rendering using the X Window System software. It offers a unique approach to skill development by leading you through basic to very advanced concepts. This book provides a guide to the Linux operating system for application development, step-by-step instruction to the correct usage and syntax of C, and a comprehensive introduction to the X Window System for interface creation and graphic rendering.

X WINDOW PROGRAMMING FROM SCRATCH
J. ROBERT BROWN
ISBN: 0-7897-2372-7
$39.99 USA/ $59.95 CAN

XML Web Documents from scratch is a road map to managing and publishing searchable XML documents on the Web. Jesse Liberty walks the reader through the real-world business problems and then shows the XML solutions. Readers learn by building BiblioTech, a Web-based book reader that displays topics, a collapsible outline, and full text search capabilities.

XML WEB DOCUMENTS FROM SCRATCH
JESSE LIBERTY; MIKE KRALEY
ISBN: 0-7897-2316-6
$34.99 USA/$52.95 CAN

Visual Basic 6 from scratch is designed to walk novice programmers through the analysis, design, and implementation of a functioning application using Visual Basic. Readers will learn all the critical programming concepts and techniques associated with the language in the context of creating a functioning online database application.

VISUAL BASIC 6 FROM SCRATCH
ROBERT P. DONALD; GABRIEL OANCEA
ISBN: 0-7897-2119-8
$34.99 USA/$52.95 CAN

GNU GENERAL PUBLIC LICENSE

Version 2, June 1991

Preamble

The licenses for most software are designed to take away your freedom to share and change it. By contrast, the GNU General Public License is intended to guarantee your freedom to share and change free software—to make sure the software is free for all its users. This General Public License applies to most of the Free Software Foundation's software and to any other program whose authors commit to using it. (Some other Free Software Foundation software is covered by the GNU Library General Public License instead.) You can apply it to your programs, too.

When we speak of free software, we are referring to freedom, not price. Our General Public Licenses are designed to make sure that you have the freedom to distribute copies of free software (and charge for this service if you wish), that you receive source code or can get it if you want it, that you can change the software or use pieces of it in new free programs; and that you know you can do these things.

To protect your rights, we need to make restrictions that forbid anyone to deny you these rights or to ask you to surrender the rights. These restrictions translate to certain responsibilities for you if you distribute copies of the software, or if you modify it.

For example, if you distribute copies of such a program, whether gratis or for a fee, you must give the recipients all the rights that you have. You must make sure that they, too, receive or can get the source code. And you must show them these terms so they know their rights.

We protect your rights with two steps: (1) copyright the software, and (2) offer you this license which gives you legal permission to copy, distribute and/or modify the software.

Also, for each author's protection and ours, we want to make certain that everyone understands that there is no warranty for this free software. If the software is modified by someone else and passed on, we want its recipients to know that what they have is not the original, so that any problems introduced by others will not reflect on the original authors' reputations.

Finally, any free program is threatened constantly by software patents. We wish to avoid the danger that redistributors of a free program will individually obtain patent licenses, in effect making the program proprietary. To prevent this, we have made it clear that any patent must be licensed for everyone's free use or not licensed at all.

The precise terms and conditions for copying, distribution and modification follow.

GNU General Public License

Terms and Conditions for Copying, Distribution and Modification

0. This License applies to any program or other work which contains a notice placed by the copyright holder saying it may be distributed under the terms of this General Public License. The "Program", below, refers to any such program or work, and a "work based on the Program" means either the Program or any derivative work under copyright law: that is to say, a work containing the Program or a portion of it, either verbatim or with modifications and/or translated into another language. (Hereinafter, translation is included without limitation in the term "modification".) Each licensee is addressed as "you".

    Activities other than copying, distribution and modification are not covered by this License; they are outside its scope. The act of running the Program is not restricted, and the output from the Program is covered only if its contents constitute a work based on the Program (independent of having been made by running the Program). Whether that is true depends on what the Program does.

1. You may copy and distribute verbatim copies of the Program's source code as you receive it, in any medium, provided that you conspicuously and appropriately publish on each copy an appropriate copyright notice and disclaimer of warranty; keep intact all the notices that refer to this License and to the absence of any warranty; and give any other recipients of the Program a copy of this License along with the Program.

    You may charge a fee for the physical act of transferring a copy, and you may at your option offer warranty protection in exchange for a fee.

2. You may modify your copy or copies of the Program or any portion of it, thus forming a work based on the Program, and copy and distribute such modifications or work under the terms of Section 1 above, provided that you also meet all of these conditions:

    a) You must cause the modified files to carry prominent notices stating that you changed the files and the date of any change.

    b) You must cause any work that you distribute or publish, that in whole or in part contains or is derived from the Program or any part thereof, to be licensed as a whole at no charge to all third parties under the terms of this License.

c) If the modified program normally reads commands interactively when run, you must cause it, when started running for such interactive use in the most ordinary way, to print or display an announcement including an appropriate copyright notice and a notice that there is no warranty (or else, saying that you provide a warranty) and that users may redistribute the program under these conditions, and telling the user how to view a copy of this License. (Exception: if the Program itself is interactive but does not normally print such an announcement, your work based on the Program is not required to print an announcement.)

These requirements apply to the modified work as a whole. If identifiable sections of that work are not derived from the Program, and can be reasonably considered independent and separate works in themselves, then this License, and its terms, do not apply to those sections when you distribute them as separate works. But when you distribute the same sections as part of a whole which is a work based on the Program, the distribution of the whole must be on the terms of this License, whose permissions for other licensees extend to the entire whole, and thus to each and every part regardless of who wrote it.

Thus, it is not the intent of this section to claim rights or contest your rights to work written entirely by you; rather, the intent is to exercise the right to control the distribution of derivative or collective works based on the Program.

In addition, mere aggregation of another work not based on the Program with the Program (or with a work based on the Program) on a volume of a storage or distribution medium does not bring the other work under the scope of this License.

3. You may copy and distribute the Program (or a work based on it, under Section 2) in object code or executable form under the terms of Sections 1 and 2 above provided that you also do one of the following:

a) Accompany it with the complete corresponding machine-readable source code, which must be distributed under the terms of Sections 1 and 2 above on a medium customarily used for software interchange; or,

b) Accompany it with a written offer, valid for at least three years, to give any third party, for a charge no more than your cost of physically performing source distribution, a complete machine-readable copy of the corresponding source code, to be distributed under the terms of Sections 1 and 2 above on a medium customarily used for software interchange; or,

c) Accompany it with the information you received as to the offer to distribute corresponding source code. (This alternative is allowed only for noncommercial distribution and only if you received the program in object code or executable form with such an offer, in accord with Subsection b above.)

The source code for a work means the preferred form of the work for making modifications to it. For an executable work, complete source code means all the source code for all modules it contains, plus any associated interface definition files, plus the scripts used to control compilation and installation of the executable. However, as a special exception, the source code distributed need not include anything that is normally distributed (in either source or binary form) with the major components (compiler, kernel, and so on) of the operating system on which the executable runs, unless that component itself accompanies the executable.

If distribution of executable or object code is made by offering access to copy from a designated place, then offering equivalent access to copy the source code from the same place counts as distribution of the source code, even though third parties are not compelled to copy the source along with the object code.

4. You may not copy, modify, sublicense, or distribute the Program except as expressly provided under this License. Any attempt otherwise to copy, modify, sublicense or distribute the Program is void, and will automatically terminate your rights under this License. However, parties who have received copies, or rights, from you under this License will not have their licenses terminated so long as such parties remain in full compliance.

5. You are not required to accept this License, since you have not signed it. However, nothing else grants you permission to modify or distribute the Program or its derivative works. These actions are prohibited by law if you do not accept this License. Therefore, by modifying or distributing the Program (or any work based on the Program), you indicate your acceptance of this License to do so, and all its terms and conditions for copying, distributing or modifying the Program or works based on it.

6. Each time you redistribute the Program (or any work based on the Program), the recipient automatically receives a license from the original licensor to copy, distribute or modify the Program subject to these terms and conditions. You may not impose any further restrictions on the recipients' exercise of the rights granted herein. You are not responsible for enforcing compliance by third parties to this License.

7. If, as a consequence of a court judgment or allegation of patent infringement or for any other reason (not limited to patent issues), conditions are imposed on you (whether by court order, agreement or otherwise) that contradict the conditions of this License, they do not excuse you from the conditions of this License. If you cannot distribute so as to satisfy simultaneously your obligations under this License and any other pertinent obligations, then as a consequence you may not distribute the Program at all. For example, if a patent license would not permit royalty-free redistribution of the Program by all those who receive copies directly or indirectly through you, then the only way you could satisfy both it and this License would be to refrain entirely from distribution of the Program.

If any portion of this section is held invalid or unenforceable under any particular circumstance, the balance of the section is intended to apply and the section as a whole is intended to apply in other circumstances.

It is not the purpose of this section to induce you to infringe any patents or other property right claims or to contest validity of any such claims; this section has the sole purpose of protecting the integrity of the free software distribution system, which is implemented by public license practices. Many people have made generous contributions to the wide range of software distributed through that system in reliance on consistent application of that system; it is up to the author/donor to decide if he or she is willing to distribute software through any other system and a licensee cannot impose that choice.

This section is intended to make thoroughly clear what is believed to be a consequence of the rest of this License.

8. If the distribution and/or use of the Program is restricted in certain countries either by patents or by copyrighted interfaces, the original copyright holder who places the Program under this License may add an explicit geographical distribution limitation excluding those countries, so that distribution is permitted only in or among countries not thus excluded. In such case, this License incorporates the limitation as if written in the body of this License.

9. The Free Software Foundation may publish revised and/or new versions of the General Public License from time to time. Such new versions will be similar in spirit to the present version, but may differ in detail to address new problems or concerns.

   Each version is given a distinguishing version number. If the Program specifies a version number of this License which applies to it and "any later version", you have the option of following the terms and conditions either of that version or of any later version published by the Free Software Foundation. If the Program does not specify a version number of this License, you may choose any version ever published by the Free Software Foundation.

10. If you wish to incorporate parts of the Program into other free programs whose distribution conditions are different, write to the author to ask for permission. For software which is copyrighted by the Free Software Foundation, write to the Free Software Foundation; we sometimes make exceptions for this. Our decision will be guided by the two goals of preserving the free status of all derivatives of our free software and of promoting the sharing and reuse of software generally.

No Warranty

11. BECAUSE THE PROGRAM IS LICENSED FREE OF CHARGE, THERE IS NO WARRANTY FOR THE PROGRAM, TO THE EXTENT PERMITTED BY APPLICABLE LAW. EXCEPT WHEN OTHERWISE STATED IN WRITING THE COPYRIGHT HOLDERS AND/OR OTHER PARTIES PROVIDE THE PROGRAM "AS IS" WITHOUT WARRANTY OF ANY KIND, EITHER EXPRESSED OR IMPLIED, INCLUDING, BUT NOT LIMITED TO, THE IMPLIED WARRANTIES OF MERCHANTABILITY AND FITNESS FOR A PARTICULAR PURPOSE. THE ENTIRE RISK AS TO THE QUALITY AND PERFORMANCE OF THE PROGRAM IS WITH YOU. SHOULD THE PROGRAM PROVE DEFECTIVE, YOU ASSUME THE COST OF ALL NECESSARY SERVICING, REPAIR OR CORRECTION.

12. IN NO EVENT UNLESS REQUIRED BY APPLICABLE LAW OR AGREED TO IN WRITING WILL ANY COPYRIGHT HOLDER, OR ANY OTHER PARTY WHO MAY MODIFY AND/OR REDISTRIBUTE THE PROGRAM AS PERMITTED ABOVE, BE LIABLE TO YOU FOR DAMAGES, INCLUDING ANY GENERAL, SPECIAL, INCIDENTAL OR CONSEQUENTIAL DAMAGES ARISING OUT OF THE USE OR INABILITY TO USE THE PROGRAM (INCLUDING BUT NOT LIMITED TO LOSS OF DATA OR DATA BEING RENDERED INACCURATE OR LOSSES SUSTAINED BY YOU OR THIRD PARTIES OR A FAILURE OF THE PROGRAM TO OPERATE WITH ANY OTHER PROGRAMS), EVEN IF SUCH HOLDER OR OTHER PARTY HAS BEEN ADVISED OF THE POSSIBILITY OF SUCH DAMAGES.

END OF TERMS AND CONDITIONS

MySQL FREE PUBLIC LICENSE (Version 4, March 5, 1995)

NOTE: This license is not the same as any of the GNU Licenses published by the Free Software Foundation. Its terms are substantially different from those of the GNU Licenses. If you are familiar with the GNU Licenses, please read this license with extra care.

This License applies to the computer program known as "MySQL". The "Program", below, refers to such program, and a "work based on the Program" means either the Program or any derivative work of the Program, as defined in the United States Copyright Act of 1976, such as a translation or a modification. The Program is a copyrighted work whose copyright is held by TcX Datakonsult AB and Monty Program KB and Detron HB.

This License does not apply when running "MySQL" on any Microsoft operating system. Microsoft operating systems include all versions of Microsoft Windows NT and Microsoft Windows.

BY MODIFYING OR DISTRIBUTING THE PROGRAM (OR ANY WORK BASED ON THE PROGRAM), YOU INDICATE YOUR ACCEPTANCE OF THIS LICENSE TO DO SO, AND ALL ITS TERMS AND CONDITIONS FOR COPYING, DISTRIBUTING OR MODIFYING THE PROGRAM OR WORKS BASED ON IT. NOTHING OTHER THAN THIS LICENSE GRANTS YOU PERMISSION TO MODIFY OR DISTRIBUTE THE PROGRAM OR ITS DERIVATIVE WORKS. THESE ACTIONS ARE PROHIBITED BY LAW. IF YOU DO NOT ACCEPT THESE TERMS AND CONDITIONS, DO NOT MODIFY OR DISTRIBUTE THE PROGRAM.

1. **Licenses.** Licensor hereby grants you the following rights, provided that you comply with all of the restrictions set forth in this License and provided, further, that you distribute an unmodified copy of this License with the Program:

    1. You may copy and distribute literal (i.e., verbatim) copies of the Program's source code as you receive it throughout the world, in any medium.

    2. You may modify the Program, create works based on the Program and distribute copies of such throughout the world, in any medium.

2. **Restrictions.** This license is subject to the following restrictions:

   1. Distribution of the Program or any work based on the Program by a commercial organization to any third party is prohibited if any payment is made in connection with such distribution, whether directly (as in payment for a copy of the Program) or indirectly (as in payment for some service related to the Program, or payment for some product or service that includes a copy of the Program "without charge"; these are only examples, and not an exhaustive enumeration of prohibited activities). However, the following methods of distribution involving payment shall not in and of themselves be a violation of this restriction:

      1. Posting the Program on a public access information storage and retrieval service for which a fee is received for retrieving information (such as an on-line service), provided that the fee is not content-dependent (i.e., the fee would be the same for retrieving the same volume of information consisting of random data).

      2. Distributing the Program on a CD-ROM, provided that the files containing the Program are reproduced entirely and verbatim on such CD-ROM, and provided further that all information on such CD-ROM be redistributable for non-commercial purposes without charge.

   2. Activities other than copying, distribution and modification of the Program are not subject to this License and they are outside its scope. Functional use (running) of the Program is not restricted, and any output produced through the use of the Program is subject to this license only if its contents constitute a work based on the Program (independent of having been made by running the Program).

   3. You must meet all of the following conditions with respect to the distribution of any work based on the Program:

      1. If you have modified the Program, you must cause your work to carry prominent notices stating that you have modified the Program's files and the date of any change;

      2. You must cause any work that you distribute or publish, that in whole or in part contains or is derived from the Program or any part thereof, to be licensed as a whole and at no charge to all third parties under the terms of this License;

      3. If the modified program normally reads commands interactively when run, you must cause it, at each time the modified program commences operation, to print or display an announcement including an appropriate copyright notice and a notice that there is no warranty (or else, saying that you provide a warranty). Such notice must also state that

users may redistribute the Program only under the conditions of this License and tell the user how to view the copy of this License included with the Program. (Exception: if the Program itself is interactive but does not normally print such an announcement, your work based on the Program is not required to print an announcement.);

4. You must accompany any such work based on the Program with the complete corresponding machine-readable source code, delivered on a medium customarily used for software interchange. The source code for a work means the preferred form of the work for making modifications to it. For an executable work, complete source code means all the source code for all modules it contains, plus any associated interface definition files, plus the scripts used to control compilation and installation of the executable code. However,the source code distributed need not include anything that is normally distributed (in either source or binary form) with the major components (compiler, kernel, and so on) of the operating system on which the executable runs, unless that component itself accompanies the executable code;

5. If you distribute any written or printed material at all with the Program or any work based on the Program, such material must include either a written copy of this License, or a prominent written indication that the Program or the work based on the Program is covered by this License and written instructions for printing and/or displaying the copy of the License on the distribution medium;

6. You may not impose any further restrictions on the recipient's exercise of the rights granted herein. If distribution of executable or object code is made by offering the equivalent ability to copy from a designated place, then offering equivalent ability to copy the source code from the same place counts as distribution of the source code, even though third parties are not compelled to copy the source code along with the object code.

3. **Reservation of Rights.** No rights are granted to the Program except as expressly set forth herein. You may not copy, modify, sublicense, or distribute the Program except as expressly provided under this License. Any attempt otherwise to copy, modify, sublicense or distribute the Program is void, and will automatically terminate your rights under this License. However, parties who have received copies, or rights, from you under this License will not have their licenses terminated so long as such parties remain in full compliance.

4. **Other Restrictions.** If the distribution and/or use of the Program is restricted in certain countries for any reason, Licensor may add an explicit geographical distribution limitation excluding those countries, so that distribution is permitted only

in or among countries not thus excluded. In such case, this License incorporates the limitation as if written in the body of this License.

5. **Limitations.** THE PROGRAM IS PROVIDED TO YOU "AS IS," WITHOUT WARRANTY. THERE IS NO WARRANTY FOR THE PROGRAM, EITHER EXPRESSED OR IMPLIED, INCLUDING, BUT NOT LIMITED TO, THE IMPLIED WARRANTIES OF MERCHANTABILITY AND FITNESS FOR A PARTICULAR PURPOSE AND NONINFRINGEMENT OF THIRD PARTY RIGHTS. THE ENTIRE RISK AS TO THE QUALITY AND PERFORMANCE OF THE PROGRAM IS WITH YOU. SHOULD THE PROGRAM PROVE DEFECTIVE, YOU ASSUME THE COST OF ALL NECESSARY SERVICING, REPAIR OR CORRECTION. IN NO EVENT UNLESS REQUIRED BY APPLICABLE LAW OR AGREED TO IN WRITING WILL LICENSOR, OR ANY OTHER PARTY WHO MAY MODIFY AND/OR REDISTRIBUTE THE PROGRAM AS PERMITTED ABOVE, BE LIABLE TO YOU FOR DAMAGES, INCLUDING ANY GENERAL, SPECIAL, INCIDENTAL OR CONSEQUENTIAL DAMAGES ARISING OUT OF THE USE OR INABILITY TO USE THE PROGRAM (INCLUDING BUT NOT LIMITED TO LOSS OF DATA OR DATA BEING RENDERED INACCURATE OR LOSSES SUSTAINED BY YOU OR THIRD PARTIES OR A FAILURE OF THE PROGRAM TO OPERATE WITH ANY OTHER PROGRAMS), EVEN IF SUCH HOLDER OR OTHER PARTY HAS BEEN ADVISED OF THE POSSIBILITY OF SUCH DAMAGES.